WORKER PRODUCTIVITY

Volume 137, Sage Library of Social Research

RECENT VOLUMES IN
SAGE LIBRARY OF SOCIAL RESEARCH

WORKER PRODUCTIVITY
Myths and Reality

David Macarov

1982

Volume 137
SAGE LIBRARY OF
SOCIAL RESEARCH

SAGE PUBLICATIONS
Beverly Hills / London / New Delhi

Copyright © 1982 by Sage Publications, Inc.

For information address:

SAGE Publications, Inc.
275 South Beverly Drive
Beverly Hills, California 90212

SAGE Publications India Pvt. Ltd.
C-236 Defence Colony
New Delhi 110 024, India

SAGE Publications Ltd
28 Banner Street
London EC1Y 8QE, England

Printed in the United States of America

Library of Congress Cataloging in Publication Data

Macarov, David.
    Worker productivity.

    (Sage library of social research ; v. 137)
    Bibliography: p.
    Includes indexes.
    1. Labor productivity.   2. Job satisfaction.
I. Title.   II. Series.
HD57.M19 1982   331.11'8   81-18499
ISBN 0-8039-1774-0
ISBN 0-8039-1775-9 (pbk.)   AACR2

FIRST PRINTING

CONTENTS

To the memory of
Eileen Blackey,
social worker beyond compare;
educator par excellence;
mentor, colleague,
and friend.

PREFACE

A Hebrew saying holds that all beginnings are difficult. Mounting an investigation into the roots of worker productivity involved many conceptual, methodological, and technical problems, especially concerning that area that has hardly been studied—work as a relatively stable personality element. To my great good fortune, a number of people contributed to easing my task—too many, in fact, to name them all. The first step along the way (although at that time I did not know where it would lead me) was the conceptualization of the problem and an understanding of its importance. That step resulted in a book, *Incentives to Work,* in which I was greatly helped by advice and encouragement on the part of Charles Schottland, Wyatt C. Jones, and Morris S. Schwartz, all of the Brandeis University faculty. Outlining the dimensions and implications of the problem resulted in a second book—*Work and Welfare: The Unholy Alliance*—which benefited from contact with Felice Perlmutter, Max Kaplan, and those present at the NATO Conference in Thessaloniki in 1979, among others. In the publication of that book, a major part was played by Joseph L. Vigilante.

The empirical study of work patterns in a kibbutz owes a great deal to Aryeh, who smoothed the way for me, both through the negotiations leading to the study, and during the process. Unfortunately, he can be identified no further, in deference to the promise of anonymity given the kibbutz in question. Thanks for that study are also due to Haviva Schmerling Ber, who headed the research team with verve and understanding; to Norman Grover, who made the computer sit up and talk; to the Fritz Naphtali Fund and its chairman, Akiva Levinsky; and to the student research team, who showed devotion beyond the call of the classroom.

The factory studies mentioned in this book were made possible by the cooperation of Benno Cohen, Yisrael Tor, and Tami Perry, among others, and were carried out by students of the Paul Baerwald School of Social Work as part of a research seminar. The research committee of the same school made available funds to cover some of the technical handling costs.

I am also grateful to the participants in the seminar on "Approaches to Social Development," which took place in The Hague in 1981, and to those at the Second International Congress on Social Economics, which was held in Jerusalem during the same year, for the feedback I received concerning some of the ideas discussed at greater length in this book.

During the period when I felt wedded to the typewriter and the computer, my wife, Frieda, carried the burden of family responsibilities with her usual grace. However, it would be less than fair not to mention that the pain and joy of my writing comes from her flesh and nerves no less than my own. In fact, my delight in being committed to writing a book is lessened only by the certain knowledge of what this requires of her. Consequently, double thanks to her for easing the way.

To all these, and many more, I am truly grateful, and hereby absolve them of any responsibility for errors of omission and commission in this book. I made the decisions, and I alone am responsible.

I

INTRODUCTION

That people in general should work harder than they do seems to have been an article of societal faith since the beginnings of recorded time. Whether one goes back to work as punishment for eating the forbidden apple, or examines the proverbs, parables, proclamations, and fables of the past, or examines popular and scientific literature, the necessity and desirability of hard work is a continuing and recurrent theme. Today, the major, basic, ubiquitous value of modern westernized society is work, and, as such, work surpasses honesty, education, and religion as the keystone of, and touch-stone for, societal activities and evaluation. Consequently, it is not surprising that the search for ways to induce people to work harder occupies a large place in research, experimentation, and practice.

The major impetus for the emphasis on hard work has almost always been the presumed need for maximum (or, at least, greater) productivity on the part of persons, firms, and countries; and the assumption that worker productivity is synonymous with and positively related to human inputs. This view is buttressed by the opinion that work is physically and mentally good for the person involved; that work is a social obligation owed by each person to others; that work constitutes normalcy, and nonwork, deviance; that work is a moral act, and not working, immoral; and that work is a religious act, as desired or commanded by God. However, despite the undoubted importance of these subsidiary views, there is little question but that it is the desire for more and more production, and hence greater worker productivity, which is the underlying rationale for the great bulk of studies focused on incentives to work.

Existing incentive studies can be roughly divided into five areas. First, there are those that focus on workers' satisfactions, on the assumption that satisfied workers work harder or produce more. With growing evidence that this assumption is unfounded—at least as a generalization—the field of satisfaction studies has widened to include a search for worker satisfactions as important in themselves. The second area of research is subsumed under the heading "job redesign," and is intended to increase productivity without regard for, or parallel with, satisfactions. Then there are the so-called process theories that deal primarily with presumed motivators. The fourth area, relatively neglected in incentive research, concerns work personalities, and the fifth area is devoted to direct incentives—money, discipline, promotion, and fringe benefits. This book will review these areas of what has been tried, written, and is known, and what is still unknown, concerning the roots of human productivity.

Perhaps it would be wise to point out here, as will be noted several times further on, that in modern production the amount or quality of human labor is a relatively small element as compared to the impact of changes in methods, machines, and materials. In fact, it has been estimated that human labor is responsible for only 10 percent to 25 percent of productivity.[1] As Anthony points out:

> The simple equation between work and production is no longer so obvious; machines, rather than human effort, produce goods; chemical plants, rather than their human occupants, refine and synthesize materials; sensing equipment, rather than human sense, supervise and inspect production processes; computers, rather than managers, control and direct manufacture and assembly.[2]

Nevertheless, heavy emphasis continues to be placed on per-person productivity in modern industrial society, for three reasons. First, it is difficult to divest oneself of the notion—sanctified by history, tradition, morality, and cultural lag—that productivity is rooted in human effort. Second, it seems easier and more efficient to induce people to work harder than it is to move toward higher technology. The costs of research and development, capital costs, retooling and retraining needs, the opposition of labor unions to the loss of jobs, the resistance of individual workers, and the disruption to society caused by unemployment or even by the need to shorten hours—all make the path of least resistance a search for work incentives. Finally, regardless of the proportion of productivity made up by human labor, any increase—however small—means some gain in total production. For these reasons, and perhaps others, industrial research continues to devote considerable attention to the area of worker productivity, and it is with this subject, rather than with the impact of changes in methods, materials, or machines, that this book is concerned.

However, worker productivity may be defined and measured in a number of ways. For example, absenteeism, tardiness, turnover, amount of work, quality of work, and production as a surrogate for work have all been used in different studies. Consequently, a few words of definition may be in order.

DEFINITIONS

WORK

Much hard work has gone into efforts to define the very word *work*. The Oxford English Dictionary devotes nine full pages to the effort, and Webster's Unabridged, twelve. Given the fact that any definition may be used in different ways and for various purposes, it is no wonder that a word as ubiquitous as *work* is subject to many meanings and usages.

Some of the definitions offered are relatively simple, but too broad for usefulness in incentive research, such as, "Any expenditure of energy." Others are more complex, but contain subjective elements: "An obligatory economic action involving physical energy with the intention of perfecting or bettering something, which is useful and respectable."[3] Hannah Arendt goes a step further, distinguishing between labor and work: Labor is related to the cyclical and biological nature of man which produces articles that are immediately consumed and need to be renewed, while work results in products which are lasting and a source of satisfaction in themselves.[4] Unfortunately, this distinction, although conceptually elegant, is empirically useless, since under its terms spraying a fruit tree is laboring, while spraying an ornamental tree is working—to which many similarly absurd examples could be added.

As definitions become more complicated, they move toward less measurable phenomena. Neulinger, for example, distinguishes among work, jobs, and leisure in terms of presence of perceived freedom and constraint, and instrinsic versus extrinsic motivation. Under this formula, leisure, work, and job—and various combinations thereof—become purely states of mind.[5] Again, this is conceptually interesting, but of little use in defining workers vis-à-vis nonworkers for purposes of studying incentives and patterns.

Since studies of motivation, satisfaction, productivity, and other aspects of labor relations have included engineers, accountants, hospital cleaning personnel, assembly line workers, and many others, a usable definition for such studies might be *those activities in which people engage in order to acquire material necessities and luxuries*. Admittedly, this definition does not distinguish between physical and intellectual activities, or between those that are legal and illegal, socially useful and socially destructive; nor does it distinguish between self-employment and working for others. It also specifically excludes activities undertaken for emotional, psychological, or social ends alone, such as volunteer work, rehabilitation workshops, and leisure-time activities, and thus permits concentration on industrial, indirect service, and direct service workers in a pragmatic fashion. This definition has proved functional in the kibbutz study to be discussed later, in the factories studies, and in some later studies among teachers, street-gang workers, clerks, and others, which will be referred to, and in almost all of the studies present in the literature.

HARD WORK

Despite the difficulties of arriving at a functional definition of work, defining hard work presents even more problems. Part of the difficulty arises from the fact that work—and especially hard work—may mean different things to workers, to foremen, managers, and employers, and to researchers. In these connections, Strauss warns that workers have different interests from those of management,[6] and Boisvert points out that workers and researchers define the quality of working life differently[7]—facts which may well lead to different definitions of hard work.

Hard work as a concept seems to contain at least three elements. The first and most obvious is the amount of effort expended. Physical effort is the most obvious and perhaps most easily measurable, but there is also mental or intellectual effort, as in solving a problem, and—especially in the service vocations—psychic energy, as in attempting to convey feelings of concern and support. The second element in hard work is the carefulness of the work; in short, quality. The third element is the factor of reliability, dependability, responsibility—getting the job done, even in spite of difficulties. These various elements may be present in varying degrees in any subjective description of hard work.

Differences in emphasis become clear in the kibbutz and factories studies discussed later. Pretesting of the instrument to be used in the kibbutz indicated that kibbutz members saw good workers as those who were reliable and responsible. Factory workers, however, defined hard work as physical effort in over 50 percent of their responses; 27 percent gave long hours or overtime as their definition; while 15 percent mentioned "investing oneself" and intellectual effort in their answers. On the other hand, the factory in question includes 9 elements in their definition of a good worker (not, it should be noted, good work), including somewhat peripheral items, such as safety-mindedness and identification with the firm. In general, workers stress inputs of effort, time, and thought in their definitions, while management tends to stress outputs. These may include, in varying proportions, elements of direct production, that is, number of units; elements of behavior assumed to affect production indirectly, such as absenteeism, tardiness, and turnover; and—although rarely—elements of quality, such as the number of rejects.

The criteria used by most researchers are closer to those of management than to those of workers—perhaps because much research requires prior agreement on the part of management, if it is not actually management-sponsored. However, researchers have a tendency to add, or even to dwell upon, through-put items—satisfactions, participation, reinforcement, achieved expectancy, and so on. There is decided neglect of inputs—effort, hours, and personal investment.

One reason for this may be that most researchers study total results, in terms of productivity increases (if any), rather than individual work patterns, and hence have little need to define hard work. A partial exception to this is the work of Zaleznik and his associates. In discussing stereotypes associated with successful careers, they comment that "one characteristic, 'drive and aggressiveness,' refers generally to how hard a person works, in addition to his persistence and assertiveness."[8] Similarly, a Russian study distinguishes between "honest and conscientious toilers" and "progressive workers," holding that the latter show initiative, overfulfillment of work assignments, and excellent quality of product. (Both of these categories, incidentally, are distinguished from "undisciplined young workers," who amounted to 21 percent of the sample.)[9]

These distinctions are not simply pedantic. Research results may vary as one studies inputs, through-puts, or outputs. In addition, some people may work hard and well; others may work hard, but with little regard for quality; still others may be very precise, but limited in their total productivity; while still others may work neither hard nor well. Even on a pragmatic basis, there may be settings in which one outcome is more important or desirable than another. It has been reported, for example, that a rejection rate as high as 75 percent can be tolerated in the manufacture of silicon chips, because of the inexpensiveness of the manufacturing process once established, as compared to the cost of repairing defective chips, or retooling or retraining for greater accuracy.[10] Contrariwise, the diamond-polishing industry is highly intolerant of errors—they can be extremely costly and irremediable.

Consequently, it would be desirable that a book about worker productivity distinguish among the roots of physical, mental, and psychic effort, and among quantity, quality, and dependability. Unfortunately, despite more than fifty years in pursuit of worker productivity, these distinctions are rarely taken into account. Hence, the entire area must be viewed as underconceptualized and underoperationalized. When the term *hard work* is used in the literature, it contains a congeries of subtle variations, usually not recognized. Since, however, just as policy makers are said to operate in the absence of sufficient information,[11] so a book on worker productivity must define—at least operationally—the meaning attached to the term.

Examination of many of the studies taken into account here, and others not mentioned, indicates that most of them could be understood through a definition of hard work as *the amount of effort exerted in relation to the amount the worker could presumably exert,* and it is therefore this operational definition which is adopted in this book.

PRODUCTIVITY

Whereas the term *production* is usually used to indicate the gross output of the factory, firm, or service involved, *productivity* usually refers to the per-person output. Since increased productivity is felt to lead to increased production—in the absence of countervailing factors—most incentive studies dwell on productivity, although, as pointed out previously, this may be a minor factor in production growth or decline.

On the face of it, measuring individual worker productivity presents few difficulties. Those situations in which the worker is paid on a piecework basis have obviously arrived at a solution, and even in those situations in which individual production records are kept for purposes other than payment, the major method involves record keeping and counting. When a broader view of productivity is taken, however, problems arrive. Huizinga, in an attempt to apply Maslow's need hierarchy to the work situation, gives up on defining productivity, saying: "It is very difficult, if not impossible, to obtain adequate approximations for productivity because it has so many short range and long range aspects, of which hourly output, creative ideas, turnover, absenteeism, and waste are only a few." He consequently does not establish productivity as a variable in his research.[12]

When the element of quality enters into productivity definitions and measurements, the problem becomes more complicated. Allowances must be made for rejects, and this rests upon the tolerances that are permitted, the quality of supervision, and so on. It is when services, rather than material items, are at issue, however, that definitional and measurement problems multiply. For example, one attempt to measure productivity in the service sector simply divides the dollars used by the numbers employed.[13] Such quantification of what are essentially qualitative goals not only results in distortions in the research, but—if applied—in the services. Greenberg points out that, if efficiency is the sole goal, it is possible to perform the Minute Waltz in 46 seconds.[14] Etzioni has found that when there is a heavy emphasis on countable items, there is a tendency to perform those services which generate countable items.[15] Take, for example, the report on the attempt to streamline the Human Resources Administration of New York City. Productivity results reported include a 15 percent increase in rejection rate of welfare applicants, and removal of 13,000 clients from the rolls. There is no reference to previously unaided cases discovered or helped, or to greater success in rehabilitating those cases that remained on the rolls.[16]

In social work in particular, many attempts to evaluate the effectiveness of services—even when offered on a massive, experimental basis—indicate no difference between experimental and control groups, or even inverse relationships between treatment and success.[17] It is for such reasons that Drucker contends that service organizations cannot succeed,[18] since success is generally defined as acquiring a continuing or larger budget, rather than in terms of successful services. Gross, in an insightful article, points out the various ways in which both costs and benefits are calculated in the human services—methods that make many studies noncomparable.[19]

Fortunately or unfortunately, these knotty definitional problems have had little influence on productivity reporting or on incentive studies, since only the rare case attempts to measure the productivity of each individual under study. Almost invariably, productivity figures (as reported to and by the International Labour Office, for example)[20] are derived from gross production divided by the number of employees, hours worked, and, sometimes, salaries paid. Further, the assumption in almost every incentive study is that increased per-person productivity is linked to changes in human work patterns, or—in simpler language—that people work harder. Consequently, *productive* and *hard work,* or *increased productivity* and *harder work* are used almost synonymously in most of the literature, and therefore must be used similarly here in reporting on those studies. In the original research reported in this book, however, in which individual differences were the focus, reputations as hard workers, or as other categories of workers, are used as surrogates for individual production records—for this reason, as well as for others which will be explained.

OVERVIEW

The chapter following this Introduction traces the history of work and its influence on almost every phase of human society, as an indication of the importance of the subject. Chapter 3 outlines the ways in which increased human productivity has been sought during the last century—mainly through efforts to increase worker satisfaction. Chapter 4 discusses some false starts in the search for greater human productivity. Chapter 5 is the account of research done by this author in an Israeli kibbutz, in an effort to overcome the effects of differential payments on work patterns and to seek connections between satisfactions and hard work.

Chapter 6 deals with worker satisfactions as such, including some comments on the quality of working life movement. Chapter 7 reviews the evidence concerning a satisfaction/productivity link, while Chapter 8 reviews both job redesign experiments and process theories. Chapter 9 moves into the relatively uncharted area of work personalities as stable attributes of the person, and Chapter 10 discusses the impact of other incentives. The final chapter is a summing up, with some comments by the author on the uses to which he hopes the research results will be put.

APPLICATIONS

As noted, the ethics of incentive research will be discussed in some detail at the end of this book. However, it should be mentioned here, from the outset, that the purpose of studying work incentives is not necessarily to induce people to work more or harder. Indeed, as has been explicated elsewhere, it is the hope of this writer that greater understanding of the roots of hard work will facilitate the creation of a new social and economic order in which values other than those of hard work will be encouraged, accepted, and aggrandized. In any case, whether deeper understanding of work incentives will lead to more exploitation, more production, more prosperity, or more problems, or whether it will lead to more efficiency, more leisure, more creativity, and more happiness, or to any other sequence or combination, are ideological and/or political questions. Why some men and women work harder than others, however, is an empirical problem, and it is to that area that this book is addressed.

NOTES

1. J. M. Rosow, "Human Values in the Work Place Support Growth of Productivity." *World of Work Report* 2 (1977): 62.

2. P. D. Anthony, *The Ideology of Work* (London: Tavistock, 1977), p. 9.

3. P. Schrecker, *Work and History: An Essay on the Structure of Civilization* (Gloucester, MA: Peter Smith, 1967).

4. H. Arendt, *The Human Condition* (Chicago: University of Chicago Press, 1958).

5. J. Neulinger, "The Need for and the Implications of a Psychological Conception of Leisure." *Ontario Psychologist* 8 (1976): 13-20.

6. G. Strauss, "Book Review of I. Berg, M. Freedman, and M. Freeman, *Managers and Work Reform: A Limited Engagement.* New York: Free Press, 1978." *American Journal of Sociology* 85 (1980): 1467-1469.

7. M. P. Boisvert, "The Quality of Working Life: An Analysis." *Human Relations* 30 (1977): 155-160.

8. A. Zaleznik, G. W. Dalton, and L. B. Barnes, *Orientation and Conflict in Career* (Boston: Harvard, 1970).

9. A. G. Zdravomyslov, V. P. Rozhin, and V. A. Iadov, *Man and His Work* (White Plains, NY: International Arts and Sciences Press, 1967; S. P. Dunn, trans.).

10. British Broadcasting Corporation, *The Chips Are Down,* television documentary film, 1979.

11. N. Gilbert and H. Specht, *Dimensions of Social Welfare Policy* (Englewood Cliffs, NJ: Prentice-Hall, 1974).

12. G. Huizinga, *Maslow's Need Hierarchy in the Work Situation* (Gronigen: Wolters-Noordhoff, 1970).

13. V. R. Fuchs and J. A. Wilburn, *Productivity Differences Within the Service Sector* (New York: Columbia University Press, 1967).

14. L. Greenberg, *A Practical Guide to Productivity Measurement.* (Washington, DC: Bureau of National Affairs, 1973), p. 45.

15. A. Etzioni, *Modern Organizations* (Englewood Cliffs, NJ: Prentice-Hall, 1964), p. 9.

16. R. A. Katzell, P. Bienstock, and P. H. Faerstein, *A Guide to Worker Productivity Experiments in the United States 1971-1975* (New York: New York University Press, 1977), p. 87.

17. J. Fischer, "Is Casework Effective? A Review." *Social Work* 18 (1973): 5-20; and "Has Mighty Casework Struck Out?" *Social Work* 18 (1973): 107-110; G. E. Brown (ed.), *The*

Multi-Problem Dilemma: A Social Research Demonstration with Multi-Problem Families (Metheun: Scarecrow, 1968); H. J. Meyer, E. F. Borgatta, and W. C. Jones, *Girls at Vocational High* (New York: Russell Sage, 1965); E. Power, *The Cambridge-Somerville Youth Study* (New York: Columbia, 1951).

18. P. F. Drucker, *Management: Tasks, Responsibilities, Practices* (New York: Harper and Row, 1973), pp. 137-147.

19. A. M. Gross, "Appropriate Cost Reporting: An Indispensable Link to Accountability." *Administration in Social Work* 4 (1980): 31-41.

20. See various editions of the *Yearbook of Labour Statistics* (Geneva: International Labour Organization).

2

THE IMPORTANCE OF WORK

A recent cartoon in a popular magazine shows a doctor saying to a listless, unhappy young man: "You must work harder, drink more, and start smoking." The humor of the cartoon, of course, arises from its reversal of expected norms—overworking, like drinking and smoking to excess, is almost always viewed by the medical profession as a danger. The compulsive worker—the "workaholic"—is often seen as having or exhibiting a problem, if not as actually psychopathological.

With these exceptions, however, society as a whole views hard work—even the abnormally hard work of the workaholic[1]—with approbation. Even the doctor who liberally prescribes "taking it easier" may be working himself to death as he does so. In fact, "hard worker," or "good worker," is one of the highest accolades that society can bestow on an individual, while its antonym, "lazy" (often suffixed with "bum"), is one of the most pejorative terms in the societal lexicon.

The emphasis placed on work in western society has a number of sources in history. One of the most important bases for current work emphasis, though not the only one, was the Protestant Revolution and the religious significance which this gave to work.[2] When Martin Luther nailed his 95 theses to the door of the church in Wittenberg in 1517, religious duties began to shift—at least for the adherents of the new church—from the good works of Catholicism to the good work of Protestantism. Working hard was serving God, and not only were religious people expected to work (and, as added by Calvin, without regard for the material rewards), but in many cases they were expected to be grateful for opportunities to work, that is, to their employers. Labor unrest of various kinds thus became heresy, and nonworkers, sinners.

Together with the religious aspect, work took on a social visage with the philosophy of Adam Smith. In Smith's theory of economics, laissez-faire, the total weal was dependent upon each competing with all. Anyone who did not try to improve his or her position harmed the entire economy, and thus other people. Work became a matter of social responsibility, and those who did not work, or who did not work as hard as they could, were drags on their fellows.[3]

The philosophy and policy of mercantilism added still another dimension to the work ethic.[4] As countries tried to become richer by acquiring raw materials as cheaply as possible, usually abroad, and selling manufactured articles for as much as possible, preferably to another country, efforts to maintain such a favorable balance of trade required labor costs at the lowest possible level. Working hard thus became a patriotic duty, by which the home country was enabled to outstrip its rivals and its enemies. One who did not work hard, or as hard as he or she could, thereby became not only irreligious (or, at least, immoral) and a bad neighbor, but also a poor citizen. When the social welfare system began supporting people who could not, should not, or did not work, such people were looked upon as parasites, living off the work of others. Consequently, in one way or another, the work ethos penetrated the fields of education, religion, family, leisure, politics, national defense, the criminal justice system, the area of therapy and rehabilitation, and—to a striking extent—the social welfare system.

WORK AND EDUCATION

The impact of work as an ideology on the educational system is observable on several levels. Semantically, lessons performed in the school are classroom *work,* while those done outside are home*work.* A successful test or paper may be graded as "good work." Often, children are told that they must learn to work together, rather than to learn together or to live together. Both parents and teachers urge children to work hard in school, or at their schoolwork.

On an activity level, emphasis is usually on punctuality, behavior, and following the rules, rather than on creativity, neighborliness, or even intellectual ability, since it is the former traits, and not the latter, which are looked upon as necessary for successful job holding or careers. Toffler puts it like this:

> Employers wanted workers who were obedient, punctual, and willing to perform rote tasks. The corresponding traits were fostered by the schools and rewarded by the corporation.[5]

Perhaps it is for this reason that so much competition is generated within the classroom, and not just for grades. Caplow remarks that the potato race at the nursery school is operated in much closer conformity to the principles of pure competition than is the insurance business.[6] Anthony remarks that education in Britain seems to be increasingly regarded as preparation for work. He waxes particularly caustic over the oft-voiced criticism that excellent training in schools is no longer sufficient:

A brochure published by the University of Warwick in 1967 said that British universities "have traditionally provided training which, while excellent in itself," (isn't that enough?) "has not developed the type of mental discipline in its graduates needed for the problems which they subsequently face in industry and commerce." It was clearly the intention at Warwick that the unfortunate tendency should be corrected.[7]

In grammar and high schools as well, the subordination of education to a process of psychological preparation for work is evident in the teachers who regard themselves, and speak of themselves, not as teachers, tutors, mentors, or role models, but as "managers of educational resources."[8] Herzberg notes the intrusion of the business ethos into the university, where the scholarly professor is passed over in favor of the professorial tycoon.[9] O'Toole criticizes the American system of education because it "seems bent on training young people to meet current, ephemeral employment demands and cyclical economic circumstances," rather than forecasting future employment demands and needs and preparing students for them. He does not relate at all to the role of education in terms other than job holding.[10]

Similarly, Schumacher answers his own question, "How do we prepare young people for the future world of work?" by suggesting they be taught to distinguish good work from bad work.[11] Ginzberg, commenting on Berg's approach to education, holds that education is important, not for what it contributes to an individual's productivity, but how it helps him get a better-paying job.[12] Even the commission appointed by the president of the United States to examine work in America found, in part:

> The market value of education has driven out its other values. . . . The schools themselves are a workplace, influenced by, and influencing, other workplaces.[13]

Indeed, changes in schooling, it is charged, are designed to overcome the dissatisfactions of blue- and white-collar workers.[14]

Perhaps the most cogent and best documented account of the subjugation of the educational system to the world of work is that by Bowles and Gintis. Inter alia, they point out that "particularly dramatic is the statistically verifiable congruence between the personality traits conducive to proper work performance on the job and those which are rewarded with high grades in the classroom."[15] They further charge that educational policy has only two goals: the production of labor power and the reproduction of those institutions and social relationships which facilitate the translation of labor power into profits.[16]

On a less formal educational level, Rodgers has done a masterful job of analyzing children's literature (or, more correctly, literature written for children) between 1850 and 1920. His introduction to the theme must serve as a summary here:

> The storytellers could not avoid themes of work and duty. They could not evade the task of setting forth the ethical formulas a child would need to carry with him into the snares and responsibilities of adult life. The career of work values, accordingly, is not all to be found in volumes of social economy. One facet of it is spread out, dusty, knee-high, on children's bookshelves.[17]

The relationship between work and education is not all one-sided, however. Just as the work ethos invaded the educational arena, so there are those who regard education as a panacea for all that is wrong with the industrial system, the world of work, and the lives of workers. Education is said to add both to the wealth of the nation and to the wealth of the worker.[18] Unemployment is attributed, at least in part, to lack of educational preparation for the technological society.[19] Employment, via education, is held to be the answer to poverty.

There are, it is true, dissenting voices. More education for everyone will simply assure a more educated unemployed group, in one view. Education as an answer to poverty has a dismal record, as most of the poor are not in the labor force.[20] Technology requires more education only up to a certain point, after which the tasks are technical, requiring—at best—training rather than education.

Despite these demurrers, the interaction between education and the world of work has been and remains ubiquitous, deep, and pervasive.

WORK AND WELFARE

The Elizabethan Poor Laws of the beginning of the seventeenth century codified the intuitive restraints of charity as practiced by individuals, families, churches, and voluntary groups, by differentiating between the deserving poor, that is, those who could not work, and the undeserving poor, that is, those who presumably could. The former were entitled to help, while the latter were "less eligible." Relief therefore was administered at various times via work tests, workhouses, and work relief.[21] With the advent of insurance-type social welfare programs, the emphasis upon work records or current employment as criteria for benefits was continued. In 1977, of 114 countries reporting insurance-type old-age pensions, 101 specified that benefits were only for employees (and, in some cases, for the self-employed). Of the remaining 13 countries, 6 paid additional benefits to workers, and 2 required payments to have been made into the scheme, thereby linking benefits to former incomes, meaning, in effect, former work. Of the remaining 5 countries, 2 seem to assume that one will have worked and saved money, since their payments are limited to those in need. Only Iceland, Australia,

New Zealand, and Israel report universal, noncontributory, non-means-tested old-age pensions; but one must be 67 years old and a resident for 40 years in Iceland, and 70 years old for a non-means-tested pension in Australia and in Israel.[22] Thus, 97 percent of old-age and survivors' insurance plans throughout the world are linked to previous work records.

Similarly, of 72 countries reporting sickness and maternity benefit programs in 1977, only 8 were not work-related—a rate of 89 percent work-relatedness. Of medical care programs, 74 percent are for employees only. Of the 65 family allowance programs, 47 are for employees, and—of course—work disability and unemployment programs are only for those who are or have been working. Thus, from 72 percent to 100 percent of the various social insurance programs throughout the world are linked to, based upon, or limited by work records.

The sequence in which programs are adopted is further evidence of the strong connection between work and welfare. Workmen's compensation programs, which are intended to induce people to join the labor force and to continue working by assuring them that any work-connected injury or illness will be compensated, and that the worker will be rehabilitated, is always the first social security measure adopted in any country, and in some it is the only branch of social security.[23] Work-injury payments are usually much higher than ordinary sickness payments,[24] and even higher than invalidity pensions arising from nonwork causes.[25]

Contrariwise, unemployment insurance is usually one of the last social welfare programs to be instituted, if at all. Just as the justification for early, wide, and substantial insurance against work injuries arises from the desire to keep people at work, so the lag in initiation, coverage, and amounts of unemployment insurance reflects widespread suspicion, or fear, that payments in lieu of work will induce people to stop working, or to stop looking for work. Consequently, historically and currently, unemployment compensation has always been the least numerous of insurance programs, except for the relatively new family allowance programs, which have already outstripped unemployment compensation in rate of growth and in absolute numbers.

There is good reason to believe that "unemployment compensation . . . has been less popular and has evoked more disagreement than have other programs to aid the needy."[26] In a nationwide poll, support for unemployment compensation ranked seventh on a list of 9 domestic programs.[27] While 70 percent of the population favored more expenditures for help for older people and 60 percent supported more help for needy people, only 29 percent favored higher unemployment benefits. Further, whatever support there may have been at one time for unemployment benefits—say, at its inception—seems to have gradually decreased.[28]

Not only have these programs usually been late, but many of them are highly restrictive. Some are for building workers only; some are for, or not for, government employees; there are programs for members of trade unions only, for employees of firms of a certain minimum size, not for domestic workers, and so on. In fact, about half the programs throughout the world cover only workers in industry and commerce.

Insurance-type programs are not alone in being tied to work records and efforts. Those programs which simply give out money to the needy are similarly conditioned, in many instances, on the recipient seeking work. The Work Incentive Program (WIN) added to Aid to Families of Dependent Children (AFDC) conditions the aid given parents of small children on their willingness to undergo job training, and subsequently to accept almost any job offered.

Even in-kind programs, which provide items and services other than money, are tied into the work syndrome. The largest in-kind program in the United States, the food stamp program, makes such stamps legally available only to people who register for work.[29] Similarly, the spreading network of child-care facilities is available, in many cases, only to working mothers. The latter is also true in countries where there are camps, sightseeing trips, and other benefits available to working mothers, but not to mothers who stay home with their children.

Finally, the "personal" social services—in contradistinction to payments and other material items—are geared in large measure to using work for socialization and resocialization, for therapy, and for rehabilitation.[30] As pointed out previously, the measure of success is rarely anything other than the rate of return to the world of work. Even this is sometimes justified, not in terms of the normalcy involved for the person, but as an increase in productivity. In this way, upgrading of poor schools, or day-care programs for small children, are proposed as instruments to improve the future work abilities of those involved.[31] This may even be costed out in order to prove that rehabilitation repays society in terms of future income taxes received.[32]

Social workers "on the line," in face-to-face contact with clients, spend enormous amounts of their time trying to induce clients to go to work, helping them find work, directing them to courses to prepare them for work, helping solve problems which deter them from working, and solving problems arising from work.

The connections between work and the welfare system outlined above would be of only academic or pedantic interest if it were not for the fact that they guide the welfare system in its operations, and thereby contribute to producing and continuing poverty. There are four aspects of the dynamics of the work-welfare link responsible for this situation.

DYNAMICS OF THE WORK-WELFARE LINK

Limited Coverage

In over 90 percent of all insurance-type programs in all countries, coverage is specified as only for "employed persons," "employees," or "wage earners." This excludes from benefits, *a priori,* two large groups: the self-employed, and housewives (or, more correctly, nonworking wives and single parents). Nor does designation as a worker or employee necessarily guarantee coverage. In 58 of the existing 114 old-age programs, for example, certain groups of workers are excluded from possible coverage. These are usually agricultural workers, domestic workers, and casual workers. Some countries do not include school leavers as unemployed or entitled to sickness benefits, since they have not yet held jobs.

In grant programs the designation as unwilling, rather than unable, to work is reason enough to deny help. People who do not accept jobs found for them, or even those for whom it is difficult to find jobs, are often labeled "uncooperative," or "unable to use help," and dropped from the rolls or service.

Vestedness

Being eligible for coverage in a work-linked program does not necessarily result in coverage. Most insurance-type programs require a certain amount of prior work time as a condition for enjoying benefits; and benefit amounts and duration are often proportional to time worked. The prior time required for old-age pensions varies from 5 to 45 years, with 15 years the period most often specified.[33] Even family allowances may be affected by work records—in the Federal Republic of Germany such allowances may be paid for 9 years past the statutory limit of 18 if the person is an apprentice or in a vocational school.[34]

At the other end of the vestedness scale, payments are often limited to a certain period of time, or they are proportional to the amount of time worked previously.[35]

Administrative Regulations

Although administration is sometimes thought of as a value-free technology,[36] the ideology of the institution must be reflected in the regulations and practices for administration to be effective. Thus the influence of the link between work and welfare can also be seen in the minutiae of technical arrangements.

Take, again, the differences between work-disability programs and unemployment compensation, on an administrative level. No minimum qualifying period of employment or insurance is ordinarily required for entitlement to work-injury benefits. Temporary benefits are usually payable from the start of an incapacity, and this is replaced by permanent benefits if the incapacity lasts. For unemployment benefits, however, the worker is ordinarily required to have completed a specified minimum qualifying period of work—usually six months. Then a waiting period, often between three and seven days, is required. In practice, this waiting period is usually much longer. The "seven day" waiting period in Australia has been found to last seventeen days in most cases.[37] Again, injured workers have their benefits based on their salaries at the time of injury; other programs pay in proportion to salaries earned long ago, often at rates which inflation makes unrealistic. Many insurance programs require registration for benefits only once—when one becomes aged, sick, injured, or has a child—after which payments are made automatically until the condition changes. Unemployment compensation, however, is paid almost everywhere only if the worker continues to report regularly to an employment office.[38] There is, of course, no more difficulty in having the unemployed person register once and continue to receive payments until he or she is notified of a job opening than there is in continuing payments to the injured, but in this way the historic concept of work tests continues to surface.

The limitation of coverage, vestedness, and administration, based upon the work records, results in the Iron Law of Social Welfare: Those who need the most get the least. Those who have been able to work and provide for themselves at an adequate level usually receive the highest benefits. Those who have worked, but in jobs where they never made much money, receive less. And those who have never been able to work much, and are therefore in the greatest need, receive the least. As a matter of fact, the least well-off have benefited the least from social insurance; the position of the poor relative to the rest of the population has hardly altered in spite of these programs.[39] For example, in 1935, when the American Social Security Act was passed, it was felt that the direct assistance program to the aged would be phased out as the former extended coverage to the recipients of the latter. But forty years later, almost two million people were still in need of the assistance program.[40]

It is difficult to determine how many people are excluded from welfare programs or benefits through limitations of coverage, vestedness, and administration. One possible index is the difference between the number of people found to be unemployed through surveys, compared to the number officially listed as unemployed, and further compared to the number actually drawing benefits. In Australia in 1977, surveys indicated 334,800 unemployed. At the same time, there were only 326,500 registered unemployed, and only 236,400 drawing unemployment benefits.[41] The surveyed unemployed were 14 percent more numerous than the registered unemployed in

Japan in 1975, 38 percent greater in Ireland at the same time, and 83 percent greater in Sweden.[42] In Britain in 1971, the registered unemployed accounted for only 77 percent of all unemployed persons, and in 1972, over 26 percent of the unemployed failed to register for benefits.[43] In this way work-linked regulations exclude large numbers of needy persons from enjoying benefits.

The Wage-Stop

No combination of work-linked factors more effectively limits social welfare benefits than does the concept and practice of the wage-stop alone. The idea that anyone should get from welfare more than someone else gets from working seems so morally repugnant to most people[44] that provisions against such a contingency have been written into almost every social welfare program in the world, including the most inappropriate instances. It is almost universally axiomatic in social welfare policies that benefits are pegged, explicitly or implicitly, at a level so far below income from work that no one would, or could afford to, elect welfare payments over earned income. In this manner, the Elizabethan principle of "less eligibility" is retained in modern programs.

The actual effect of the link between work and welfare is graphically illustrated when one compares the total amount lost in salaries by those who reach pensionable age and the total amount of payments made to them. The following figures are from the United States in 1978:

single persons	52 percent of minimum wage
couples	78 percent of minimum wage
single persons	41 percent of average wage
couples	62 percent of average wage[45]
single persons (1973)	30 percent of recent earnings
couples (1973)	45 percent of recent earnings[46]

Benefits from other programs, and in other countries, reflect substantially the same gap between income lost and welfare payments received.[47]

Noninsurance payments are also limited by the wage-stop. In the AFDC program, grants are less than 50 percent of the level established by the states themselves, in more than half the states.[48] And, throughout the world, the ratio of payments to earnings, incomes, average salaries, or minimum salaries seems to be getting smaller.[49]

EFFECTS OF THE WORK-WELFARE LINK

The total effect of limitations of coverage, vestedness, administrative measures, and the wage-stop is to thrust into and hold in poverty millions of people who depend upon social welfare as the major or only source of their incomes.[50] In the United States, approximately 12 percent of the population lives under the officially designated poverty line.[51] In Australia, 10 percent of the population is defined as very poor, with another 7.7 percent called poor.[52] In England, the number of people living at or below the poverty line has steadily increased in the postwar world, reaching 12 percent in 1976.[53]

In 1975, the United States federal SSI standard for aged individuals with no other income was 73 percent of the official poverty threshold for unrelated persons 65 and over residing in non-farm areas. The comparable figure for aged couples was 87 percent. Only 7 states provided supplements sufficient to abolish poverty for single recipients.[54] Even when other income is taken into account, it produces no dramatic change: Taking into account all income, about 14 percent of retired social security beneficiaries were living below the official poverty level in 1976.[55] Methods of determining poverty lines and formulae for benefits may differ, but from 10 percent to 13.5 percent of the populations of the United States, Australia, and England are below the poverty line.

The irony of the situation is that the fear of work disincentives which gives rise to the wage-stop, which in turn makes it impossible to link benefits to needs rather than to work records, operates mainly on those who cannot work or should not work. In all of the western countries, the overwhelming bulk of poor people are too old to work, too young to work, too disabled to work, or unable to find work; or, social policy has specifically indicated that they should not work, as in the case of single parents of young children. Thus, their incentives to work are really irrelevant, but they are nevertheless barred from sufficient income by the work-welfare link.

The importance of work as a societal institution is nowhere more clear than as regards social welfare. The system established to defend people (mostly workers) against the exigencies inherent in work-centered societies has become a handmaiden, supporter, and defender not only of the system, but of its lacunae. Through limitations imposed on coverage, the requirements of vestedness, administrative regulations, and—above all—the wage-stop, benefits are deliberately pegged below salaries, regardless of need. The result is that millions of people—most of whom cannot or should not work—are held hostage to ensure that others will work. As was pointed out at a recent international conference of social workers, what is shocking about this situation is that the results of social welfare "are not due to the failure of the methods, but to the methods themselves."[56]

WORK AND RELIGION

The connection between religion and work is almost coeval, and reciprocal, with the work ethos affecting religious values and structures, and with religion shaping and supporting the ideology of work. Predating the expulsion from the Garden of Eden and the designation of work as repentence was the report that "God took the man, and put him into the garden of Eden to dress it and to keep it." Commentaries on this fact include the sentence: "Not indolence but congenial work is Man's divinely allotted portion."[57] Perhaps as a consequence, the rites in which the Hebrew Priests and Levites engaged during the days of the two Temples—in effect, "dressing and keeping" the faith—are referred to in the Hebrew Bible as *avodah,* one of the dictionary definitions of which is simply "work." Later, Jesus found it necessary to admonish Martha, who evidently was continuing with established values in believing that carrying on with her housework was more important than the "laziness" of simply sitting and listening.

From a structural point of view, almost every western religion was organized on hierarchical lines, anticipating and laying a basis for later bureaucracy as described by Weber. This structure involved the division of labor and specialization, beginning with Jethro's famous advice to his son-in-law Moses,[58] continuing into the fixed hierarchy of the Catholic Church (among others), down to priests who specialize—in pastoral counseling, in preaching, in theological disputation, in social action, or in other areas. The principles of business organization and religious organization are thoroughly intermingled.

The church as business is further evidenced by the property holdings and investments of many church groups, which not only require that they engage in complicated business dealings, but also give them power to determine economic policies. In some cases this is in a limited area, as when buying up slum property in the neighborhood of the church to maintain property values, or to rehabilitate the neighborhood, or to raze it, or as a future investment, thereby affecting the quality of life and—to some extent—the standard of living of the neighborhood dwellers. In other cases this power may be considerable: Early in the twentieth century the Greek Orthodox Church owned vast tracts of land in and around Jerusalem, which partially determined property values and the pattern of urban growth. There are even those who hold that fund-raising ability among clergy affects upward mobility within the hierarchy.[59]

On a semantic level, acts of charity are, as noted previously, known as good works. Preachers, priests, and laymen speak of doing the Lord's work. Clerics "work in the vineyard of the Lord." Henry Ward Beecher exhorted men to "work" with God, the "great Worker," in "hammering out" their salvation.[60] God was presented as presiding over his "toiling" creation,[61] and pictured as the "supreme Supervisor" of workers.[62] Even today, church groups engage in "mergers," rather than combining or joining together.[63]

Insofar as activities are concerned, the emergence of "worker-priests" further indicates the interpenetration of religion and work. Similarly, one of the bases of the Zionist movement was to "invert the economic pyramid," which was felt to be top-heavy with intellectuals and merchants, in order to create a base of farmers and laborers. In this vein, an early pioneer in the Holy Land traveled the length and breadth of the country, preaching "The Religion of Labor"—a theology that proved particularly appealing to the emancipated, revolutionary, non- or antireligious youth who made up the bulk of the early pioneers. Contrariwise, in medieval Europe there were heretical sects who emphasized work as painful and humiliating, and therefore a desirable scourge for the pride of the flesh.[64]

However, it was without question the emergence of the Protestant Ethic, through the activities of Luther and Calvin, which not only gave work religion's official stamp of approval, but which saw in work the fulfillment of God's will, and almost the only divinely inspired, approved, and required activity on the part of man. The emergence and the influence of the Protestant Ethic has been too fully and too well described to warrant repetition here,[65] so suffice it to say that the concept of work as carrying out God's will became deeply rooted, not only in Protestant countries, but in Catholic ones as well; thereby acquiring a moral value which transcended the purely instrumental aspects of working for a living. Among the values ascribed to work, one was an antidote against religious doubts and against sexual temptations: "Along with a moderate vegetable diet and cold baths . . . work hard in your calling."[66] Hard work was also recommended as a remedy for sedition.[67] Perhaps more important, work was a preventative for adultery: "Pains in a calling will consume a great part of that superfluous nourishment that yields matter to this sin. It will turn the blood and spirits another way."[68] In short:

> Work had every advantage. It was good in itself. It satisfied the selfish economic interest of the growing number of small employers or self-employed. It was a social duty, it contributed to a good reputation among one's fellows, and to an assured position in the eyes of God. Work was becoming a standard, a cliche, cure-all.[69]

Among other things, the Protestant Ethic helped create a mass of sober, conscientious, and unusually industrious workmen,[70] who precisely fitted the needs of the nascent Industrial Revolution. Conversely, employers saw themselves (or, at least, said they saw themselves) as offering people an opportunity to serve God. Hence, those who refused to work, or to work under the conditions offered, were sinners. Similarly, the formation of labor unions, strikes, and other forms of labor unrest were not seen as protective actions on the part of workers, but as rebelliousness against God's natural order. Anthony points out that employers contribute to the production of various statements which set out the worker's duty in religious terms.[71] It is no wonder, then, that "Christian institutions have constantly adjusted . . . so that the independence of their values have been sacrificed to the need to continue to achieve influence over economic drives,"[72] and that some ministers complain that they would be better off with a degree in business administration instead of the traditional degree in religion.[73] Calvin Coolidge, when president, said: "The man who builds a factory builds a temple, and the man who works there worships there." Bruce Barton said that if Jesus were alive today he would be an account executive in an advertising agency.[74]

There has also been a carry-over from the world of religion to the world of work in terms of rites and values displayed in the work place, and even in industrial disputes. Catholic workers have been known to kiss the cross when swearing not to scab during a strike; Jewish workers under similar circumstances have taken an oath derived from Psalm 137, including the penalty, "May my right hand wither . . . " As late as 1910 a mine boss and alleged labor spy was physically crucified while wearing a crown of thorns, in Pennsylvania.[75]

It is possible to view many of the rites and traditions of the world of work as neoreligious manifestations without resorting to such hyperbole as serving in the Temple of Mammon. There are symbols ranging from the hard hat to the attache case; the omnipresent and incorruptible time clock; the pocket calculator of varying degrees of complexity; and even, in some places, rank established by smoking cigarettes, cigars, or pipes, or being a nonsmoker. There are holy places, including executive lunchrooms, elevators, and parking places, as well as entire parking lots; with the office of Top Brass referred to, only half-jocularly, as the Holy of Holies. Middle management often serve as priests, mediating between supplicants and unseen deities. There are rites too numerous to list: coffee breaks, retirement ceremonies, orientation, Christmas parties, and so on. And, finally, one tithes—to Social Security, union funds, pension funds, charity check-offs, and the like. In short, as Vernon holds, the boundaries between business and religion have not yet been definitely and finally drawn.[76]

WORK AND THE FAMILY

The world of work also has impact in various ways on the family. "In all societies, the family system and the occupational system are closely related. The family prepares the individual for work and is the immediate beneficiary of his labor."[77] Further, the move from the traditional extended family to the modern nuclear family was brought about, in large measure, by the needs of modern industrialization. Indeed, there are definitions of work as that which is *not* done in the family setting.[78]

Hofstede points out that many firms and industries start out as family businesses,[79] and these necessitate family arrangements usually dictated by the necessities of the business. Indeed, successful careers are said to always involve a trade-off between the demands of the career and those of family life.[80] The extent to which these demands are met in favor of the career, rather than the family, are both culturally and temporally determined. In one survey, German respondents increased their responses that when the job demands it the family should be prepared to come second from 1973 to 1977, with male respondents so answering in over 50 percent of the cases.[81] In the United States, however, there seems to be an increasing tendency to refuse promotions that involve uprooting the family or require being away from them for long periods.

The deleterious effect of prolonged unemployment on family relationships has been noted in a number of places, and detailed in some. These include family disorganization, poorer school grades for children, diminished sexual drive coupled with a high rate of illegitimacy, a high level of mother-headed families, and a lower rate of remarriages among the divorced women.[82] On the other hand, leisure as such has not been found to have a negative effect on family relationships, at least insofar as married couples are concerned. On the contrary, time spent at home is an extraordinarily strong factor in marital cohesion.[83]

One of the areas of strong impact of the work world on the family in recent years has been occasioned by the increasing entry of women into the labor force. The necessity that women go to work, and the desire on the part of some of them to do so, has had its impact in the women's liberation movement to the point that there are demands from a number of quarters that housework be redefined as "real" or "market" work, and/or paid, so that it can give status to the person engaged in it.[84] As increasing numbers of women join the labor force, however, attention is being turned to the possible effects of this movement on family life. Rossi discusses the possible conflicts revolving around the role of the mother in such cases,[85] while Hoffman and Nye point out that the entry of women into the labor force is made possible by decreasing demands for child care and care of the elderly at home, due to growth of alternative arrangements.[86] It is possible, however, that the growth of alternative arrangements is made necessary by the desire of many women to work. In any case, one of the growth industries in the United States for years has been that of homes for the aged and child-care facilities. Hoffman and Nye discuss working mothers from point of view of the possible effects on children, on power and division in the family, on husband-wife relationships, and on the wife as mother.[87] A further influence of work on families is the fact that working women tend to have fewer children[88]—a fact that is welcomed and encouraged in some areas as an answer to the population problem, and viewed with alarm in others. Finally, there are the dilemmas, stresses, and strains of the dual-career families, in which both husband and wife pursue their own vocations.[89]

Not only does work intrude on family structure and relationships—there is also a reverse effect. This is reflected in the phenomenon of children following, or rejecting, the parent's field or job; the parent as role model of a worker; and adolescent revolt being directed against employers rather than parents. In any case, the reciprocal influence of work and family is no less obvious and important than the other areas discussed above.[90]

WORK AND LEISURE

The area of leisure is, by definition, linked closely to the world of work. Cheek holds that it is difficult to define leisure rigorously, as it is a cafeteria concept residual to work.[91] However, Neulinger distinguishes between leisure, the job, and work;[92] Csikszentimihalyi introduces the concept of "flow" at work as being a type of leisure;[93] De Grazia distinguishes between leisure and free time;[94] and Kaplan notes and examines given elements in definitions of leisure.[95] Despite such analytic exercises, to the person in the street, leisure is seen as freedom from work (as defined previously).

Not only does work operate to define leisure, but the content of leisure-time activities are said to be related to work. One view holds that there is a spillover effect from work—the quality of a person's work experiences are considered to spill over and affect the quality of experiences away from work.[96] In effect, this says that one who has become accustomed to doing precise, time-consuming tasks at work, for example, will seek the same kind of activity in his or her leisure time. Or, one who is a member of a close work group will seek leisure-time experiences within groups. The opposite view—and there is little empirical evidence on either side—is that leisure is a kind of compensatory activity that repays employees for stultifying job experiences.[97] By extension, people seek in leisure the kinds of experiences they cannot get at work.

Be that as it may, the fact remains that leisure time has become enlarged almost entirely as a result of work time being reduced. It is interesting in this connection that leisure-time experts and professionals, who probably really do see leisure as a social good, have been strangely silent as regards demanding or trying to bring about more leisure. Leisure is accepted, as it were, as scraps from the table of work.

The relationship between leisure and work has been traced by Argyle,[98] who finds similarities between them as regards so-called constructive leisure, cultural pursuits, family-centered leisure, and pure relaxation. Only sport is found to be unrelated to work, but this is true only in regard to amateur sports—an increasingly endangered species. Even here company teams, uniforms provided as advertising, and "subsidies" and "scholarships" mark the invasion of the world of work into the area of sports.

So completely has the work ethic captured other aspects of society that it is held that leisure, to be satisfying in any important sense, must be a kind of "moral equivalent of work."[99] Herzberg goes further, and says that leisure, *above all other segments of life,* has become captive to the industrial complex.[100] Levy details the size of the leisure industry (note the terminology): In 1972 expenditures for leisure were $100 billion more than the cost of national defense.[101]

Kateb, writing about the enemies of utopia, balances the ills that arise from working with those that arise from leisure, and concludes that the pains associated with unlimited leisure would be far less awful than the pains banished from such a utopia.[102]

In these ways the world of leisure is limited by, takes its meaning from, and serves the world of work.

WORK AND OTHER AREAS OF LIFE

The impact of the work ethic on the world of politics is reported from Britain, where industry appears to have permanently occupied the field of politics.[103] The process of communicating an ideology of work has become an important part of the business of government,[104] and both capitalism and communism exhibit a deep commitment to an ideology of work, issuing appeals that work should be undertaken willingly.[105] Indeed, the constitution of supposedly anti- or irreligious Russia (or, more correctly, the Soviet Union) quotes directly from the New Testament: "He who will not work shall not eat."[106] An enormous amount of time is given over by the parliaments and executives of western countries to discussions and decisions concerning manpower policies, full employment, increasing the labor force, labor mobility, and the like.[107]

National defense also partakes of the rhetoric of work—"Give us the tools and we will do the job," for example; or recruitment efforts which emphasize learning a useful trade in the service, rather than defending the country. Even the criminal justice system partakes of the work syndrome. The workhouse—that predecessor of the prison—offered the threat of incarceration at hard labor as its chief deterrent. In a further development, punishment for the petty criminal necessitated a structure to force inmates to labor, and the institution's designers believed it could be used for setting the idle to work.[108] The influence of work on the criminal justice system is evidenced by sentences which include the words "at hard labor," on the one hand, and prison workshops used to keep prisoners busy, to make them happy, to rehabilitate them for the world of work, to offer them a chance to earn some money, to earn money for the institution, or to make them "useful," on the other.[109] Probation and parole often require not just evidence of a crime-free life, but make holding a job a condition for continued freedom.

Therapy, and particularly rehabilitation, depends heavily upon work both as a means, and as the (often sole) criterion of success.[110] Returning the incapacitated to the world of work usually takes precedence over evidence of improved family functioning, better relationships with others, improved self-images, greater physical abilities, and personal happiness. For example, the highly skilled, independent technician who is injured, but "rehabilitated" to the point that he or she can work as time checker might be a success story from a statistical point of view, but is hardly so from a personal one.

As Anthony points out, "There is no theoretical challenge to the system of values which maintains and is supported by an ideology of work [because] . . . alternative systems of values have been virtually destroyed."[111] For example, in 1883 Karl Marx's son-in-law, Paul Lafargue, proclaimed for the working class the "right to be lazy."[112] Although he was not against labor as a concept, but only opposed the monotonous, unpleasant, exploitative work to which laborers were being subjected, this fine distinction was washed out by the triumph of the Revolution, as was any recognition of the right to live without working. Emphasis on work as a national duty, a civic virtue, and an ennobling experience for the individual is a steadfast article of faith in communist states. In this respect, at least, there is very little difference between communist and capitalist societies. Indeed, Anthony speaks of a convergence of the two systems.[113] Throughout the modern West there is an almost overwhelming emphasis on the importance and desirability of work.[114] Thus, both the religious and the nonreligious, communists and capitalists, agree on work as a societal value of the highest order.

SUMMARY

The impact of the work ethic on various aspects of society, as pointed out above, is to socialize people into believing that work in and of itself is both necessary and desirable; that it is required for society and for the individual; that there is no better way to structure time, distribute resources, and create happiness; and that to work is to be a good citizen, a good neighbor, and a normal, moral, religious person. Consequently, the goal of every societal institution—as well illustrated by social welfare—is to persuade, coerce, cajole, and force people to work, and to attempt to get them to work more or to work harder.[115] The pursuit of productivity has been more than a thread—indeed, a veritable rope—running throughout history, and woven into that thread has been the search for practical, reliable, generalizable incentives that will result in harder work on the part of individuals. It is to this pursuit that we turn in the next chapter.

NOTES

1. M. M. Machlowitz, "The Workaholic." Yale University, 1976 (mimeo).

2. Engnell holds that in Biblical days emphasis was nowhere placed upon work for its own sake: "The evaluation of work is entirely negative." Gartner speaks of the New Testament: "The Sabbath is sometimes represented . . . as a foretaste of the world to come. . . . The Messianic age will be a blessed age in which there will be no work." I. Engnell, "The Biblical Attitude to Work: Work in the Old Testament"; B. Gartner, "Work in the New Testament"; *Svensk Exegetisk Aarsbak* 26 (1961): 5-18; quoted by K. Stendahl, "Religion, Mysticism, and the Institutional Church," in D. Bell (ed.) *Toward the Year 2000: Work in Progress* (Boston: Beacon, 1967). See also D. Macarov, *The Design of Social Welfare* (New York: Holt, Rinehart & Winston, 1978).

3. Macarov, ibid.

4. D. Macarov, "Social Welfare as a By-Product: The Effect of Neo-Mercantilism." *Journal of Sociology and Social Welfare* 4 (November 1977): 1135-1144.

5. A. Toffler, *The Third Wave* (New York: Bantam, 1980), p. 384.

6. T. Caplow, *The Sociology of Work* (New York: McGraw-Hill, 1954), p. 274.

7. P. D. Anthony, *The Ideology of Work* (London: Tavistock, 1978), p. 156.

8. Ibid.

9. F. Herzberg, *Work and the Nature of Man* (Cleveland: World, 1966).

10. J. O'Toole, *Work, Learning, and the American Future* (San Francisco: Jossey-Bass, 1977), p. 34.

11. E. F. Schumacher, *Good Work* (New York: Harper & Row, 1979), p. 118.

12. I. Berg, *Education and Jobs: The Great Training Robbery* (Boston: Beacon, 1971), p. xii.

13. U. S. Department of Health, Education and Welfare, *Work in America* (Cambridge: MIT Press, 1973), p. 134.

14. G. Hunnius, "On the Nature of Capitalist-Initiated Innovations in the Workplace," in T. R. Burns, L. E. Karlsson and V. Rus (eds.) *Work and Power: The Liberation of Work and the Control of Political Power* (Beverly Hills, CA: Sage, 1979), p. 302.

15. S. Bowles and H. Gintis, *Schooling in Capitalist America: Educational Reform and the Contradictions of Economic Life* (New York: Basic Books, 1976), p. 9.

16. Ibid., p. 129.

17. D. T. Rodgers, *The Work Ethic in Industrial America 1850-1920* (Chicago: University of Chicago Press, 1974), p. 128.

18. W. A. Westley and M. W. Westley, *The Emerging Worker: Equality and Conflict in the Mass Consumption Society* (Montreal: McGill-Queen's University Press, 1971), p. 26.

19. "Technology introduced another and increasingly ominous distinction: unlike the nineteenth century type of industry, which had an almost unlimited demand for men and women without any qualification except strength and willingness, the technology of the mid-twentieth century has less and less use for them." E. J. Hobsbawn, *Industry and Empire: An Economic History of Britain Since 1750* (London: Weidenfeld and Nicolson, 1968), p. 245; "Large numbers of slum youngsters cannot qualify for employment in an increasingly automated society." A. B. Shostak, "Educational Reforms and Poverty," in A. B. Shostak and W. Gomberg (eds.) *New Perspectives on Poverty* (Englewood Cliffs, NJ: Prentice-Hall, 1965), p. 64.

20. See D. Macarov, *Work and Welfare: The Unholy Alliance* (Beverly Hills, CA: Sage, 1980), pp. 77-78.

21. For a fuller explanation, see Macarov, *The Design of Social Welfare*, op. cit., pp. 206-211.

22. U.S. Department of Health, Education, and Welfare, *Social Security Programs Throughout the World 1977* (Washington, DC: Author, 1977).

23. Ibid.

24. Ibid.

25. Ibid.

26. L. P. Adams, *Public Attitudes Toward Unemployment Insurance: A Historical Account with Reference to Alleged Abuse* (Kalamazoo: Upjohn, 1971), p. 21.

27. Ibid.

28. M. E. Schiltz, *Public Attitudes Toward Social Security 1935-1965* (Washington, DC: Department of Health, Education, and Welfare, 1970), p. 93.

29. R. C. Lampman, "Employment versus Income Maintenance," in Ginzberg, E. (ed.) *Jobs for Americans* (Englewood Cliffs, NJ: Prentice-Hall, 1976), pp. 163-183.

30. Sommer, for example, holds that work as a clinical goal can be a valid focus for treatment. J. J. Sommer, "Work as a Therapeutic Goal: Union-Management Clinical Contribution to a Mental Health Program." *Mental Hygiene* 53 (1969): 263-268.

31. J. A. Kershaw, "The Attack on Poverty," in M. S. Gordon (ed.) *Poverty in America* (San Francisco: Chandler, 1965), p. 56.

32. B. J. Black, "Vocational Rehabilitation," in *Encyclopedia of Social Work* (New York: National Association of Social Workers, 1965), pp. 819-820.

33. U. S. Department of Health, Education, and Welfare, *Social Security Programs . . .* , op. cit., p. xiii.

34. Ibid., p. xxii.

35. Ibid.

36. D. Macarov, "Management in the Social Work Curriculum." *Administration in Social Work* 1 (1977): 135.

37. D. Griffiths, *The Waiting Poor: An Argument for Abolition of the Waiting Period on Unemployment and Sickness Benefits* (Fitzroy, Victoria, Australia: Brotherhood of Saint Laurence, 1974), p. 3.

38. U.S. Department of Health, Education, and Welfare, *Social Security Programs . . .* , op. cit., p. xx.

39. M. Bruce, "Thirty Years on the Politics of Welfare." *Social Service Quarterly* 52 (1978): 5-8.

40. Macarov, *The Design of Social Welfare*, op. cit., p. 121.

41. *Employment and Unemployment, May 1977* (Canberra: Bureau of Statistics, 1977), pp. 10-13.

42. Organisation for Economic Co-operation and Development, *Main Economic Indicators: Historical Statistics, 1955-1971* (Paris: Author); also *Supplements 1, 2, and 3,* May, August, and November, 1977.

43. F. Field, "Making Sense of the Unemployment Figures," in F. Field, *The Conscript Army* (London: Routledge & Kegan Paul, 1977).

44. This position is clearly expressed by Plattner, taking issue with the idea that "the person who works harder is entitled to nothing more, while the person who works less hard gains a greater claim over what others have produced. The moral absurdity of this view is transparent." M. F. Plattner, "The Welfare State *vs.* the Redistributive State." *Public Interest* 55 (1979): 28-48.

45. R. M. Ball, *Social Security Today and Tomorrow* (New York: Columbia University Press, 1978), p. 23.

46. M. G. Arnold and G. Rosenbaum, *The Crime of Poverty* (Skokie, IL: National Textbook, 1973), 242-266.

47. For comparative purposes: Vestedness for old-age payments in the Soviet Union and Eastern Europe vary from 10 to 25 years. Payments to single individuals vary from 38 percent to 75 percent of the average annual wage, and 47 percent to 85 percent for couples. J. L. Porket, "Old Age Pension Schemes in the Soviet Union and Eastern Europe." *Social Policy and Administration* 13 (1979): 22-36.

48. N. Gottlieb, *The Welfare Bind* (New York: Columbia, 1974), p. 19.

49. M. N. Ozawa, "Issues in Welfare Reform." *Social Service Review* 52 (1978): 37.

50. Despite the mythology of other income, only 20 percent of the people over 65 in the United States in 1973 had any type of supplementary benefits, such as private insurance or private pension plans, and only about 30 percent in 1975. J. Galper, "Private Pensions and Public Policy." *Social Work* 18 (1973): 5-22; Ball, op. cit., p. 390.

51. U.S. Department of Health, Education, and Welfare, *Social Security Bulletin, Annual Statistical Supplement, 1975* (Washington: Author, 1975).

52. R. F. Henderson, *Poverty in Australia,* Volume One (Canberra: Australian Government Printing Service, 1975), p. 13.

53. *Poverty* 39 (1978): 7.

54. D. L. Grimaldi, "Distributive and Fiscal Impacts of the Supplemental Security Income Program." *Review of Social Economy* 26 (1978): 175-196.

55. Ball, op. cit., p. 27.

56. S. Dasgupta, "Facing the New Era: A Plea for a New Approach to Human Well-Being," in *Human Well-Being: The Challenge of Continuity and Change* (New York: International Council on Social Welfare, 1978), p. 52.

57. J. H. Hertz (ed.), *The Pentateuch and Haftorahs* (Philadelphia: Jewish Publication Society, 1917), p. 8.

58. In summary: "Moses chose capable men . . . and appointed them heads over the people—chiefs of thousands, hundreds, fifties, and tens. And they exercised authority over the people at all times: the difficult matters they would bring to Moses, and all the minor matters they would decide themselves." *Exodus* 18:13-27.

59. See, for example, the fictional priest in C. McCullough, *The Thorn Birds* (New York: Harper & Row, 1977).

60. Rodgers, op. cit., p. 97.

61. Ibid., p. 101.

62. Anthony, op. cit., p. 43.

63. G. M. Vernon, "Religion as a Social Problem," in E. O. Smigel (ed.) *Handbook on the Study of Social Problems* (Chicago: Rand-McNally, 1971), p. 390.

64. A. Parker, *The Future of Work and Leisure* (New York: Praeger, 1971), p. 35.

65. The classical treatise is that of M. Weber, *The Protestant Ethic and the Spirit of Capitalism* (New York: Scribners, 1952).

66. Anthony, op. cit., p. 42.

67. Ibid., p. 43.

68. Ibid., p. 44.

69. Ibid.

70. Ibid., pp. 42-43.

71. Ibid., p. 302.

72. Ibid., p. 274.

73. Herzberg, op. cit., p. 4.

74. W. Manchester, *The Glory and the Dream* (Boston: Little, Brown, 1973), p. 25.

75. H. G. Gutman, *Work, Culture and Society in Industrializing America* (New York: Knopf, 1976), pp. 65-66.

76. Vernon, op. cit., p. 387.

77. Caplow, op. cit., p. 248.

78. G. Hofstede, *Culture's Consequences: International Differences in Work-Related Values* (Beverly Hills, CA: Sage, 1980), p. 163.

79. Ibid., p. 390.

80. Ibid., p. 376.

81. Ibid., p. 370.

82. O'Toole, op. cit., pp. 20-21.

83. K. Varga, "Marital Cohesion as Reflected in Time-Budgets," in A. Szalai (ed.) *The Use of Time* (The Hague: Mouton, 1972).

84. H. J. Weiner and S. H. Akabas, *Work in America: The View from Industrial Social Welfare* (New York: Columbia University School of Social Work, Industrial Social Welfare Center, 1974), p. 7; and D. G. Gil, *Unravelling Social Policy* (Cambridge, MA: Schenkman, 1973).

85. A. S. Rossi, "Equality Between the Sexes: An Immodest Proposal," in R. L. Coser (ed.) *Life Cycle and Achievement in America* (New York: Harper & Row, 1969), p. 153.

86. L. W. Hoffman and F. I. Nye, *Working Mothers* (San Francisco: Jossey-Bass, 1975).

87. Ibid.

88. Ibid., p. 81.

89. M. P. Fogarty, R. Rapoport, and R. P. Rapoport, "Dual-career Families," in D. Weir (ed.) *Men and Work in Modern Britain* (Bungay, Suffolk: Fontana, 1973), pp. 181-192.

90. "The reference to the company as a family . . . has become a management cliche." D. Katz and R. L. Kahn, *The Social Psychology of Organizations* (New York: John Wiley, 1978), p. 377.

91. N. H. Cheek, Jr., "Toward a Sociology of Not-Work," in T. B. Johannis, Jr., and C. N. Bull (eds.) *Sociology of Leisure* (Beverly Hills, CA: Sage, 1971), pp. 7-20.

92. J. Neulinger, *The Psychology of Leisure: Research Approaches to the Study of Leisure* (Springfield, IL: Charles C Thomas, 1974).

93. M. Csikszentimihalyi, *Beyond Boredom and Anxiety* (San Francisco: Jossey-Bass, 1975).

94. S. De Grazia, *Of Time, Work and Leisure* (New York: Twentieth Century Fund, 1962).

95. M. Kaplan, *Leisure: Theory and Policy* (New York: John Wiley, 1975), p. 29.

96. J. E. Champoux, "The World of Nonwork: Some Implications for Job Re-Design Efforts." *Personnel Psychology* 33 (1980): 61-75.

97. I. Berg, "Foreword," in S. Parker, *The Future of Work and Leisure* (New York: Praeger, 1971), p. 4.

98. M. Argyle, *The Social Psychology of Work* (Harmondsworth: Penguin, 1972), p. 258.

99. Ibid., p. 260.

100. Herzberg, op. cit.

101. J. Levy, *Play Behavior* (New York: John Wiley, 1978), p. 41.

102. G. Kateb, *Utopia and Its Enemies* (New York: Schocken, 1963), p. 137.

103. Anthony, op. cit., p. 301.

104. Ibid., p. 303.

105. Ibid., p. 8.

106. *Constitution of the Union of Soviet Socialist Republics 1936,* Article 12; *Thessalonians* 3:10. The Russian attitude to work is exemplified in a statement which must have received official approval: "Labor is the foundation of human existence, the main connecting rod of the history of society; together with nature, it is the source of all wealth and of the values of human culture. . . . Labor is the foundation of the existence of any society in the sense that all social relationships . . . develop in the sphere of labor, or else relative to labor and its results. Labor . . . is the foundation of the structure of society." A. G. Zdravomyslov, V. P. Rozhin, and V. A. Iadov, *Man and His Work* (White Plains, NY: International Arts and Sciences Press, 1967; translated from the Russian by S. P. Dunn).

107. See D. Macarov, "Work and the Prospect of Social Development: In the West and Elsewhere." Paper presented at the Seminar on Social Development, Institute of Social Studies, The Hague, Netherlands, May 1981.

108. D. J. Rothman, *The Discovery of the Asylum* (Boston: Little, Brown, 1971), pp. 25-26.

109. At the moment of writing, the magazine section of the *Jerusalem Post* contains an article entitled "Productivity in the Prisons." *Jerusalem Post,* July 17, 1981.

110. B. J. Black, "Vocational Rehabilitation," in *Encyclopedia of Social Work* (New York: National Association of Social Workers, 1965), pp. 819-820. See also J. F. Garrett and B. W. Griffis, "The Economic Benefits of Rehabilitation for the Mentally Retarded." *Welfare in Review* 9 (1971): 1-7.

111. Anthony, op. cit., p. 273.

112. M. R. Marrus (ed.), *The Emergence of Leisure* (New York: Harper & Row, 1974).

113. Anthony, op. cit., p. 8.

114. Sarason interprets *The Death of a Salesman* in this manner: "If anything is clear in this play . . . it is how the experience of work is inevitably affected by and affects all other significant areas of living." S. B. Sarason, *Work, Aging and Social Change: Professionals and the One-Life One-Career Imperative* (New York: Free Press, 1977), p. 64.

115. R. Segalman, "The Protestant Ethic and Social Welfare." *Journal of Social Issues* 24 (1968): 125-141.

3

THE PURSUIT OF PRODUCTIVITY

REDUCING HUMAN LABOR

People have been seeking ways to increase productivity since the beginnings of recorded history. In some cases the goal is to increase output, and in others it is to reduce the amount of human labor needed, but the desire for greater output, or the same amount for less input—both of which spell productivity—has deep historical roots. When primitive society divided work between the old and the young, or between men and women, this rudimentary division of labor resulted in specialization and greater returns. When human effort was augmented or replaced by animal power, the result was less human work and more production. Technical advances, from the wheel to computers, either reduced the amount of human energy necessary, increased the amount of production, or did both.

In the preindustrial world, however, there was a natural barrier to increased production. When a farmer produced as much as he and his family needed, there was little reason to work for a surplus. This was due not only to the absence of storage (and particularly refrigeration) facilities and transportation, but also to the fact that there was no societal structure for converting surplus crops into other items. In the absence of a money economy, time and effort invested in producing more agricultural products than the farmer's family could use were—with the exception of the small amount that could be bartered for other items—simply wasted.

During the feudal period additional produce simply went to the ruling lord. He may have pressed his peasants to work harder, but there was little gain for themselves in doing so, which was hardly an incentive to work harder. Nor is the amount of agricultural produce primarily determined by the quality or the quantity of human labor—agriculture is affected to a much greater extent by relatively uncontrollable events, such as rain or its lack, sun, soil quality, and the presence of pests, than it is by the amount of human work. Finally, there is the fact that farm work is mostly drudgery—hard, monotonous, wearying labor—as many foreign volunteers to Israeli kibbutzim, and many city dwellers who decide to become farmers, learn to their dismay.

It is no wonder, then, that the average farmer in the West had more than a hundred holidays a year.[1] Indeed, such days off, in the form of saints' days, other religious holidays, the king's birthday, and local events, were often deliberately provided to keep the population occupied and happy, and on the assumption that not only does the Devil find work for idle hands, but that social unrest is germinated and nurtured among people with nothing else to do.

There is a good deal of tangential evidence to support the thesis that people did not see more production as a goal in itself, and consequently did not work hard of their own volition. For example, when the Israelites in ancient Egypt complained about the lack of straw for brick making, they were not concerned about production as such, but rather with the punishment imposed for not meeting quotas. Mendelssohn holds that the building of the later pyramids had no goal other than that of providing employment, and thereby subsistence to workers—the pyramids themselves were not needed or wanted.[2] Incidentally, he also holds that, contrary to popular belief, the pyramids were not built by slave labor, but by Egyptians who saw in their work a religious content (thereby anticipating Luther by many centuries). The reforms of Diocletian, in the third century, which required sons to continue in their fathers' occupations, were made necessary by the growing practice among young people to seek easier work.[3]

Even today there are places where increased production by the individual farmer brings little personal return, for reasons ranging from a shortage of jute bags in which to pack the surplus[4] to absentee landlords who literally confiscate the additional produce.[5] In such situations, workers or farmers seek new tools and new methods more for greater comfort than for greater productivity, except where increased productivity immediately and directly results in shorter hours or easier living.[6]

The desire to avoid work, or not to work hard, is further evidenced by the numerous exhortations on the part of rulers, moralists, prophets, and priests that people should work hard: the fables, such as that of the grasshopper and the ant; proverbs, such as "Look to the ant, thou sluggard"; and even modern epigrams, such as "Nobody ever died of hard work." All of these indicate a societal need to spur people on—a need which would not have existed if people had not been avoiding work. Indeed, much later Sigmund Freud arrived at the conclusion, after much delving into the unconscious thoughts, feelings, and motivations of his clients, that there exists a natural human aversion to work.[7]

It is not surprising that this is so. The ubiquitous myth of the happy preindustrial farmer, responding to the seasons and getting active satisfaction from being attuned to nature, has been seriously questioned by objective research.[8] Indeed, there is the view that, to most people, work has always been ugly, crippling, and dangerous.[9] Consequently, until the advent of the

Industrial Revolution, attempts to improve productivity have probably been more in the direction of reducing human effort than in the direction of acquiring greater output.

One of the first uses of cybernation, or self-regulating machines, and an important contribution to the beginnings of the Industrial Revolution, was due to the boredom and/or laziness of one Humphrey Potter. In 1713, 12-year-old Humphrey was hired by Thomas Newcomen, who had invented a steam engine (50 years before Watt's) used to drain the water from mine pits, to open the valves on the engine whenever the steam pressure reached a dangerous point, and to close them again when the pressure subsided. Soon tiring of the monotonous task of opening and closing the valves, young Potter rigged up an ingenious arrangement of strings and levers by which the steam pressure itself opened the valve, allowing it to close again as the pressure dropped. Unfortunately for the history of work and productivity, we are not told whether Newcomen gave Potter a bonus for his invention and let him go, shifted him to other tasks, or, perhaps, gave him a laboratory to work on other inventions; or whether he boxed his ears for being a lazy lout and fired him. We can be reasonably sure, however, that Newcomen did not continue Potter on salary just to stand and watch his invention work. The day of changes in work patterns purely for personal ease was coming to an end.

INCREASING OUTPUT

With the rise of guilds, and the emergence of a stratum of craftsmen and tradesmen, surplus agricultural products began to be of some value, but insofar as the great bulk of society—the farmers—was concerned, finding ways to work less hard, rather than working harder, remained the goal of the individual. It was only with the beginnings of industrialization and a widespread money economy that increasing the output of goods became more important than decreasing the input of labor, and then more in the eyes of the country's rulers, or the owners of industries, than in the view of the workers. At one time the accepted role of profits was to pay the country's soldiers, and later the previously mentioned concept of mercantilism came into play, wherein the wealth of the country was seen as more important than the welfare of individuals.[10]

The importance ascribed productivity during and after the Industrial Revolution is epitomized in Adam Smith's seminal treatise, *Inquiry into the Nature and Causes of the Wealth of Nations,* in which there appears a chapter devoted to "The Causes of the Improvement in the Productive Powers of Labour." Among other things, Smith was very impressed with the results of the division of labor and specialization, as he saw them in a pin factory:

One man draws out the wire, another straights it, a third cuts it, a fourth points it, a fifth grinds it at the top for receiving the head; to make the head requires two or three distinct operations; to put it on is a peculiar business; to whiten the pins is another; it is even a trade by itself to put them into the paper. . . . Ten persons . . . could make among them upwards of forty-eight thousand pins in a day. . . . But if they had all wrought separately and independently, . . . they certainly could not each of them have made twenty, perhaps not one pin in a day.[11]

Smith saw three advantages arising from this system. One was that workmen became more skilled in doing their single jobs; another was that the workers were able to stay in one place, with the material coming to them instead of having to move around (thus portending the later assembly line); and the third was that the simplicity of each job facilitated the invention and use of machines to do the various tasks. Insofar as the latter point is concerned, it might be well to let Smith speak for himself:

A great part of the machines made use of in those manufactures in which labor is most subdivided were originally the invention of common workmen who, being each of them employed in some very simple operation, naturally turned their thoughts toward finding out easier and readier methods of performing it.[12]

Smith, it will be noted, did not speak of the necessity for people to work harder, nor did he suggest reducing labor by means of his suggested changes. The changes which he advocated were to attain greater output with the same labor. The changes in machines and methods which followed during and after the next century had basically the same goal. It is obviously impossible to list or discuss all of them, but two will serve as the prototypes.

Eli Whitney, who had made ladies' hat pins at one time, was asked to devise a machine to separate cotton lint from the seeds—a job so difficult for human hands that it made the growth of cotton unprofitable. Using a series of hooks—which are basically bent pins—he increased output tremendously. In the area of new methods, it was also Eli Whitney who devised interchangeable parts for rifles, which reinforced the utility of division of labor and specialization. Invention followed invention—sewing machines, typewriters, reapers and binders, locomotives—and method change followed method change: Movable rollers with which to handle and transfer beef carcasses in slaughterhouses evolved into Ransom E. Olds's first automobile assembly line, in 1899.

Most of these inventions and changes were designed to increase production, and were not used to diminish or even to humanize labor as such, despite the conditions depicted by Dickens in England, and those existing in the sweatshops of the American east coast. On the contrary, the shortage of labor itself led to many inventions. Take, for example, the mechanical cotton picker. It was an article of faith in the American South for generations that no machine could be devised to pick cotton—how could a machine determine the difference between the cotton, the boll, a leaf, or the stem? It was not until the great exodus of southern black farmers to the cities and to the North created a desperate shortage of cottonpickers that the fancied difficulties were overcome and the mechanical cotton picker hove into sight.

Whether contemporary automation and cybernation arise from a desire to increase production, to reduce labor, from labor shortages, or from labor difficulties is a moot question. In many cases, there is probably a combination of these elements present.

Insofar as the history of the pursuit of productivity is concerned, two periods—scientific management and human relations in industry—are clearly demarcated, while the third—the structuralist approach—is more difficult to bound.

THE SCIENTIFIC MANAGEMENT SCHOOL

The forebears of the scientific management school include de Lahire, in France, who studied men lifting, carrying, and pulling weights, and decided that the force exerted depended upon the method used. This study was published in 1699. In 1781, M. Charles Augustus Coulomb, in France, published a study of the interaction of force, speed, and time to furnish the greatest quantity of action. Charles Babbage, in England, also studied "a fair day's work."[13] It is the name of Frederick W. Taylor, however, that is more generally connected with the idea of scientific management (a phrase coined by Justice Brandeis). When Taylor began searching for more efficient methods in American industrial settings at the end of the nineteenth century, he was clearly within the tradition of attempting to increase production, rather than of reducing labor. A successful manager himself, Taylor attempted to find the best fit among the worker, the tools, and the job. By studying the smallest possible fraction of each job, Taylor tried to find ways of better performing that fraction. This involved redesigning tools and reinstructing workers. Faced with the problem of shoveling pig iron, for example, Taylor experimented with different weights and shapes of shovels, different lengths of shovel handles, gripping the handle at various places and in different ways, the movement of arms, legs, and body, and myriad other aspects. This was seen as the application of science to what had been a hit-or-miss procedure, and became widely known as "scientific management."

Taylor was completely unconcerned about making the work easier for the laborer, except insofar as this might emerge as incidental to an increase in productive methods. For most jobs, he saw the worker as basically another tool, to be manipulated as needed for desired results. For some jobs, he declared, the more like an ox the worker was, the better—he was not only not required to think, to understand, to initiate, or to question, but was forbidden to try. As Taylor said: "What I demand of the worker is not to produce any longer by his own initiative, but to execute punctiliously the orders given, down to their minutest details."[14] This did not mean that Taylor ignored or disliked people. On the contrary, he was concerned about them, but felt that, to quote Drucker, "the ability to fill the belly comes first."[15]

Taylor's investigative methods for determining the one best way to do a job usually involved a stopwatch, and came to be known as "time-motion studies." Once workers began to recognize that the result of Taylor's work was more productivity for the company, but no gain for themselves, they began to resent and to resist the idea of time-motion studies, and the "speedup" which it almost invariably involved for the workers. Unions were, and in many cases continue to be, particularly watchful of and opposed to anything that seems to be a speedup.

Despite such resistance, Taylor's methods often resulted in dramatic increases in production. In other cases, however, the increase was never as high as prior calculations predicted. Even when increased productivity was shared somewhat with the workers, the predicted figures were not reached. Nevertheless, in many cases Taylor's methods increased productivity, although little attempt was made to increase the amount of effort or the energy that was being exerted by the worker of his or her own free will.

One result of Taylorism—stemming from Adam Smith's division of labor—was the division of jobs into smaller and smaller fragments. With each reduction in complexity, it was thought, there would arise greater specialized skill. It was Emile Durkheim, the French sociologist, who recognized the danger in such fragmentation of tasks, and predicted that the result would be alienation of workers from one another, resulting in anomie, or lack of norms and values, which would affect the mental health of the worker. In later years, with the advantage of hindsight, George Homans pointed out that the division of labor also reaches the point where it doesn't pay: The costs of introducing the scheme, training the workers, supervising such fragmentary tasks, keeping production records, and so on, may outweigh the gains in productivity.[16]

THE HUMAN RELATIONS SCHOOL

Despite such caveats, it was while trying to apply Taylor's methods that a group of researchers literally stumbled into what was to be the second important period in the pursuit of productivity, generally referred to as the human relations school. This is the method which takes into consideration workers' feelings, desires, and relationships with one another, and attempts to exploit them in the service of greater productivity.

The seminal study was conducted at the Hawthorne plant of the Western Electric Company, which began with the purpose of seeking ways to increase production by changing some of the physical conditions of work. There were, in total, fifteen experimental periods. They began in 1924, and for three years were devoted to changes in illumination in the work room to study the effect on productivity. As a matter of fact, the experiments were devoted to lowering illumination, but, to the surprise of the investigators, no amount of lowered illumination seemed to affect output.

Consequently, a second set of inquiries was begun in 1927, and lasted for five years. During this period the subjects were six women—all experienced operators—five of whom were engaged in assembling telephone relays, while the sixth brought and distributed the necessary parts.[17] Before any proposed change in conditions was instituted, it was discussed with the women, and initiated only with their agreement. The first change consisted of paying the subjects piece rates based on the output of the group of six, rather than as part of a group of one-hundred, as had been the case previously. Total output of the group then increased.

In the next experimental period, the group was given two rest pauses of five minutes each, one in the morning and one in the afternoon. There was a definite rise in output after institution of the rest periods. The rest periods were next changed to ten minutes each, and again output went up. During the next phase, there were six five-minute rest periods each day, but the women expressed some dislike for this pattern, and it was discontinued. In the seventh period, the workers were provided, at company expense, with light refreshments during the morning break. Production again increased. Further changes included stopping work a half-hour earlier, followed by a remarkable rise in output, then stopping another half-hour earlier, and introduction of a five-day week. Each of these changes resulted in higher output.

The experimenters then began varying the conditions—taking away some already instituted, substituting some for others, and finally returning to the conditions which existed at the beginning of the inquiry. This situation was continued for 12 weeks, and the daily and weekly output rose to a point higher than at any other time. Some of the previous changes were then reinstituted for 31 weeks—and output rose to even greater heights.[18]

The conclusion at which the experimenters, and many who followed them, arrived was that what had actually changed was the attitude of the workers, that is, that "measured experimental variables had little effect, but that the unmeasured quality of human relations . . . was responsible for most output improvements."[19] In other words, the relations between the workers, between the workers and their supervisors, and between the workers and the researchers, brought about by their participation in decision making, were responsible for the continuous growth in production. Having been treated like tools for years, the experience of being considered thinking, feeling human beings was responded to in the direction that they felt the researchers, or the company, wanted. So goes the explanation. The reasons for the overoptimism in Taylor's predictions concerning increased production by increased efficiency began to come clear to the researchers—the workers were affected in their work by their feelings.

It is hard to overestimate, or even to describe, the influence of these findings on incentive research, labor relations, organizational psychology, administration, and many other fields concerned with work and with productivity. The human relations school took over from scientific management, and concern for the workers' feelings and relationships became the focus of attention. There followed literally thousands of studies investigating relations between workers, group cohesiveness, the effect of organizational size on employee relationships, and similar human-relations-in-industry studies. Between 1946 and 1958 alone, 406 such studies were identified, and this number rose to over 3000 by 1976,[20] despite the fact that no review includes all the studies, and that the great bulk of studies, experiences, and experiments never find their way into print.[21] Taylor's concern for fit among workers, tools, and jobs was deemphasized, and concern with keeping employees happy with their fellow employees, their supervisors, and their own feelings became the name of the game. In some cases this resulted in company teams, games, outings, parties, and other comfort- and friendship-inducing procedures, to the point of giving the impression that the industry or service was being operated for the pleasure of the employees, rather than for the output of their activities. Social workers were employed by industries to help iron out interpersonal problems that cropped up at work. Suggestion boxes, opinion polls, worker participation in decision making—all stemmed from the desire to keep workers happy in the knowledge that management was concerned about them. Herzberg summed up this viewpoint succinctly, saying: "A supervisor is successful to the degree to which he focuses on the needs of his subordinates as individuals rather than on the goals of production."[22]

HERZBERG-TYPE STUDIES

Within that school of thought which holds that workers' satisfactions are important to production, no study or series of studies has resulted in the same impact as did Frederick Herzberg's investigation into the causes of worker satisfaction or dissatisfaction.[23] Herzberg's method was simplicity itself (and has been the root of some criticism of his findings): He simply asked workers to think of a time when they were very satisfied at work, and to relate the causes for such satisfaction; conversely, he asked the same workers to think of a time when they were very dissatisfied at work, and to name the causes. Herzberg replicated his original study in a number of different settings, and others have done the same, including (using a somewhat different methodology) a study in an Israeli kibbutz. The rather surprising finding from most of these studies is that satisfactions and dissatisfactions are not the obverse of one another. That is, satisfactions do not arise from lack of factors which cause dissatisfaction; and dissatisfaction is not a result of lack of satisfactions. In light of Herzberg's finding, different factors cause satisfactions and dissatisfactions. Satisfactions arise from feelings of achievement, recognition, the work itself, responsibility, and advancement; dissatisfactions come from company policy or administration, technical supervision, salary, interpersonal relationships (including those with supervisors), and working conditions. Hence, one may remove dissatisfactions without increasing satisfactions or increase satisfactions without affecting dissatisfactions.

Herzberg first termed his two categories "satisfactions" and "dissatisfactions," but later changed the former to "motivators" and the latter to "hygiene factors." Both logic and commonsense supported Herzberg's thesis that satisfiers are motivators, and, as a result, there began a search for those factors which give or increase the satisfactions of people at work. Such studies number, literally, in the thousands, and at almost regular intervals reviews of such studies are published.[24] One such review categorizes incentive studies into those that deal with

(1) participative supervision;
(2) opportunity to interact with peers;
(3) varied duties;
(4) high pay;
(5) promotional opportunities; and
(6) control over work methods and pace.[25]

Herzberg's experiments and findings have been subject to a number of criticisms, both methodological and substantive, while the critics have themselves been criticized.[26] One of the criticisms of Herzberg-type studies is that there is a marked uncertainty in the ways in which the money factor—wages, salaries, bonuses, premium payments, increases, and decreases—is handled. Herzberg himself wrote that "the . . . factor of salary is indeed complex,"[27] and, whereas in his initial study salary was listed as an item in its own right, it appears in the tables describing his subsequent studies only among housekeeping workers in a hospital—a notoriously underpaid group. In other cases it seems to be used as an indicator of recognition and achievement. Other researchers in this tradition have the same problem: "The subject of money is extremely complex and its exact influence is hard to determine . . . considering the manifold uses of money and the meaning it imparts to men [*sic*], it is little wonder that precise statements of its incentive effects are difficult."[28]

The difficulty of controlling for the effect of salary in incentive studies is evidenced by the fact that studies of salary as a work motivator in itself have found that it differs in its effect on various kinds of workers, such as unskilled, semiskilled, and highly skilled;[29] between the relatively well paid[30] and the clearly underpaid;[31] and between workers in affluent societies and those in countries with lower living standards.[32] It changes in its effect over time;[33] takes on symbolic meanings;[34] is affected by considerations of equity as well as of equality;[35] and may affect other variables in a manner not always observed or understood. It was for this reason, among others, that the research in an Israeli kibbutz, where money is not and cannot be a factor, was undertaken. That research is described in Chapter 5.

THE STRUCTURALIST SCHOOL

That the human relations approach increased workers' satisfactions in many areas can be deduced both from the reports of many experiments and from the reported experiences of many workers and industries. The effect upon productivity, however, as will be explicated later, was more questionable. Hence, within the relatively recent past there has begun a swing back from human relations as a panacea to a combination of scientific management and human relations, which is referred to as the structuralist approach.

The approach uses the principles of Taylorism in fitting the worker and the tools to the job, while at the same time being concerned with the workers' satisfactions. This process is referred to in many places as job redesign, that is, redividing, redefining, and reassigning jobs both on the basis of fit and on the basis of preference of the worker. In some cases the attempt to satisfy workers exhibits itself by allowing their participation in the planning of the redesign. This participation, in turn, may be accomplished through direct worker involvement in planning meetings, through representatives of groups of workers, having worker representatives on company boards, and in a number of other ways.

Perhaps the ideal type of the structuralist school, and certainly the most discussed and quoted, is the Scanlon Plan.[36] Named for Joseph Scanlon, this plan is virtually a blueprint for restructuring industries, or, at least, their decision-making processes. Basically, the Scanlon Plan consists of employee groups, or employee-foremen groups, who discuss methods and make suggestions for improvements in the productivity of the company. These suggestions are then evaluated by a joint management-worker committee, and those that are accepted are put into effect. Increased profits— sometimes involving intricate calculations as to what should be considered—are then shared with the workers. In some cases the profits are shared with all the workers, in others with the workers in the department concerned, or in the group making the accepted suggestion.

The Scanlon Plan is admittedly not easy to initiate, nor is it successful in every instance.[37] However, it is an example of the attempt to combine technical advance with concern for workers' feelings, which is the hallmark of the structuralist school.

In summary: Before the Industrial Revolution, the pursuit of productivity was basically a desire to reduce human labor as much as possible; it then became a search for greater output; today it contains both of these elements, although not always in the same proportion. Similarly, the scientific management school gave way to the human relations school, while the current structuralist approach attempts a synthesis of both. What has been the result of this long pursuit of greater productivity?

THE INCREASE IN PRODUCTIVITY

There can be little question but that over the long span—a century, a generation, or even a decade—productivity has consistently risen. Even when this is not viewed in totals, like the Gross National Product, but is examined in terms of person-hour production, there can be little serious debate.

From 1956 to 1964 the per-person productivity in the major industrial nations increased by 41 percent; from 1966 to 1975, by 37 percent. Using 1970 as the base of 100, there was a 17 percent growth in productivity by 1976.[38] Between 1950 and 1978, the output per hour of all persons in the private business sector almost doubled.[39] The rate of productivity increases in the major western industrialized countries in 1978 were:

United States	2.5
Canada	4.2
France	4.9
Germany	3.7
Italy	2.9
United Kingdom	1.6[40]

Industrial productivity was matched by agricultural productivity. In 1776, 1 American farmer provided food for 3 people; in 1976, 1 farmer provided food for 57 people.[41] In the United States, agricultural output per unit of land increased on the average by 80 percent in 1971-1975, as compared to 1941-1945. Crop yields of wheat have increased by 90 percent, and of corn, 2.8 times during the same period.[42] In Europe, employment on the farms declined about 40 percent in the last decade.[43]

Seen on a longer term, there has been an average of 3 percent annual increase in productivity on the part of all persons in the private sector, from 1947 to 1973.[44] Since 1974, however, the United States has had lower rates of growth of productivity than before that time. In fact, there are those who hold that in 1979-1980 this reached an absolute decline in productivity, and not just in the rate of growth.[45] The reasons offered for this drop range from lack of investment in research and development and lack of investment in technology, through the effects of the postwar baby boom, to the entry of women and minority groups into the labor force.[46] Each of these factors is generally seen as temporary, to be overcome within a relatively short time.

PRODUCTIVITY IN SERVICES

It will be noted that much of the previous discussion of productivity has been concerned with the industrial sector, and this is because most studies of work patterns are conducted in such settings. However, in the United States, service employment accounts for two-thirds to three-quarters of all employment, and the same situation holds true in most of the western world.

In attempting to take into account the service sector, one obvious problem concerns a definition of services:

> An adequate conceptualization of services that are productive does not exist.
> . . . A tentative way of looking at the issue of productivity is two-fold: The first kind of production activity is one that contributes to labor power, in the sense that it makes people work more effectively . . . The second kind of productive activity is one that contributes directly to well-being.[47]

In this connection, Gershuny points out that about half of the so-called service jobs are in support of production.[48] Bookkeepers, drivers, warehouse personnel, typists, and many others work to support production as a goal. In 1971, less than a quarter of the working population in the United Kingdom—23.1 percent—"was involved in providing for the final consumption of services."[49] This kind of service is hard to measure in terms of productivity:

> The measurement of productivity worsens as the service sector in the national economy increases relative to the manufacturing sector, resulting in a probable downward bias as a whole. Because of the intrinsic difficulty in measuring the output of service-oriented activities, data for the service sector are relatively weak and probably result in an under-estimation of output. This is also true of the wholesale and retail trade sectors. Also, there are no available measures of productivity for the government and nonprofit sectors on a continuing basis, again because of the inherent difficulty of arriving at an independent measure of final output.[50]

Despite such lack of overall productivity figures in the service sector, there are nevertheless productivity figures for specific areas and activities.

Some of these appear periodically in the *Monthly Labor Review*. Thus, output in the laundry and cleaning services grew at an annual rate of 1.6 percent between 1958 and 1976.[51] In the retail food industry, output increased by 2.4 percent annually in the same period.[52] With 1967 considered as 100, productivity in eating and drinking places grew from 91.3 in 1958 to 103.2 in 1976.[53] Between 1960 and 1977, productivity in the telecommunications industry rose 5.5 percent annually.[54] Even new car dealers reported impressive long-term gains in productivity.[55]

As is obvious, the trend and direction in almost all such studies and reports is in the direction of productivity increases. The introduction of computerized machine methods into many service trades parallels the trend toward automation in manufacturing industry.[56] These trends are easily confirmed by simple observation of technological improvements in services, ranging from teaching via television, through computerized library methods, to medical body scanners, each of which makes the personnel involved immensely more productive.

REDUCTION IN WORK HOURS

Increases in productivity are not solely reflected in more output; much of this gain has gone into more leisure time. Patruchev points out that

> during the past 100 years the annual amount of spare time of the working people has increased four to five times. The annual amount of working time among the employed in the United States dropped from about 3,300 hours in 1870 to 1,950 hours in 1965, and spare time increased from about 360 hours to 1,700 hours. The annual amount of spare time of Soviet working people reaches . . . 1,500-1,900 hours, i.e., close or equal to the annual balance of working time.[59]

5×8 + 4 SAT   5×10 + 3 SAT

The average workweek in the United States shrank from 53 hours in 1900 to 44 hours in 1946,[58] and in 1979 the average workweek for production and nonsupervisory workers in private industry was 35.5 hours.[59] From 1957 to 1965, hours of work in manufacturing in all the developed economies decreased by 2.14 percent,[60] and from 1972 to 1978 hours of industry changed as follows:

	1972	*1978*
Italy	1900	1851
Belgium	1934	1820
Germany	1863	1820
United Kingdom	1794	1827
Luxemburg	1869	1630
France	2011	1886[61]

In the developed economies, basic paid holidays for manual workers increased from 1.75 weeks 25 years ago to 3.5 weeks in 1977;[62] paid holidays in the metropolitan areas of the United States increased by 1.3 days a year from 1968 to 1979.[63] In short, over the past half-century, labor hours per unit of output have been reduced about 3 percent per year, and average hours worked per year have been reduced by close to .5 percent per annum.[64]

Where services are concerned, data concerning hours are more available than those concerning productivity. Not only are there studies of specific industries—for example, in the laundry and cleaning services, hours dropped at an average annual rate of 3.1 percent between 1958 and 1976,[65] and dropped from 35.6 to 28 in eating and drinking places during the same period[66]—there are also monthly reports by the Department of Labor. Weekly hours of work in services dropped from 32.8 in 1978 to 32.7 in 1979, and to 32.6 in November 1980.[67]

The amount of leisure time available to people in the United States today is only 2.75 per week less than work, even when second jobs are included,[68] and this gap is rapidly narrowing. Leisure time will outweigh work time very shortly. The average American has 4 more hours of leisure a day than his or her grandparents had,[69] and if the ratio of reduction in work hours continues as it has since 1880, before today's children retire, the workweek will be halved again.[70] As the workweek has contracted and life expectancy has been extended, the average American has added about 22 years of leisure to life,[71] and if workers had their way, average work hours would drop to 1517 by 1990.[72] 30 W/wk   52 wks/YR

It should be noted that there are those who view the decrease in work hours cynically, secure in the belief that as normal hours decrease, overtime and/or second-job hours increase. However, the figures given in the *Yearbook of Labour Statistics* of the International Labour Organization are based upon "all hours worked during normal periods of work," and specifically include overtime.[73] Further, while normal hours of work were declining rapidly from 1968 to 1979, there was no increase in overtime.[74] Finally, the multiple jobholding rate holds reasonably steady at around 5 percent.[75]

It has been pointed out previously that the proportion of production or productivity increases that can be attributed to human labor is small—perhaps between 10 and 25 percent.[76] Further, labor was responsible for only 11 percent of the growth of national income per person from 1948 to 1973; and 9 percent from 1973 to 1976.[77] Nevertheless, the desire to increase the inputs of working people continues, perhaps spurred on by the facts that people generally work at about 44 percent of their capacity[78] and that 54 percent of all people could work harder than they do.[79] Of course, it is not generally recognized that low labor productivity is more a function of the job requirements than of the person—"Keeping a job usually requires performance far short of the potential of the worker,"[80] and that phenomenon is growing. Hours actually worked relative to hours paid for have declined significantly in the past decades—unproductive work time has been increasing.[81]

Consequently, the search for ways to induce people to work harder continues along the lines outlined previously, and explicated later. Part of the difficulty of designing definitive research into the reasons that people work, or work hard, is the existence of contradictory theories and conflicting theories. Three sets of such theories or beliefs are set forth below.

THEORIES, BELIEFS, AND ASSUMPTIONS
ABOUT WORK MOTIVATIONS

One way of categorizing widespread beliefs about work incentives is to distinguish among those which hold that there is an instinctive, or bodily, need to work, those which see people as working primarily for material motives, and those which put social, emotional, and relationship drives at the head of the list.[82] In Maslow's theory of a hierarchy of human needs, work enters on many levels: physiological, security, acceptance, self-esteem, and self-actualization.[83] Consequently, instinctual, material, and social needs are separated out here purely for heuristic purposes, since there are many combinations among these categories, and a constant dynamic interchange among them.

INSTINCTS OR BODILY NEEDS

The instinctive school of thought holds that people have an innate need to work; or, more precisely, an innate need for bodily or muscular activity, for which work is the easiest, most accessible, outlet: "Inactivity . . . is a torment to a healthy human being. Every muscle is alive with the impulse to activity. The normal form of this activity is: in the child, play: in the adult, work."[84] Others propose an "activity drive" which expresses itself, when necessary, in proportion to the time during which the organism has been forced to be inactive.[85] Similarly, Parrington speaks of a common instinct of acquisitiveness, at least insofar as the English middle class is concerned,[86] and Tawney speaks of the acquisitive society—both of which would ordinarily lead to work in some sense.[87] Freud added great weight to the instinctual school, without terming it such, with his famous prescription for happiness: "To love and to work."[88] Then there are those who believe that the need to work—without recognizing it as the Protestant Ethic as such—is implanted by God, either as punishment or as a way to achieve grace, or simply as a human attribute.

MATERIAL NEEDS

The "material satisfiers" school of thought sees work as a response to tangible needs. People work primarily for money, and the major incentive to work is financial. Although money may not be seen as a sufficient motivation for work, it is viewed as a necessary one: Remove money, goes this argument, and you'll see how few people keep working. The role of money or material items as work incentives continues to its inexorable conclusion concerning the insatiability of human wants, which holds, in effect, that there will never be a time when individuals or societies will say, "Hold, that's enough." Further, when needs are seen as either relative or normative, rather than as absolute, they can reach their end only in an absolutely egalitarian situation, since the presence of inequality will inevitably generate feelings of relative need.[89] Finally, the theory of material needs as work incentives makes no distinction between needs and wants—people presumably work as hard as they do to acquire the things they want, regardless of whether they or others define these as "real" needs.[90]

The entire network of social welfare, as discussed in the previous chapter, rests basically upon the idea that people work primarily to acquire money, and thereby material goods; and that income from work must be maintained at a higher level than income from welfare to appeal to this need, thus assuring continuing work.

SOCIAL/EMOTIONAL NEEDS

Social or emotional needs to work arise from the very structure of society. According to this view, work regulates life activity by structuring the day, week, month, and year; provides a means of identification ("What do you do?"); offers a setting for sustained association with others; and adds meaningful experiences to life.[91] This school speaks of psychic rewards from work, such as sense of achievement, responsibility, and growth, recognition by others, and power, authority, and status.[92] Work thus takes on moral, religious, and mystical overtones, leading to discussion of work and incentive questions in terms that are very heavily emotion-laden. These become struggles over deep psychic and cultural commitments.[93]

Although the three schools of thought regarding work motivations described above account for the force of the thrust toward work in modern society, there are nevertheless counterbeliefs and theories that are equally widespread. The instinctive theory is opposed by the postulation of an avoidance instinct, by which people attempt to avoid work, or physical energy generally, insofar as possible.[94] Indeed, there seems to be a law of parsimony in work efforts—the desire to do as little work as possible in achieving desired ends. People do not seem to work overtime for the sheer joy of working, or to choose to work longer hours for the same remuneration as they receive for shorter hours. Seeking easier methods, using labor-saving devices, and utilizing resources in new ways are not only seen as legitimate, but are considered desirable traits. Indeed, many companies pay bonuses to workers who suggest methods of reducing work. Even Freud, who held that work is indispensable for human happiness, also said that "as a path to happiness work is not valued very highly by men."[95]

—The "material satisfiers" school also comes under attack, mostly on the basis mentioned previously, that needs are artificially created; and that the amount of human labor demanded is in excess of the amount actually necessary to produce the same amount of satisfiers than are now being made. In this way, work to acquire material satisfiers becomes an artifact of the economic system, and not an innate need of individuals.

The social and emotional motivators to work are questioned, if not denied, by those who hold that people receive their major satisfactions from leisure rather than from work;[96] that their central life interests are outside the work place;[97] and that their friendship patterns are based on nonwork associations.[98] This viewpoint holds that work is basically alienating, anomic, and unsatisfying.

These contradictory but widely held theories about work result in deep societal ambivalences, which have been summed up as follows:

People work in order to satisfy instinctual and biological needs and drives, and are unhappy to the point of sickness if they are denied such opportunity—
People are inherently lazy; no one wants to work or does so unless he or she has to; and efforts to avoid work are the basis for all social and mechanical progress.

People work basically to achieve material ends, and any other supposed motivations are rationalizations which would not support work motivations if material needs were provided by other means—
People work even when their material needs are satisfied, because of personal needs and social pressures.

Only people whose sustenance needs are unmet are motivated by the need to work; other people must be stimulated by advertising, social pressure, and other devices, or else they would be satisfied—
People's needs are insatiable, and therefore people will always work to achieve more material items.

People work because of the satisfactions inherent in working: the sense of creativity, fulfillment, productivity, and performing an expected and useful social role—
Most people find their work boring, unsatisfying, and uncreative, and constantly seek to reduce the hours they must spend at it.

People work because in their work groups they find primary group relationships, companionship, enjoyment, status, and recognition—

The major focus of people's lives is outside their work places; major interests center on nonwork activities; and most satisfying personal relationships are not found with fellow workers.

People work because of the social identity that work offers them, the regulation of daily life activity it entails, and the way it defines them to the rest of society— People define themselves and are defined according to their leisure-time activities, their interests and expertise, and their familial and ethnic backgrounds.[99]

As a result of such widely held contradictions and ambivalences concerning work and its incentives, empirical studies take on even greater value. It is doubly distressing, therefore, to entertain the view that some of the most seminal of incentive research studies were methodologically badly flawed, and gave a false lead to years of additional work. The next chapter reviews the evidence that this is so.

NOTES

1. W. Buckingham, *Automation* (New York: Mentor, 1961).

2. K. Mendelssohn, *The Riddle of the Pyramids* (London: Sphere, 1977).

3. M. Kranzberg and J. Gies, *By the Sweat of Thy Brow* (New York: Putnam, 1975), p. 42.

4. S. Samant, S. Sawant, and B. Talati, *Distribution of Fertilizers in Ralnagiri (India) District* (Tel Aviv: Foreign Training Department, Ministry of Agriculture, 1970), p. 6 (mimeo). In this connection, see D. Macarov and G. Fradkin, *The Short Course in Development Training* (Ramat Gan, Israel: Massadah, 1973).

5. It is for such reasons that it has been reported that despite the successes of the so-called Green Revolution, the number of hungry people in the world has risen during the last 10 years from about 600 million to 900 million.

6. This does not happen automatically. Many studies of the results of an increased GNP indicate small absolute gains on the part of the lowest economic stratum of the population, and actual losses when poverty is measured in a relative fashion.

7. S. Freud, *Civilization and Its Discontents* (New York: Paperback, 1958).

8. A. Clayre, *Work and Play: Ideas and Experience of Work and Leisure* (New York: Harper & Row, 1974).

9. P. D. Anthony, *The Ideology of Work* (London: Tavistock, 1978), p. 277.

10. D. Macarov, "Social Welfare as a By-Product: The Effect of Neo-Mercantilism." *Journal of Sociology and Social Welfare* 4 (1977): 1135-1144.

11. Kranzberg and Gies, op. cit., pp. 93-94.

12. B. Mazlish, *The Wealth of Nations: Representative Selections* (New York: Bobbs-Merrill, 1961), p. 5.

13. J. H. Hoagland, "Charles Babbage: His Life and Works in the Historical Evolution of Management Concepts." Ph.D. dissertation Ohio State University, 1954; quoted in E. Dale (ed.) *Readings in Management: Landmarks and New Frontiers* (New York: McGraw-Hill, 1975).

14. F. W. Taylor, *The Principles of Scientific Management* (New York: Harper & Row, 1911).

15. P. F. Drucker, "Frederick W. Taylor: The Professional Management Pioneer." in Dale, op. cit., pp. 98-100.

16. G. C. Homans, *The Human Group* (New York: Harcourt Brace Jovanovich, 1950), p. 102.

17. Although the group consisted of six, no production records were kept, for obvious reasons, concerning the person who distributed supplies. Hence, subsequent discussion concerns only five persons.

18. E. Mayo, *The Human Problems of an Industrial Civilization* (New York: Viking, 1933).

19. R. H. Franke and J. D. Kaul, "The Hawthorne Experiments: First Statistical Interpretation." *American Sociological Review* 43 (1978): 623-643.

20. E. Locke, "The Nature and Causes of Job Satisfaction," in M. D. Dunnette (ed.) *Handbook of Industrial and Organizational Psychology* (Chicago: Rand-McNally, 1976).

21. "One wonders how many other failures were never written up for publication." R. A. Katzell, P. Bienstock, and P. H. Faerstein, *A Guide to Worker Productivity Experiments in the United States 1971-1975* (New York: New York University Press, 1977), p. 39.

22. F. Herzberg, B. Mausner, and B. B. Snyderman, *The Motivation to Work* (New York: John Wiley, 1959), p. 10.

23. Ibid.; and F. Herzberg, *Work and the Nature of Man* (Cleveland: World, 1966).

24. Katzell et al., op. cit.

25. B. K. Scanlan, "Determinants of Job Satisfaction and Productivity." *Personnel Journal* 55 (1976): 12.

26. R. J. House and L. A. Wigdor, "Herzberg's Dual-Factor Theory of Job Satisfaction and Motivation: A Review of the Evidence and a Criticism." *Personnel Psychology* 20 (1967): 369; and D. A. Whitsett and E. K. Winslow, "An Analysis of Studies Critical of the Motivator-Hygiene Theory." *Personnel Psychology* 20 (1967): 391.

27. Herzberg, *Work and the Nature of Man*, op. cit.

28. B. W. Bass and G. V. Barrett, *Man, Work, and Organizations: An Introduction to Industrial and Organizational Psychology* (Boston: Allyn & Bacon, 1972).

29. J. H. Goldthorpe, D. Lockwood, F. Bechhofer, and J. Platt, *The Affluent Worker: Industrial Attitudes and Behaviour* (Cambridge: University Press, 1968).

30. R. Barlow, "Motivation of the Affluent," in G. G. Somers (ed.) *Manpower and Its Motivation* (New York: Industrial Relations Research Association, 1967).

31. S. E. Bernard, *Fatherless Families: Their Economic and Social Adjustment* (Waltham, MA: Brandeis University, 1964).

32. A. L. Opsahl and M. D. Dunnette, "The Role of Financial Compensation." *Psychological Bulletin* 66 (1966): 94-118.

33. M. Hare, E. E. Ghiselli, and M. E. Gordon, "A Psychological Study of Pay." *Journal of Applied Psychology Monograph* 51 (1967); W. F. Whyte, *Organisational Behaviour: Theory and Application* (Homewood, IL: Dorsey, 1969).

34. W. F. Whyte, *Money and Motivation* (New York: Harper & Row, 1955).

35. Bass and Barrett, op. cit.

36. For a fuller description, see D. McGregor, *The Human Side of Enterprise* (New York: McGraw-Hill, 1960).

37. T. Q. Gilson and M. J. Lefcowitz, "A Plant Wide Productivity Bonus in a Small Factory: Study of an Unsuccessful Case." *Industrial and Labor Relations Review* 10 (1957): 284-296.

38. *Yearbook of Labour Statistics: Sixteenth Edition: Twenty-Sixth Edition: Thirty-Sixth Edition* (Geneva: International Labour Organization, 1956, 1966, 1976).

39. *Monthly Labor Review,* 102 (March 1979): 91, 107.

40. *World of Work Report,* 4 (August 1979): 59.

41. U.S. Department of Agriculture, *The Secret of Affluence* (Washington, DC: Author: 1976).

42. W. Leontiff, "The Future of the World Economy." *Socio-Economic Planning Sciences* 2 (1977): 171-182.

43. Organisation for Economic Co-operation and Development, *Work in a Changing Industrial Society* (Paris: Author, 1975), p. 22.

44. R. E. Kutscher, J. A. Mark, and J. R. Norsworthy, "The Productivity Slowdown and the Outlook to 1985." *Monthly Labor Review* 100 (May 1977): 3-8.

45. E. F. Denison, *Accounting for Slower Economic Growth: The United States in the 1970s* (Washington DC: Brookings, 1979).

46. *World of Work Report*, 6 (May 1981): 38.

47. S. M. Miller, "Productivity and the Paradox of Service in a Profit Economy." *Social Policy* 9 (1978): 4-6.

48. J. Gershuny, *After Industrial Society: The Emerging Self-Service Economy* (London: Macmillan, 1978), p. 98.

49. Ibid.

50. K. Chandrasekar, "Productivity and Social Indicators," *Annals of the American Academy of Political and Social Science* 453 (1981): 153-167.

51. R. B. Carnes, "Laundry and Cleaning Services Pressed to Post Productivity Gains," *Monthly Labor Review* 101 (1978): 38-42.

52. J. L. Carey and P. F. Otto, "Output per Unit of Labor Input in the Retail Food Store Industry." *Monthly Labor Review* 100 (January 1977): 42-47.

53. R. B. Carnes and H. Band, "Productivity and New Technology in Eating and Drinking Places." *Monthly Labor Review* 100 (September 1977): 9-15.

54. M. D. Dymmel, "Technology in Telecommunications: Its Effect on Labor and Skills." *Monthly Labor Review* 102 (1979): 13-19.

55. J. Duke, "New Car Dealers Experience Long-Term Gain in Productivity." *Monthly Labor Review* 100 (March 1977): 29-33.

56. A. E. Mussan, "Technological Change and Manpower: An Historical Perspective." *International Journal of Manpower* 1 (1980): 2-5.

57. V. A. Patruchev, "The Problem of Organizing Spare Time of Society in Conditions of the Scientific and Technological Revolution," in M. R. Haug and J. Dofny (eds.) *Work and Technology* (Beverly Hills, CA: Sage, 1977), pp. 231-237.

58. *World of Work Report*, 5 (1980): 53.

59. Ibid.

60. *Yearbook of Labour Statistics*, op. cit.

61. *Le Monde*, May, 28, 1981.

62. D. Bell, "The Future That Never Was." *Public Interest* 51 (1978): 35-73.

63. *World of Work Report*, 5 (1980): 53.

64. J. W. Kendrick, *Understanding Productivity: An Introduction to the Dynamics of Productivity Change* (Baltimore: Johns Hopkins University Press, 1977), pp. 5-6.

65. Carnes, op. cit.

66. Carnes and Band, op. cit.

67. *Monthly Labor Review*, "Current Labor Statistics." 104 (January 1981): 103.

68. A. Szalai (ed.), *The Use of Time* (The Hague: Mouton, 1972).

69. M. Kaplan, *Leisure in America: A Social Inquiry* (New York: John Wiley, 1960).

70. W. Buckingham, *Automation* (New York: Mentor, 1961).

71. R. L. Cunnngham, *The Philosophy of Work* (New York: National Association of Manufacturers, 1964).

72. *World of Work Report*, 5 (December 1980): 86.

73. *Yearbook of Labour Statistics* (Geneva: International Labour Organization, 1978), p. 319.

74. *World of Work Report*, 5 (1980): 53.

75. K. Michelotti, "Multiple Jobholding Rate Remained Unchanged in 1976." *Monthly Labor Review*, 100 (June 1977): 44-48; A. Rees, *The Economics of Work and Pay* (New York: Harper & Row, 1979), p. 19, puts the rate at 4.5 percent.

Kreps raises the question as to how long the economy can continue to pay the same salaries for reduced work time, particularly in declining industrial sectors, and sees this as a constraint on reduction of weekly work hours, while admitting that longer vacations and earlier retirement will continue. J. M. Kreps, "Some Time Dimensions of Manpower Policy," in E. Ginzberg (ed.) *Jobs for Americans* (Englewood Cliffs, NJ: Prentice-Hall, 1976).

76. J. M. Rosow, "Human Values in the Work Place Support Growth of Productivity." *World of Work Report* 2 (June 1977): 62.

77. Chandrasekar, op. cit., p. 160

78. M. Walbank, "Effort in Motivated Work Behavior," in K. D. Duncan, M. M. Gruneberg, and D. Wallis (eds.) *Changes in Working Life* (Chichester: Wiley, 1980), pp. 403-422.

79. I. Berg, M. Freedman, and M. Freeman, *Managers and Work Reform: A Limited Engagement* (New York: Free Press, 1978), p. 37.

80. Ibid.

81. J. W. Kendrick, "Productivity Trends and the Recent Slowdown," in W. E. Fellner (ed.) *Contemporary Economic Problems* (Washington DC: American Enterprise Institute, 1979), p. 45.

82. D. Macarov, *Incentives to Work* (San Francisco: Jossey-Bass, 1970).

83. A. H. Maslow, *Motivation and Personality* (New York: Harper & Row, 1954).

84. V. H. Vroom, *Work and Motivation*. New York: John Wiley, 1964.

85. W. F. Hill, "Activity as an Autonomous Drive." *Journal of Comparative and Physiological Psychology* 49 (1956): 15; J. Kagan and M. Berkun, "The Reward Value of Running Activity." *Journal of Comparative and Physiological Psychology* 47 (1954): 108.

86. V. L. Parrington, *Main Currents in American Thought* (New York: Harcourt Brace Jovanovich, 1927).

87. R. H. Tawney, *The Acquisitive Society* (New York: Harcourt Brace Jovanovich, 1948).

88. Freud, op. cit.

89. For the distinction among relative, normative, and absolute needs, see D. Macarov, *The Design of Social Welfare* (New York: Holt, Rinehart & Winston, 1978).

90. For the problem of distinguishing between needs and wants, see E. Allardt, *Dimensions of Welfare in a Comparative Scandinavian Study* (Helsinki: University of Helsinki, 1975).

91. E. A. Friedmann and R. J. Havighurst, *The Meaning of Work and Retirement* (Chicago: University of Chicago Press, 1954).

92. R. Barlow, H. E. Brazer, and J. N. Morgan, *Economic Behavior of the Affluent* (Washington DC: Brookings, 1966); R. Dubin, *The World of Work* (Englewood Cliffs, NJ: Prentice-Hall, 1958).

93. J. M. Martin, *Lower-Class Delinquency and Work Programs* (New York: New York University Press, 1966).

94. Vroom, op. cit.

95. Freud, op. cit.

96. M. Kaplan, *Leisure in America: A Social Inquiry* (New York: John Wiley, 1960).

97. H. Kornhauser, *Mental Health of the Industrial Worker* (New York: John Wiley, 1965).

98. Dubin, op. cit.

99. Macarov, *Incentives to Work,* op. cit.

4

FALSE STARTS ON THE ROAD
TO PRODUCTIVITY

HAWTHORNE AND HUMAN RELATIONS

The Hawthorne experiments opened an entirely new era in the history of the pursuit of productivity. Studies, experiments, articles, and books poured out in profusion, all based upon the Hawthorne findings that the relationships between people in the work place and workers' feelings of being consulted and appreciated were the important missing elements in achieving greater production. These studies, incidentally, also had an impact on research methodology as such. The so-called Hawthorne effect is the change that being a research object creates in the person being studied.

The Hawthorne studies covered a period of eight years. Consequently, an enormous amount of data was generated. Obviously, not every piece of the data could be, or was, given equal weight in evaluating and interpreting the results. Those findings that were published, however, and the manner in which they were interpreted, managed to communicate the excitement of the researchers concerning this previously neglected phenomenon, which came to be called human relations in industry.[1] The amount, width, and depth of the documentation, research, and experiments concerning human relations that then followed are staggering.[2] Entire industries—indeed, almost the entire field of labor relations—were restructured to take this new factor into consideration.

Despite the almost universal uncritical acceptance of the findings of the Hawthorne research, there were some observers who expressed caveats. In 1967 Alex Carey published that which he termed a radical criticism of the Hawthorne findings.[3] Three of his most salient observations concerned control groups, reporting, and changes in the experimental group.

Carey pointed out that, with a single short-lived exception, no control groups had been used. Consequently, it is possible that the differences in productivity achieved by the experimental group were also being achieved by other groups without the experimental conditions, or by the factory as a whole. In fact, productivity in the factory *had* risen by about 7 percent in the 2 years preceding the experiment. Carey's concern about lack of control groups was heightened by the results of the control group that was utilized. When the 5 women in the experimental group were changed from a payment system based upon the output of a group of 100 workers to one in which they were paid according to their own group's output, another group of 5 women, who experienced none of the other experimental changes, had the basis of their pay changed in a similar manner. Like the experimental group, their productivity promptly rose. However, their situation caused so much jealously among the other workers that they were put back on the original payment formula—whereupon their productivity dropped. Yet the importance of the new payment incentive was hardly taken into account when reasons for productivity increases were sought. In Carey's words, the comparison between the control group and the experimental group, and the similar influence of the new pay system on them, "appears not to have made any impression on the investigators' confidence about the superior importance of social factors."

A second criticism leveled at the Hawthorne studies concerns the anecdotal, impressionistic method by which conclusions were reached. Carey points out that when the researchers' assumptions or theories were at stake, they were accepted if no "conclusive evidence" was found against them. When counterassumptions or theories were examined, they were rejected unless "conclusive evidence" was found for them. Carey refers to this as "the scientifically illiterate procedure of dismissing non-preferred explanations."

Perhaps the most cogent of Carey's objections is to the fact that the experimental group had its composition changed during the experiment, obviously in order to give the research a better chance to achieve the desired results. Two women of the original five were replaced eight months after the beginning of the study. The manner of replacement, and its reason, raised important questions about the reported results of the experiment.

Twelve weeks after the beginning of the study, four of the five women were reprimanded by their foreman for talking too much on the job. Efforts to control the women's talking continued. Two of the women, when reprimanded, retorted that they had been told to work as they felt like (which was indeed the purpose of the study), and they felt like talking. It was decided that none of the women was being very cooperative with the research, and pressure on them to stop talking and work better continued, up to the point that there was a threat that their free lunches would be discontinued. For two of the women the threats and pressure seemed inoperative—one of them was reproved for her "low output and behavior" almost daily. Finally, the two women were removed from the group for not being cooperative in the research. They were replaced by two other women, one of whom expressed her need for money, and who led the group in productivity throughout the rest of the experiment. Indeed, after the two original respondents were removed, production increases became habitual.

As mentioned, the findings of the Hawthorne study are voluminous, and some items are understandably emphasized over others. From Carey's criticisms, however, it is possible to question the reputed strength of the human relations factors—the operatives' feelings that they were being consulted and brought into the picture, their good relations with their foreman, the opportunity to create relationships with each other. To the extent that the opportunity to earn more money was operative through increased group productivity (which it was), the pressure by the foreman for more output, the continued demands for less talking, and finally the removal of two operatives for not being cooperative, that is, not producing, do not add up to better human relations as the cause of increased productivity.

Carey's criticisms of the generally accepted Hawthorne findings did not go unchallenged. Jon M. Shepard, for one, holds that the researchers did not disregard or minimize the role of financial incentives at Hawthorne, but considered them as part of a "mix" of incentives.[4] Shepard also rejected some of Carey's methods of criticism, but did not deal with the method of supervision or the firing of the two women.

Eleven years later, a new and different kind of criticism was leveled at the findings of the Hawthorne studies. Franke and Kaul held that

the massive Hawthorne experiments of some 50 years ago serve as the paradigmatic foundation of the social science of work. The insights gleaned from these experiments provide a basis for most current studies in human relations as well as for subareas such as participation, organizational development, leadership, motivation, and even organizational design. But aside from visual inspection and anecdotal comment, the complex of data obtained during the eight years of the Hawthorne experiments has never been subjected to thorough-going scientific analysis.

At the time when the Hawthorne experiments were taking place, neither the hardware nor the software available today was at hand, and consequently no sophisticated analysis of variables was undertaken. It is just this sort of analysis which Franke and Kaul computed. Their conclusion differs radically from that of the original researchers, who, according to them, found that it was the human relations factor and not the other experimental variables which accounted for the difference in output. Their—Franke and Kaul's—statistical analysis indicates that 79 percent of the improvement in productivity was due to managerial discipline (which included the impact of having removed two workers); 14 percent was due to the onset and continuation of the economic depression; and 4 percent was due to scheduled rest time. In short, this study found that close supervision, the need for money and the fear of unemployment during a depression,[6] and being rested accounted for almost all of the increase in productivity, while the much-vaunted human relations factor—feeling important, participating in decisions, and the like—was almost absent.

This reanalysis has not gone unchallenged. Wardwell, for one, argues that quantitative analysis is not appropriate, or is not sufficient, since the anecdotal material is equally convincing.[7] He also questions a number of the items in the statistical analysis. Franke, in rebuttal, defends quantitative analysis and points out that Wardwell's criticisms do not controvert the import of the statistical findings.[8]

It is almost certain that there will be further reanalyses of the mountainous Hawthorne data, using more sophisticated methods than were then available. There will probably also be criticism of these findings, especially on the part of those who have built their own research or their own labor-relations methods upon the original interpretation. However, it does seem at least possible that the importance of the human relations factor in the Hawthorne experiments was overemphasized at the expense of the supervisory discipline, the tightening economic situation and the opportunity to maintain or increase earnings within the experimental group, and even the importance of being rested. Consequently, it would seem that, from a productivity point of view, there may have been a great deal of money, time, and effort wasted in pursuing the chimera of greater productivity through better human relations.

It is possible, of course, that the results of the Hawthorne studies, even if misinterpreted, resulted in better relationships in the work place, or more satisfactions for workers. To the extent that they did, they are only to be blessed. Insofar as people want to have better relations with fellow workers and others, want to be treated with respect, and want to participate in making decisions, anything which contributes to these ends is to be welcomed. But whether this is the factor that leads to greater productivity, in contradistinction to or in place of, financial incentives, close supervision, fear of job loss, and physical rest, is a different question.

One way of examining the actual impact of the Hawthorne studies is to examine whether the introduction of human relations improvements into the work place generally resulted in greater productivity, and, if so, whether the human relations factor was the operative one. To pursue this question further, it is worthwhile to look at the Herzberg-type experiments, since they widened this question and examined it.

HERZBERG AND MOTIVATION

In 1959, Frederick Herzberg and his associates published the results of their investigations into worker satisfactions outlined in the previous chapter.[9] Both the Hawthorne and the Herzberg studies were focused on the worker as such, but whereas the Hawthorne studies dwelt mainly on relationships with others and feelings about oneself, Herzberg broadened the scope to include all of the workers' satisfactions and dissatisfactions.

As noted, there have been criticisms of Herzberg's methodology.[10] By asking workers to think of a time that they were happy at work and to adduce the reason, Herzberg assumed that life satisfactions, or out-of-work satisfactions, could be excluded from the answers, or the thinking and feeling that went into the answers. A person happy about something that happened away from work might have difficulty disassociating from the feeling, and might adduce a work-connected reason if pressed to do so. This seems to have happened in the kibbutz study described in the next chapter. Again, one person's deep satisfaction might equate with another's very slight lift of spirits, and no measure of the amount of satisfaction is contained in the studies.

It should also be noted that few incentive studies attempt to compare the level of satisfaction at work with the level of satisfaction from nonwork activities, the implications of which will be discussed in Chapter 6. Consequently, in evaluating the results of Herzberg-type studies, it would be well to keep in mind that the satisfying periods reported by workers are so designated only in relation to other work periods, and not to their total life situations.

Despite such limitations, the Herzberg methodology was replicated, sometimes with changes, in tens, if not hundreds, of additional studies, and in general the bipolarity theory stood up: Satisfactions were seen as coming from the work itself, and dissatisfactions as arising from the conditions surrounding the work, at least when the Herzberg open-ended method was used.

But a funny thing happened on the way from the findings to the interpretation. Herzberg changed the terms that he had been using. Instead of speaking of "satisfiers," as he had previously, he transmuted the term into "motivators." Similarly, he changed "dissatisfiers" into "hygiene factors." The latter change had little impact, but the former change had profound influence on later research and on thinking about productivity. Herzberg explains his venture into semantics in one sentence, saying that dissatisfiers lead to avoidance behavior while satisfiers lead to approach behavior, and "since it is in the approach sense that the term motivation is most commonly used, we designate the job-factors as the 'motivators' as opposed to the extra-job factors, which we have labeled the factors of hygiene."[11]

This linguistic, or definitional, switch from satisfiers to motivators had profound implications for the continuation of incentive research. The assumption that one who is satisfied at work is motivated to work hard, or harder, is a beguiling one. It is so logical, it agrees so well with the folklore of work, and it solves so many problems concerning productivity that it was accepted with the same eagerness and whole-heartedness as were the results of the Hawthorne studies. Yet even a moment's reflection will lead to the question of whether satisfactions create motivation. One may be reasonably well satisfied, or even very satisfied, *at* work, and accept the situation as a given, calling for and calling forth no specific action or attitude. One may also get satisfaction *from* one's work, without being motivated to work harder at it. Further, there is the finding that satisfaction itself "includes an element of indecision, vacillation, and a less resolute attitude," more than does dissatisfaction.[12]

The assumption that satisfaction leads to motivation seems to stem from a managerial *weltanschauung* that workers who are made happier, or given more satisfactions, *ought to* repay this with harder work. It is seen as ungrateful of them, if not immoral, not to do so. Satisfaction is thus seen as a sort of prepaid recompense—just as money is paid for work after it is done, increased satisfactions are given in advance, in the expectation of greater output. Workers who do not respond to these increased satisfactions are in some way cheating the company. From the managerial viewpoint, it may be hard to conceive that workers given added satisfactions can feel that these are long overdue; or are due them in any case; or are still no recompense for the work they do or the conditions under which they do it; or are illegitimate substitutes for more money or shorter hours. As noted previously, workers have different interests from those of management, and define quality of working life differently than do researchers.[13] These may be reasons that management's expectations as to the results of attempted incentives are so often disappointed. Indeed, there is very little evidence of the traditional and well-believed work ethic in the self-reports of workers on the job, and Massey raises the question as to whether America ever had such a work ethic, since the historical material is drawn almost exclusively from nonworkers.[14]

In fact, being satisfied can be seen as the very opposite of being motivated. To most people, *dis*satisfaction is the spur to a determination to make a change in the situation. Indeed, one can search the literature of anecdotal and autobiographical accounts of working people without finding a single reference to a decision or a determination to work better or harder because of something the company or the supervisor has done to make life better or easier. There are, however, numerous accounts of decisions to make a change—quit the job, not to work hard, fool the supervisor—or not to make a change—to work no harder—arising from dissatisfactions or lack of satisfactions.

The satisfier-equals-motivation assumption is almost incredibly naive. As Athanasiou says, motivation implies the willingness to work or produce, while satisfaction simply implies a positive emotional state which may be totally unrelated to productivity.[15] Motivation itself is an extremely complex subject, very incompletely understood. As Bindra and Stewart point out, "the problem of motivation has remained unchanged in its essential definition for over a hundred years."[16] Spitze and Waite note that measures of work attitudes are often post hoc and based on the behavior they are supposed to have caused.[17] There is also the case of motivation as anticipated satisfaction, rather than as an ex post reaction. One of the objections to Herzberg-type studies is that they ask only about past events, and assume that they are reacted to by changed motivation. Yet many researchers hold that motivation is created by anticipation to a much greater degree than by reaction. Indeed, according to McClelland, *all* motivated behavior depends upon the anticipation of emotionally pleasant or unpleasant outcomes.[18] Insofar as job enrichment plans are concerned, they seem to suffer from the same weakness—an assumption that once they are instituted, workers will produce more because of them. In this connection, Grant says:

> Many highly-touted job enrichment programs implemented by organizations during the past two decades have not succeeded. Enriched jobs—along with high salary, status, good working conditions, and fringe benefits—will not motivate unless the enrichment is granted as a *reward* for greater employee effort.[19]

Others agree: "In order for effort to be expended, one must first have a clear expectation that increased effort will be associated with outcomes perceived as valent."[20]

SUMMARY

The Hawthorne studies posited better human relations at work as a major factor in increasing productivity, but later reanalysis throws question on these findings.

The Herzberg studies differentiated between satisfiers and dissatisfiers, finding that these did not arise from the same sources. However, the effect of money (wages, salaries, bonuses, premiums, and so on) was not controlled for, and the studies indicate ambivalence concerning its role and importance.

The Herzberg studies investigated satisfactions, but simply assumed that satisfactions create motivation; and that satisfactions are therefore related to human productivity.

It was in order to test all three of these gray areas that the study of work patterns and satisfactions in an Israeli kibbutz, which makes up the subject matter of the next chapter, was undertaken.

NOTES

1. These experiments are reported in detail in a number of places. See, for example, E. Mayo, *The Human Problems of an Industrial Civilization* (New York: Viking, 1933); F. J. Roethlisberger and W. J. Dickson, *Management and the Worker* (Cambridge, MA: Harvard

University Press, 1939); G. C. Homans, *The Human Group* (New York: Harcourt Brace Jovanovich, 1959).

2. Kahn mentions two thousand studies on job satisfaction. R. L. Kahn, "The Meaning of Work: Interpretation and Proposals for Measurement," in A. Campbell and P. E. Converse (eds.) *The Human Meaning of Social Change* (New York: Russell Sage, 1972); Locke estimates 3350 studies, and "this must be considered a minimum figure." E. A. Locke, "The Nature and Causes of Job Satisfaction," in M. D. Dunnette (ed.) *Handbook of Industrial and Organizational Psychology* (Chicago: Rand McNally, 1976), p. 1297.

3. A. Carey, "The Hawthorne Studies: A Radical Criticism." *American Sociological Review* 32 (1967): 403-416; see also A. J. Sykes, "Economic Interest and the Hawthorne Researches: A Comment." *Human Relations* 18 (1965): 253-263.

4. J. M. Shepard, "On Alex Carey's Radical Criticism of the Hawthorne Studies." *Academy of Management Journal* 14 (1971): 23-32.

5. R. H. Franke and J. D. Kaul, "The Hawthorne Experiments: First Statistical Interpretation." *American Sociological Review* 43 (1978): 623-643.

6. On the possible effects of the deepening depression on the workers' behavior, see Thibaut and Kelley's comments about decisions to remain in a job being linked to the possibility of finding another job. J. W. Thibaut and H. H. Kelley, *The Social Psychology of Groups* (New York: John Wiley, 1959).

7. W. I. Wardwell, "Critique of a Recent Professional 'Put-Down' of the Hawthorne Research." *American Sociological Review* 44 (1979): 858-861.

8. R. H. Franke, "The Hawthorne Experiments: Re-View." *American Sociological Review* 44 (1979): 861-867.

9. F. Herzberg, B. Mausner, and B. B. Snyderman, *The Motivation to Work* (New York: John Wiley, 1959); F. Herzberg, *Work and the Nature of Man* (Cleveland: World, 1966).

10. R. J. House and L. A. Wigdor, "Herzberg's Dual-Factor Theory of Job Satisfaction and Motivation: A Review of the Evidence and a Criticism." *Personnel Psychology* 20 (1967): 369; D. A. Whitsett and E. K. Winslow, "An Analysis of Studies Critical of the Motivator-Hygiene Theory." *Personnel Psychology* 20 (1967): 391.

11. Herzberg et al., op. cit., p. 114.

12. R. Stollberg, "Job Satisfaction and Relationship to Work," in M. R. Haug and J. Dofny (eds.) *Work and Technology* (Beverly Hills, CA: Sage, 1977), pp. 107-121.

13. Hofstede points out that there is a difference in values between those who take the initiative in humanizing the work place—usually college-trained managers and professionals—and the workers involved in simple unskilled and clerical work whose jobs are to be humanized. G. Hofstede, *Culture's Consequences: International Differences in Work-Related Values* (Beverly Hills, CA: Sage, 1980), p. 387.

14. G. M. Massey, "Book Review" (reviewing D. T. Rodgers, *The Work Ethic in Industrializing America, 1850-1920*). *American Journal of Sociology* 85 (1980): 1446-1449.

15. R. Athanasiou, "Job Attitudes and Occupational Performance: A Review of Some Important Literature," in J. P. Robinson, R. Athanasiou, and K. B. Head, *Measures of Occupational Attitudes and Occupational Characteristics* (Ann Arbor: University of Michigan, Institute for Social Research, 1969), pp. 79-98. Writing in a Polish context, Kulpinska also points out that "Satisfaction consists in fulfilling the aspirations and expectations connected with work . . . the higher the aspirations the smaller the chances of achieving satisfaction." J. Kulpinska, "Workers' Attitudes Towards Work," in Haug and Dofny, op. cit., pp. 35-43. Yadov and Kissel also define satisfaction as "a psychological state setting in as a result of saturation of a certain need." Y. A. Yadov and A. A. Kissell, "Job Satisfaction: Analysis of Empirical Data and Attempt at Their Theoretical Interpretation," in Haug and Dofny, op. cit.

16. D. Bindra and J. Stewart (eds.) *Motivation* (Harmondsworth: Penguin, 1973), p. 9.

17. G. D. Spitze and L. J. Waite, "Labor Force and Work Attitudes: Young Women's Early Experiences." *Sociology of Work and Occupations* 7 (1980): 3-32.

18. P. Ribeaux and S. E. Poppleton, *Psychology and Work: An Introduction* (London: Macmillan, 1978), p. 103.

19. P. C. Grant, "A Model for Employee Motivation and Satisfaction." *Personnel* 56 (1979): 51-57.

20. L. L. Neider, "An Experimental Field Investigation Utilizing an Expectancy Theory View of Participation." *Organizational Behavior and Human Performance* 26 (1980): 425-448.

5

WORK PATTERNS AND INCENTIVES IN AN ISRAELI KIBBUTZ

As noted in the previous chapter, a survey of work incentive literature and research findings leaves three questions dangling: Are good human relations at work related to human productivity (or, for our purposes, hard work)? Do differential money payments affect responses concerning sources of satisfaction and dissatisfaction in a manner not easily recognized? Are satisfiers motivators?

In seeking a setting in which money could not affect other responses—current income, hoped-for or expected future income, reactions to past payments, changed economic needs, or the like—the Israeli kibbutz appeared to be perfect for such research.

The concept and details of the kibbutz are too well known and have been described in too many places to require more than a summary here.[1] Founded over 75 years ago, kibbutzim (the plural of kibbutz) today contain about 200,000 members in over 200 settlements. The ideological base of the kibbutz is complete equality among members, nonexploitation, and a separation between economic and social structures. Although established originally for agricultural pursuits, during the last few decades there has been a relatively heavy inclusion of industry among kibbutz projects. It should be added that kibbutz membership is completely voluntary, although membership requires a selection procedure. Any member is free to leave the kibbutz at any time, however, and in recent years has been entitled to a share of the results of his or her productive efforts to take with him or her.

The ideological basis of the kibbutz is expressed in the phrase: "From each according to his or her ability, to each according to his or her need." In practice, this means that each kibbutz member receives satisfaction of all his or her needs, at a level commensurate with the economic ability of the kibbutz. Even the economic level is not controlling, however, as young kibbutzim or those in economic difficulty receive help from other kibbutzim, from federations of kibbutzim, and from various governmental and quasi-governmental sources. Thus, kibbutz members are assured of food, clothing, housing, medical care, education, recreation, child care, care of parents, vacations (sometimes abroad), and all the other normal and abnormal needs of the individual, including pocket money. There are many other noteworthy features of the kibbutz, but the one of most relevance here is the fact that in return for this "womb to tomb" care, members contribute their work and their participation in the governance and activities of the kibbutz. There are no differences in that which members receive that are based upon the kind, amount, or style of their work.[2] No individual work or production records are kept, and no formal distinctions based upon work are or can be made. Thus, in terms of work incentive research, the influence of money as such, or as evidence of recognition, advancement, or status, does not exist. Hence, sources of work satisfaction and dissatisfaction cannot be contaminated by money considerations, and can be compared with other studies to determine whether their findings have been so contaminated.

It should be borne in mind that there is a heavy emphasis on work in the kibbutz.[3] This has ideological roots, but is strengthened by the fact that not only is there no unemployment in the kibbutz, there is usually a labor shortage. In addition, there are no employers in the kibbutz, no supervisors or managers in the usual sense of the term. General policy is decided upon by the entire membership in plenum; committees submit detailed plans; and each branch that requires one elects a "coordinator" of activities, an office that is rotated regularly.

Finally, the question as to whether kibbutz members, not subject to individual financial predicaments, work as hard as or work harder than their opposite numbers in non-kibbutz settings cannot be answered empirically, due to measurement and comparison problems. However, when kibbutz industries are compared with similar industries outside the kibbutz, the findings, stated carefully and conservatively, are that kibbutz industries are no less efficient and productive than are non-kibbutz industries.[4]

THE SETTING

when?

The kibbutz that is the setting for this study will be called here Kibbutz Biluim. It is located not far from the coast, at the head of a fertile valley. The original group of members, consisting entirely of Israelis, founded the settlement in the mid-1930s, and were later joined by a group of youngsters from Europe. Before settling permanently at the present site, the group lived in various other settlements.

At the time of the study, the kibbutz contained 7000 dunams (1 dunam = .25 acre) of arable land, and 2000 dunams of woodland. On the work roster at the time were 255 adult members. In addition, the kibbutz contained within its physical boundaries—and provided services to—the children of members, aged, retired parents of members, youth groups from other parts of Israel, some foreign volunteers, and, inevitably, some visitors. The respondents for this study were restricted to the adult members of the kibbutz.

Although the kibbutz engages in mixed farming, including field crops and vegetables, the fruit orchards provide a substantial part of its income; there is also a factory, hothouses for flowers grown for export, and a few sheep.

The members of the research team—all university students—were housed with families of the kibbutz during the week of interviews, and spent their free time, mostly with kibbutz members of the same age, in the swimming pool, nightclub, and other recreational facilities of the kibbutz. This not only helped create rapport with members, which aided subsequent interviews, but added insights that were helpful in interpreting the results.

REASONS FOR THE STUDY

The reason for the study discussed here came about through a convergence of interests between the author and some members of a kibbutz with whom he was acquainted. The author was interested in seeking answers to the three questions outlined above; the kibbutz members were interested in increasing the satisfactions in kibbutz living in general, and in learning more about members' work patterns for purposes of more realistic planning and, it was hoped, in order to increase productivity.

SOME PROBLEMS OF KIBBUTZ RESEARCH

All research, and particularly that involving human beings, contains problems which researchers attempt to solve in various ways.[5] Some of these rather classical problems become unique in the way they exist, or are expressed, in the kibbutz.

ACCESS[6]

No one in a kibbutz is in the position to sanction a research project involving the members without the consent of the members themselves. Whereas in a factory management can authorize the study without asking the workers, and whereas in a community one can enter and begin questioning residents without authority from anyone, in the kibbutz there is no body, including the secretariat, that can authorize research without the consent of the polity. This involved the author in numerous meetings with individuals, then with committees, and finally, in a presentation followed by questions and discussion at the weekly membership meeting.[7]

Among questions raised was one concerning the ultimate value of the study to the kibbutz, since many kibbutzim are surfeited and alienated by researchers who are given access, come in, collect their data, and disappear, never to be heard from again. If their findings appear in some journal, the kibbutz is not sent a copy. As one kibbutz member put it, "Too many academic careers have been made at our expense." Another group wanted assurances that the research would result in recommendations that would improve the work situation and, further, that the researcher would serve as consultant to see that the recommendations were carried out. Still others commented that the kibbutz (as a movement) had been overresearched, and ought to be let alone for a while. Then there were questions of confidentiality, and the cost to the kibbutz in work time lost. In the final analysis, each of these issues was settled, without a commitment concerning recommendations or their application. However, the process of acquiring access not only required a long time; it raised or made more poignant some other research problems.

CONFIDENTIALITY

Guarantees of confidentiality of responses and anonymity of respondents are not unique to kibbutz research, but in a relatively small group of people, who live and work together every hour of the day and night, and among whom personal feelings might be intense, not identifying individuals or groups of respondents through description or quotation becomes doubly important and doubly difficult. As one member put it, "If you speak of older people who come from the Middle East, have little formal education, and work in the child-care branch, we'll all be trying to figure out which of the two people you mean." Similarly, if the statistical findings indicated that one percent of the respondents hated their life in the kibbutz and were trying to sabotage its success (which is a purely hypothetical case—there were no such responses), that would amount to two people, and many members might be able to guess at who the two were, without previously having been aware of the strength of their unhappiness. Finally, since this study involved identifying the best and worst workers—as will be detailed later—it was terribly important that the accolade or the stigma not be "made official" through the research report.[8]

CONTAMINATION

Conversely, the very closeness of kibbutz members to one another for the entire day, sharing in many activities, including communal meals, can lead to contamination of responses as those who have already been interviewed comment on the questions and answers, or the methodology, or are asked about it by others. Indeed, the very process of acquiring access, described above, contains the problem that some members want to know in advance what will be asked during the research, as an honest effort to judge whether the research should be authorized or not. This is particularly difficult when the question is asked by research-unsophisticated people, who really do not understand why they cannot discuss the questions and possible answers among themselves before submitting to an interview.

DECEPTION

Although "deceit" is a strong word, fooling respondents to a certain extent is, as Kelman has pointed out,[9] a widespread practice in behavioral research, and has both ethical and practical implications. Deceit arises from the assumption that the respondent's awareness of exactly what subject or trait is being investigated will so affect his or her behavior, attitude, or response that valid conclusions cannot be drawn from them. In Goffman's terms, the investigator may thus be forced to study the impression that the respondent gives, rather than that which he gives off—and the latter may be the focus of the study.[10]

In the kibbutz, which has a strong work ethic, one could anticipate that questions which asked directly about attitudes toward work would result in answers indicating devotion to, and pleasure from, work. On the other hand, by asking how a successful kibbutz should use its profits, answers were obtained which could be categorized as those which called for changes in work and work conditions, and those which dealt with the nonwork aspects of kibbutz life. It is not certain that a more straightforward question, asking whether profits should be used to change work conditions or for other things, would have evoked the same response. Thus, insofar as indirect questions involve deception, some of the questions used fit into that category.

Leaving aside, for the moment, the question of how much deception was needed and used in this research, the kibbutz as a research setting involves many problems on this score. Since the respondents must agree to the research, and sometimes even want to approve the instruments used, a sophistication concerning the indirect techniques to be used can result, and the responses can thus be affected. For example, if the reason for the question concerning the use of kibbutz profits is challenged by a member who sees no connection between that and the work satisfactions being investigated, it becomes necessary to explain that all of the answers to this question will simply be categorized as concerning work or not concerning work. It would be unrealistic to then expect the same respondent to answer the question as though he or she were not aware of the categories to be used in classifying the answers.

Consequently, the question of how much the researcher can share with respondents without biasing their answers becomes a delicate one in kibbutz research. The researcher has several alternatives. He or she can deal with the small group of interested or influential members concerning details, and hope or ask that the details not be shared outside the group—a violation of kibbutz principles, but possible in practice. In effect, then, the members of the small group become his or her co-conspirators. He or she can then exclude them from the interviews—and thereby perhaps lose some of the most important respondents in the kibbutz—or include them, using various rationalizations.

Or, the investigator can, presumably, deceive even the small group, giving them good reasons, but not the real reasons, for the item. As Kelman points out, a widening circle of such duped (and therefore increasingly sophisticated) subjects makes subsequent research more difficult and more suspect.[11] Finally, the researcher can attempt to go into as little detail as possible concerning the actual research instruments, asking the respondents—as it were—to trust him or her.

It was this last method which was used in the more serious piece of deception which this study contained. This involved the delicate problem of identifying overworkers and underworkers. Exploratory discussions and pretests had indicated that, while members were willing to identify overworkers in the kibbutz, requests for the names of underworkers were indignantly refused. It was quite obvious that identifying fellow members as poor workers to an outsider, and by name, was a serious violation of kibbutz mores. Foreknowledge that this study would attempt such identification might have resulted in denial of access or refusals to participate if access were granted, and in responses influenced by feelings concerning this aspect of the study. On the other hand, confidential knowledge on the part of the researcher as to overworkers and underworkers made it possible to examine the two groups for similarities and differences—an important part of the findings for the kibbutz as well as for theory.

Again, it is the nature of the kibbutz which made this such an acute problem. Not only were kibbutz norms involved—the persons with whom the question would be discussed were the same as those who would be asked to identify—and might be identified as—over- and underworkers. In other settings, the question would have been discussed with management, union, or agency executive, and then used with workers or clients. In the present case, the researcher mentioned to the small group that was interested in the research that an attempt would be made to distinguish between over- and underworkers, but no details of the methodology were discussed. His manner, in fact, asked that he be trusted and not pressed for too much detail. The group discussed the idea, and although various viewpoints were expressed, the consensus was, "We all know who works hard and who doesn't. If he can find it out, and doesn't identify anyone publicly, why not?" Subsequently, the discussion centered on the methods for safeguarding confidentiality to be used.

It should be noted, however, that greater deception was deemed necessary and used in discussions with the entire kibbutz membership. There the research was presented in terms of studying work patterns, and identification of over- and underworkers was not mentioned by the researcher, nor by the group who were aware of this part of the design.

In summary, the classical question of deceit in social research is particularly cogent in kibbutz research due to the collective nature of the kibbutz and the lack of division between those who must approve methodology and instruments, and the respondents.

INTERVENTION EFFECT

All research with human beings of which the subjects are aware, or later become aware, can have an intervention effect. This can range from having to think about, and/or put into words, ideas not previously consciously formulated to much more severe reactions. Not all intervention is necessarily a negative factor, however. One of the chief results in the research being described, insofar as the kibbutz is concerned, was formulated, post facto, by a member: "Regardless of anything else that comes out of this research, it made us once again aware of work as an important part of kibbutz life. We had to think about it, talk about, discuss it among ourselves—we haven't consciously discussed work as a subject in almost twenty years. It was time we did."

THE INSTRUMENTS

There were 2 instruments used in this research—a questionnaire and a card-sort. After pretesting in other kibbutzim and revisions, the questionnaire consisted of 17 demographic questions, 53 forced-choice questions, and 7 open-ended questions. Among the forced-choice questions was a set of ideal-real comparisons. That is, at one point members were asked about their work situations, and at another about their preferred work situations. Congruence between preferences and actual situations was then used as a measure of satisfaction.

The card-sort consisted of cards identifying each member of the kibbutz by number, which were sorted into 4 piles, as will be described below, labeled as the best workers, the next best workers, the average workers, and the below-average workers.

The items on the questionnaire were drawn from three sources. The first of these was the literature on work patterns, satisfactions, and influences found in the literature of industrial psychology, industrial sociology, and small-group theory. The second source was the set of studies of kibbutzim done by others. The third source consisted of exploratory discussions held by the researcher with kibbutz members and other kibbutz researchers. From the last source some intuitive, folk, and conventional ideas presented themselves.

It should be noted that gaining access for this research, as noted previously, required some compromises, and one of these was the inclusion of some quesions with no theoretical base, and of no great relevance to the hypotheses being tested, representing "pet" subjects of some kibbutz members, or information that they agreed would be "interesting."

As finally drawn, questions concerned the following:

(1) demographic material
(2) the structure of and situation in the work branch
(3) the kibbutz as a work organization
(4) views of work generally
(5) views of self
(6) personal pattern of work
(7) world view

Insofar as measures of satisfaction are concerned, the instrument approached this in three ways: open-ended questions about sources of work satisfaction, that is, a modification of Herzberg's approach; congruence questions as mentioned above; and some indirect questions, such as the use to which unexpected kibbutz profits should be put, with the answers then categorized as those which change the work situation, and those which are irrelevant to it.

METHODOLOGY

The administration of the questionnaires was straightforward, at times designated by the respondent. Insofar as the card-sort was concerned however, a word of explanation is in order.

The original intention of the card-sort was to say to respondents: "In every kibbutz there are people known as hard workers. They put all of themselves into every job. They never shirk, and can be depended upon to finish every job they undertake. Are there such people in this kibbutz?" On receipt of an affirmative answer (and every respondent answered affirmatively), the respondent was to be asked to find such people on a list, note their numbers, and then put the corresponding cards into a separate stack.

(The use of numbers on cards rather than names arose from previous experience that people are more willing to identify others through a procedure which seems anonymous than directly by name. This was also due to kibbutz tradition of referring to one named Samuel, for example, as Sammy, Samick, Shu-shu, or a number of other nicknames dating back to childhood.)

The next question was substantially the same as the first, but asked for identification of those who "usually work that way, but on some jobs, or sometimes, do not." A second stack of cards was intended to result. In this way, it was intended that each kibbutz member would rate each other member on a three-point scale, thus making it possible to distinguish between relative overworkers and underworkers.

During the beginning use of this procedure, however, interviewers were surprised by respondents who were themselves surprised that no questions were asked about people at the other end of the scale. It had not occurred to the researchers that kibbutz members would be willing to engage in such negative identification of other members, but the procedure was quickly altered, and the third question, resulting in four stack of cards, related to members who never seem to work hard, always find excuses for not working, and cannot be depended upon to complete tasks.

In this manner, scores were obtained for every member of the kibbutz, and by tallying the number of times each had been assigned to a category, which was weighted, a net score as a worker was obtained for every respondent. The results turned out to be very close to an average bell-shaped curve, which made it possible to compare reputations as workers with individual and total responses, and to compare the extreme cases.

Of the 255 adult members of the kibbutz at the time of the research, 219 were interviewed. The remainder were ill, absent, or could not be interviewed for other reasons; 18 members refused to be interviewed.

The use of peer ratings, or reputational techniques, arose from pragmatic considerations. As pointed out previously, no production records concerning individuals are kept in the kibbutz, nor would a kibbutz agree to do so. Even where there are production records, outside of kibbutz settings, this is not without its problems. For one thing, such records do not indicate to what extent the effort of the worker is involved, as compared to intelligence, dexterity, knowledge of shortcuts, or the like, as well as the influence of the previously mentioned machines, methods, and materials. Even when production records are kept, in industrial settings, these are almost invariably for purposes of paying salaries, bonuses, premiums, group incentives, and so on, which negates the goal of holding money constant in the research.

An effort was also made in the kibbutz study to elicit self-ratings of workers, although this was not used for correlational purposes. Some considerations concerning self-ratings and peer ratings follow.

SELF-RATINGS

In some research, such as motivational research, self-ratings are sometimes used as both the independent and the dependent variable. That is, workers are asked to describe themselves along some dimension, such as effort expended, and then asked to describe their feelings, aspirations, expectations, and so on. In such cases the "model" correlates higher with self-rated efforts than with effort rated by independent observers. As a consequence of such problems, Campbell and Pritchard suggest that in motivational research, at least, self-ratings of effort not be used.[12]

In both the kibbutz and the factories studies (to be described later) self-ratings of effort, or images as a worker, were solicited. The tendency for self-reports to contain more socially acceptable responses, or to be more positive, is clear in both these cases: In the kibbutz study, 18 percent of the members were categorized by their peers as excellent workers, but 28 percent felt that they would be so categorized—or were at least so seen—by others. Similarly, whereas 50 percent of the members were rated by others as better than average workers, 86 percent felt they would be so rated. Conversely, 25 percent called themselves excellent, while only 18 percent of their peers did so, and 80 percent called themselves better than average, but only 50 percent were so rated by others. In short, self-ratings differ considerably from peer ratings—in this case in the direction of social acceptability—and the choice of which to use must depend upon the goal of the research.

PEER RATINGS

When production records are not available, or are used as the basis for differential payments, peer ratings may be the measuring instrument of choice. In the case of the kibbutz study the use of peer ratings came about because, as mentioned earlier, there are neither individual production records, differential money payments, nor supervisors in the generally accepted sense in the kibbutz. This meant that the choice was basically between observation, which would have involved lengthy, and probably impossible, periods of observing each worker, and peer ratings, obtained as described. Nevertheless, peer ratings are "softer" data than production records would be.

For example, personal feelings enter into such ratings. In the kibbutz research, even those rated as very poor workers by most of the members were rated as good or very good workers by a few. A spot check indicated that the latter were usually spouses or other family members. It might also be possible that a time factor operates: There are people in the kibbutz who acquired their reputations as workers a long time ago, and who have continued in their reputations without objective justification. Similarly, a reputation might be achieved as a result of a particular incident, perhaps with high visibility, which is not representative of the worker's real role. Again, there are some tasks in the kibbutz which might have a halo effect on the members undertaking them; and there might be extra-kibbutz activities, such as army rank or role, which at least feed into the work reputation.

Flowing from this aspect, there is the additional limitation that, whereas the reported attitudes might be current, or even transient, feelings, reputations are long-lasting and subject to slow change. For example, a report that "my work requires more ability than I have," might—and in terms of the instructions contained in the study, should—refer to the work that the respondent was doing on the day of the interview. On the previous or next day, the work might be different, and thus the reported attitude different. The worker's reputation, however, would tend to remain the same on each of the three days, regardless of the work involved. Thus, the study compares long-term reputations with short-term attitudes—a limiting factor which should be kept in mind when reading the results. The severity of this limitation, however, is not as great as might be imagined, since most workers tended to do the same work every day.

Despite these limitations to peer ratings, in the research being described such ratings probably had more validity than they might have had elsewhere. Kibbutz members, as has been pointed out, live in the same area, work for the same "firm," so to speak, and intermingle during many hours of the day and night. Their ratings of each other come from a myriad of experiences, stretching over time. Consequently, when 197 of 219 respondents label someone as an excellent worker, the chances are that he really is. Similarly, when 117 of 219 respondents agree that someone is lazy, this too should be given credence. These were, indeed, the extremes in the kibbutz study.

THE FINDINGS

Given the number of questions, the differences among respondents both in terms of demographic background and work situations (branches, seniority, and so on), and possible intervening variables, an enormous amount of data was generated, and is available in the full final report of the study.[13] The results mentioned here will refer only to the three basic questions listed previously.

THE BIPOLARITY THEORY

Since the influence of money payments on other sources of satisfaction or dissatisfaction is not clear in Herzberg-type studies, one purpose of this research was to see to what extent Herzberg's findings were replicated in a moneyless environment. For this purpose, a modified type of Herzberg's question was used. Rather than ask about a certain time when the worker felt satisfied, respondents were asked: "In general, what are the things that give you satisfaction in your present work?" and "In general, what are the things which cause you dissatisfaction in your present work?"

The relative weights of the factors creating work satisfactions or dissatisfactions in the kibbutz under study, using a modified Herzberg methodology, are:

	Dissatisfactions	Satisfactions
work itself	14.8	41.9
achievement	17.0	33.0
interpersonal relations	20.5	28.0
responsibility	2.8	21.4
working conditions	28.4	18.1

The four factors which are seen to result in more satisfactions than dissatisfactions are thus seen to be the work itself, achievement, interpersonal relations, and responsibility; while the one factor resulting in more dissatisfaction than satisfaction is that of working conditions.

More specifically, dissatisfactions were expressed with physical conditions, the presence of temporary workers in the branch, a feeling of lack of cooperation on the part of other organs of the kibbutz, members' own feelings of not being permanently assigned to the branch, and a feeling that there was lack of proper planning.

Satisfactions, on the other hand, were expressed with the feeling of doing important work, fittedness to the job, pleasant work as such, profitability to the kibbutz, independence at work, suitable time schedule and pace, and the feeling of using skills properly. On the face of it, these findings replicate those of Herzberg-type studies. Further, when those sources of satisfaction or dissatisfaction which were mentioned by at least 10 percent of the respondents are grouped according to Herzberg's categories, it is clear that the bulk of dissatisfactions come from working conditions, while the bulk of satisfactions arise from the work itself and from feelings of achievement and responsibility.

On the other hand, the weights of these categories as satisfiers or dissatisfiers are not as clear-cut as in the Herzberg studies. Further, "contact with children and/or pupils" was given as a reason for satisfaction by child care workers and educators, while this category was not used by Herzberg, whose studies were mostly in industrial settings. It would be possible, of course, to subsume this under "interpersonal relations," but the manifest meaning of the latter in most studies is contact with fellow workers and sub- and super-ordinates; hence, a separate category is used here.

Only the factor of interpersonal relations, which is given much more weight in the kibbutz than in the Herzberg studies, both as a satisfier and a dissatisfier, is unique. This, however, may be a reflection of the unique nature of work and life in a kibbutz.[14] The work group and the nonwork group are made up of the same people. The work place is contiguous to the living quarters. Discussion of work matters carries over into communal meals, evening socializing, and other settings. Conversely, kibbutz matters such as child care methods or problems may be discussed throughout work time. In short, the interrelationship between work and nonwork is so close that the personal relationships and feelings about them—positive and negative—carry over into the work place and occupy a more prominent place in satisfactions or their lack than in other settings.

In summary, it was found that the findings leading to Herzberg's bipolarity theory were not so distorted by unrecognized factors stemming from money as to be invalid. Insofar as Herzberg's open-ended methodology is followed, satisfactions and dissatisfactions tend to stem from different sources, even where money is absent.

HUMAN RELATIONS AND HUMAN PRODUCTIVITY

The second question examined in the research described here has to do with the connection, if any, between human relations at work and worker productivity. In short, do people who are happy with the way they relate to other people, and the ways they are related to, work harder or produce more, as the Hawthorne studies seemed to indicate?

Questions in this area dealt with relationships with other people in the branch, the desire to work alone or with others, relationships with the branch coordinator, relationships with other kibbutz members, with how many other people the respondent considered himself or herself on good terms, and, of course, the responses concerning sources of satisfaction and dissatisfaction that were related to relationships.

In summary, it can be stated that none of these questions individually, nor all of them together, correlated with reputations as workers. That is, underworkers and overworkers all along the scale, and when considered as separate categories, were not distinguishable by their answers to questions concerning relationships. The reasons for their work patterns obviously lay elsewhere.

SATISFACTIONS AND WORK PATTERNS

The third question examined in this research concerned the relationship between work satisfaction in general, and specific sources of satisfaction, and work patterns. In short, do satisfied people work harder? This, it will be recognized, was a widening of the Hawthorne question from human relations to all satisfactions, and an attempt to determine empirically whether Herzberg's substitution of the term "motivator" for "satisfier" had a basis. For these purposes, four "congruence" questions, as noted previously, were used. Workers were asked about their current work situations insofar as individual or shared decision making was concerned, about the amount of physical labor involved in their jobs, about the size of the work group, and about their permanence in the branch. Congruence between the actual and the desired situation was considered satisfaction. Another 14 questions dealt with various assumed sources of satisfaction, such as, "The work matches my skills," instead of demanding too much or too little, assumed sources of dissatisfaction, such as physical conditions in the branch, indirect questions concerning the use of kibbutz profits and the amount of free time, direct questions about satisfaction with life generally and with happiness at work and at nonwork, and, finally, the open question about sources of work satisfactions and dissatisfactions.

Respondents ranged from the very happy, that is, those who indicated satisfaction on 16 of the possible 18 answers, to the very unhappy, who registered no satisfaction responses at all. When the range of satisfaction scores was compared with the range of work-pattern scores (that is, from best to worst worker), almost no correlation was found (.029). In other words, whether a person indicated satisfaction or dissatisfaction with his or her work situation had almost no relationship to his or her reputation as a worker.

One subsidiary question examined in connection with the kibbutz research deserves mention. "Self-actualization," as postulated by Maslow as the last, or highest, of human motivations or needs, has been adopted by many experimenters as a desirable goal,[15] and used as a rubric to encompass Herzberg's findings concerning the importance of the work itself as a satisfier (according to Herzberg, read: motivator). Taking the items from the kibbutz questionnaire which were presumed to indicate feelings of self-actualization and seeking to correlate them with reputations as workers resulted in a distinction between overworkers and underworkers. The former reported more feelings of self-actualization at work than did the latter, which seems to indicate the importance of self-actualization as a motivator. Since, however, further investigation indicated that both overworkers and underworkers were doing basically the same work, it appears that the view of work as self-actualizing is the operative variable, and not the work itself.[16]

The results of this part of the kibbutz research may be summarized as follows: Insofar as reputation as a worker indicates one's actual work pattern; and insofar as the eighteen questions were answered honestly and truly measured respondents' satisfactions or dissatisfactions at work, there is little connection between being satisfied at work and working hard.

The results of the kibbutz study discussed here[17] can be summarized as answers to the three questions posed at the beginning of this chapter:

Although the influence of interpersonal relations on worker satisfaction and dissatisfaction is greater in the kibbutz than it seems to be in the industrial settings which constitute most Herzberg-type studies, overworkers and underworkers cannot be distinguished by the satisfactions or dissatisfactions caused them by interpersonal relations.

The findings of Herzberg-type studies, that satisfactions and dissatisfactions do not arise from the same source, with the former related to the work itself and the latter to conditions surrounding the work, seem valid in a situation where money payments cannot be an intervening variable. In other words, the problem of how to deal with money in incentive research, and the various ways of solving the problem, do not distort the other findings of these studies.

Finally, insofar as reputation as a worker arising from peer ratings indicates one's actual work pattern, and insofar as the eighteen questions were answered honestly and truly measured respondents' satisfaction or dissatisfaction at work, there is little connection between being satisfied at work and working hard.

NOTES

1. See, for example, D. Leon, *The Kibbutz: A New Way of Life* (London: Pergamon, 1969); M. Weingarten, *Life in a Kibbutz* (New York: Reconstructionist Press, 1955); Y. Criden and S. Gelb, *The Kibbutz Experience: Dialogue in Kfar Blum* (New York: Herzl Press, 1974).

2. The genesis of this situation is described by Eisenstadt: "The basic criterion of status evaluation was devotion to pioneering-collective tasks with prestige in the eyes of the community the main reward. It was assumed that material rewards—and especially *differential economic* (and even prestige and power) rewards—were not only unimportant but even dangerous and potentially disruptive to the solidarity of the pioneering group." S. N. Eisenstadt, *Israeli Society* (London: Weidenfeld and Nicolson, 1967), p. 146; italics in original.

3. A succinct summary of the ideology is: "The kibbutz movement saw the ideal of physical labor as an element which . . . would give the individual a new and healthy personality." A. Arian, *Ideological Change in Israel* (Cleveland: Western Reserve University, 1968), p. 106.

4. S. Melman, "Managerial versus Cooperative Decision Making in Israel." *Studies in Comparative International Development* (New Brunswick: Rutgers), 1970.

5. For example, A. J. Vidich, J. Bensman, and M. R. Stein, *Reflections on Community Studies* (New York: John Wiley, 1964); S. T. Bruyn, *The Human Perspective in Sociology* (Englewood Cliffs, NJ: Prentice-Hall, 1966); G. Sjoberg (ed.) *Ethics, Politics and Social Research* (Cambridge, MA: Schenkman, 1967).

6. Goldner describes the problem of access in an industrial corporation. F. H. Goldner, "Role Emergence and the Ethics of Ambiguity," in Sjoberg, op. cit., p. 245.

7. On the exclusive nature of some groups, and the problems thus posed for research, see A. K. Daniels, "The Low Caste Stranger in Social Research," in Sjoberg, op. cit., p. 267.

8. See R. Colvard, "Interaction and Identification in Reporting Field Research: A Critical Reconsideration of Protective Procedures," in Sjoberg, op. cit., p. 319; on confidentiality considerations making research impossible, see D. Macarov and B. Rothman, "Confidentiality: A Constraint on Research?" *Social Work Research and Abstracts* 13 (Fall 1977): 11-16.

9. H. C. Kelman, *A Time to Speak* (San Francisco: Jossey-Bass, 1968), p. 208.

10. E. Goffman, *The Presentation of Self in Everyday Life* (Garden City, NY: Doubleday, 1959), p. 2.

11. Kelman, op. cit.

12. J. P. Campbell and R. D. Pritchard, "Motivation Theory in Industrial and Organizational Psychology," in M. D. Dunnette (ed.) *Handbook of Industrial and Organizational Psychology* (Chicago: Rand McNally, 1976), p. 93; for a thorough discussion of self-ratings, see *Personnel Psychology* 33 (1980): 259-300.

13. D. Macarov, *Work Incentives in an Israeli Kibbutz* (Jerusalem: Paul Baerwald School of Social Work, the Hebrew University, 1973; Hebrew); for a summary, see D. Macarov, "Work Without Pay: Work Incentives and Patterns in a Salaryless Environment." *International Journal of Social Economics* 2 (1975): 106-114.

14. A. Antonofsky, H. Antonofsky, and N. Biran, *Social Life in the Kibbutz* (Jerusalem: Institute for Applied Social Research, 1970; Hebrew).

15. For example: "The most striking finding which emerges . . . is that those changes which meet the worker's need for achievement and responsibility are the most crucial for increased job satisfaction. Aside from income change and interest, the job characteristics which are most highly correlated with job satisfaction are those which measure perceived challenge of the new work: chances for advancement, the opportunity to learn, being able to plan and organize one's own work, and higher skill requirements." E. Mueller, *Technological Advance in an Expanding Economy* (Ann Arbor: Institute for Social Research, University of Michigan, 1969), p. 117.

16. D. Macarov, "Reciprocity between Self-Actualization and Hard Work." *International Journal of Social Economics* 3 (1976): 39-44.

17. The questionnaire used and the "marginals" (total answers) are contained in the appendix.

6

WORKER SATISFACTIONS

Stemming from the Hawthorne studies, which seemed to indicate that satisfying human relations lead to greater productivity, and reinforced by Herzberg's contention that increased satisfactions are motivators for increased work, the overwhelming bulk of incentive studies have sought ways to increase worker satisfaction as a way of increasing productivity. Before examining the extent to which such efforts have been successful, however, it might be well to look at the extent of worker satisfaction generally, and at some attempts to humanize the work place as such.

From antiquity, there have been enjoinders that workmen—and even slaves—should be treated humanely. The Bible, for example, instructs that a daily laborer should be paid at the end of the day—evidently a reaction to what had been the common practice of withholding wages. When the Stoics in ancient Greece began to develop the idea of a natural or moral law, as distinct from the law of the state, they became concerned about the condition of slaves, as well as their existence. They solved the problem by instituting what was, in effect, a double standard. This kind of ambivalence regarding the demands of morals and of economics has continued until today, although Anthony holds that the absence of ambivalence would probably result in the total subjection of ethics to economic practice.[1] In any case, the fact that the Greeks had to grapple with the problem of slaves in defining moral law indicates a concern for their rights, too.

Efforts to humanize human labor and the work place continued under the aegis of charismatic or dedicated individuals, or organizations and movements, and of governments. In England, the Factories Regulation Act of 1833 forbade the government in textile mills of children under nine years of age, and limited the hours of older children. Similarly, the hours and type of work permitted women were regulated by law, as were the conditions of those engaged in dangerous work of various kinds. Some such reforms resulted from the descriptions of conditions publicized by individuals such as Dickens, or by governmental investigative bodies, such as the Sadler Commission. However, the great bulk of efforts to humanize the work place were undertaken by the workers themselves, through their instrumentalities: working-class political parties and labor unions. The former were strong influences in the last half of the nineteenth century and the beginnings of the twentieth century, while the latter have remained a force with which to be reckoned even today. Indeed, the difficult and often bloody history of labor unions can be read as the tracing out of the conflicting demands of productivity on the one hand and the humanization of labor on the other. As Mallet says:

> More than a political act, . . . a strike was an affirmation of individual identity. By refusing to play along, the worker showed he was still a human being. By stopping the machines which controlled his daily life patterns, he created the illusion of controlling his own destiny. The strike was the dialectical negation of the dehumanization of work.[2]

That the struggle for humanization of the work place was not a conceit or a luxury is testified to by the accident rate at the Carnegie South Works between the years 1907 and 1910. Almost *one-quarter* of the recent immigrants employed there were injured or killed during that time.[3] Such facts, tragedies like the Triangle Shirtwaist Fire, and dangerous, degrading, dehumanizing work conditions gave labor unions some of their important reasons for being.

As physical conditions at work began to be improved, both through legislation and union contracts, the major energies of labor unions passed to the fight for higher wages and shorter hours. In some cases unions were coopted by management in the drive for higher productivity,[4] in which human factor improvements were presented as deterrents. In other cases unions became institutionalized to the point that maintaining the organizational structure became more important than guarding the rights of workers. There have also been cases in which union corruption has led to neglect of concern for workers. Finally, there are cases in which management-provided improvements are opposed as weakening the attractiveness of union membership.[5] However, despite the existence of such cases, labor unions' concern for humanization of the work place is an important element in the struggle for human work conditions.

Added to the historic commitment of labor unions to humanizing the work place has been a growing concern for human rights generally, that is, for the quality of life as distinct from the standard of living. This motivation has its historic roots in the move toward greater concern for individuals, which reached the height of public expression in the 1960s. Movements for civil rights, minority rights, the right to information, the right to privacy, concern for the ecology, the student revolt, consciousness-raising groups, and the counter culture all helped establish a concern for working people, among others, and their conditions.

This concatenation of human-rights demands and movements was the cultural soil from which grew the Quality of Working Life movement.

Attitudes expressed during the student revolt in Paris, in which one placard proclaimed "Work Makes You Ugly," the Lordstown strike against the sheer inanity of much of the work required, and other such events spurred the creation and development of the movement. Basically, however, the underlying reason for the emergence of a Quality of Working Life movement was the recognition that the quality of working life was not satisfactory, despite over fifty years of effort to improve workers' satisfactions for productivity purposes.

When one considers how the work scene has changed in a century, how work and its conditions have changed and presumably "improved," why is it that so many people are unhappy about their work experience?[6]

Examining the validity of this feeling empirically requires that a number of distinctions be kept in mind. First, there is a distinction between one's attitude toward work in general and attitudes toward one's own work. Then there is the level of satisfaction related to work as compared to satisfactions from the nonwork aspects of life. Finally, attitudes toward work can be subdivided into the necessity to work as such, attitudes toward the job, reactions to conditions in the work place, and feelings about the actual work done.[7]

WORK AS THEORY
AND WORK AS PRACTICE

The concept of work is one of the most widely spread and deeply embedded elements in individual psyches, the structure of societal institutions, and the value systems of industrial civilizations. It is the measuring rod of individuals, the goal of organizations, and the linchpin of society. It is almost as encrusted with value orientations and transcendental meanings as is religion. Moreover, although there are voices, groups, countries, and even international blocs which deny the necessity for, and question the efficacy of, religion, there is no organized or unorganized body throughout the world which publicly questions or denounces the work ethic, or which has as its primary goal a reduction in the amount of labor needed or used, or which aims to strip work of its ideological mystique in order to determine objectively the extent to which it is needed or beneficial.[8]

Work as an abstract value is one of the most highly regarded and jealously held items in the societal pantheon. It is analogous to mother-love, since it is considered immoral, impolite, unsocial, and vaguely treasonable to deprecate the importance of work. The overwhelming majority of people in western countries have been socialized through all the forces of education, religion, government, the market, and the family to see work not only as necessary for individual health and societal order, but as the basic source of happiness, health, and morals. Consequently, a world without work is inconceivable to many, and, when envisioned, regarded as catastrophic.[9] Even in utopian novels, a world pictured as not needing human work is considered dystopian by many readers, and in some cases by the authors.[10]

Attempts to question the role of work as a value and as a practice are generally met with laughter, then incredulity, then derision, and finally with anger that sometimes borders on violence. Questioning the role of work seems to touch and disturb deep psychic currents, disturbing people's hard-won defenses, and stirring up doubts, questions, and hostilities that make people uncomfortable. Even respected academicians and researchers, trained to be objective and to respect data, have been known to become defensive (and sometimes offensive) when work as an ideology is seriously questioned.[11] In fact, most people would agree—at least verbally—with Brightbill's flat statement: "It is difficult to imagine being happy without work. . . . We need work quite as much as we need food."[12] There may not have been such universal consensual validation concerning any single item since everyone agreed that the earth was flat.

It is interesting that in many cases the positive value placed upon work is correlated with doubts and fears concerning increased leisure. When a relatively workless world is postulated as a future possibility, a common response is: "What will people do with all that time?" There is a fear, sometimes openly expressed, that increased leisure will lead to dissoluteness, social problems, and unhappiness. This problem, incidentally, is usually projected onto others—"they" won't know what to do with more free time. Sometimes the reaction is more positive: Leisure-time facilities and preparation will have to be increased.[13] Indeed, there are some projections, only half joking, that the anticipated increase in leisure-time industries and occupations will require so much manpower that there will be few customers for the services. In any case, the overwhelming societal attitude toward work is that it is both necessary and desirable for individuals and societies, and that large increases in leisure time are to be feared.

However, when one moves from attitudes toward work in general to individuals' attitudes regarding their own work, one hears a very different tune being sung. In this regard, researchers have learned not to depend upon the first, often facile, answers given. In all survey research there is a tendency for respondents to report satisfaction with every aspect of their lives.[14] This may be because such answers are faster, require no thought, stir up no self-doubts, do not require exposing oneself to a relative stranger, and do not move toward creation of a relationship with the questioner. The guilt that one does not feel like one is "supposed" to feel; the gaps between one's avowed norms and one's actual behavior; the fear that one may be considered a freak for expressing iconoclastic ideas—all influence responses toward the socially acceptable.

Perhaps as a consequence of this factor, many of the studies that simply ask people something like "On the whole, how satisfied are you with the work you do?"[15] or ask them to rate their work or jobs on a scale, emerge with very high satisfaction scores. Quinn and Shepard report that 90 percent of their sample was satisfied, and 52 percent reported themselves as very satisfied.[16] On the other hand, some of these studies report on lack of dissatisfactions, which, as Herzberg has shown, is not the same thing as being satisfied.[17]

However, those studies which inquire into particular facets of work satisfaction, or probe as to what causes the expressed satisfaction, or discuss work experiences on a deeper level than responses to a questionnaire, come out with different results.

Rubin, for example, found that workers originally called their situations satisfactory, but after a discussion began "confessing" that their situations were actually very unsatisfactory.[18] This is also exemplified by one of Strauss's respondents, who replied in the affirmative when asked whether he had a good job. When pressed as to what made it a good job, he replied, "Don't get me wrong. I didn't say it is a *good* job."[19]

Summaries of those studies that probe deeper than simple questions indicate that few people in all the studies reported speak of their work as challenging, exciting, or fulfilling. Those that do are almost always in the free professions, or on the upper rungs of the employment hierarchy.[20] There is a certain irony in this fact, because the people who make employment policy, or do incentive research, are almost invariably in the free professions and/or high in the organizational hierarchy. They are usually very involved in their work, spending much time at it and getting a great deal of satisfaction from it. It never enters into their consciousness, as they make policy and do research, that other people do not like to work, or do not like their work, and they make policy and base research in ignorance of this fact. For example, 93 percent of urban university professors would choose the same work again, while only 16 percent of unskilled autoworkers would; 43 percent of a cross section of white-collar workers would choose the same work again, but only 24 percent of blue-collar workers.[21] In this connection, it might be well to mention again that, according to Strauss,[22] workers have different interests than does management; and that Boisvert found that workers and researchers define the quality of working life differently.[23]

Aside from these two categories, vast numbers of people neither expect nor receive satisfactions from their work situations. Attitudes towards one's own job show up in study after study as, at best, a resigned acceptance. It seems that, accepting the fact that they must work, many people simply resign themselves to it and try to make the best of it. This reveals itself in the widespread dissatisfaction and apathy among American workers found by a presidential commission,[24] and, on a less conscious level, in the untold personal, mental, and physical problems which have their roots in the world of work.[25] Even workers reporting themselves as satisfied often mean that they have made the best bargain possible under the circumstances, which has been termed "fatalistic contentment."[26] Thus, there is said to be a "surrender process" taking place, in which workers achieve contentment by forgoing aspirations.[27]

Even in those studies which seem to show work satisfactions as growing, reanalysis of the data indicates that there is a significant *decrease* in job satisfactions among low-paid workers, which is masked by an increase in satisfaction among the higher-paid workers—that is, those who are higher in the hierarchy.[28] However, very recent evidence indicates that the malaise is creeping up the organization:

> During the past twenty years, employee satisfaction in general has been decreasing. But what Opinion Research found particularly significant is that managers—once the most satisfied of all employees—are now part of this downward trend. On virtually all counts, managers are more dissatisfied with their jobs, their companies, and their opportunities than ever before.[29]

Overall, the number of workers expressing themselves as satisfied with their jobs declined between 1973 and 1977 by large percentages, ranging from 11.3 percent to 43 percent, in all occupational groups studied.[30]

Measures of work satisfaction are not confined to survey research. The continual reduction in work hours alluded to in Chapter 3 did not come about automatically, but was the result of workers' demands, usually expressed through their labor unions. Individual behavior also supports the thesis that most people do not enjoy their work. Absenteeism, tardiness, loafing on the job, and similar problems which industry spends millions of dollars to reduce are also symptoms of the same lack of satisfaction. Further, over 70 percent of the people retiring on Social Security in the United States today have opted for early retirement, despite the lower benefits that it brings. Limitations on Social Security payment amounts, and on postretirement income, make it unlikely that such retirees have not undergone a reduction in income—but they have elected to retire nevertheless. When Peugot, in France, made it possible for workers to retire at age 56 on 70 percent of the retiree's last wage, they were overwhelmed with applications. And not just from the work floor: "An incredible 79 percent of all engineers and senior management wanted to leave, as did 86 percent of technicians and 91 percent of shopfloor workers." The same phenomenon occurred at other French automobile companies and in other industries.[31] Finally, despite the mythology to the contrary, retirees who do not have financial problems are mainly enjoying life, are glad they retired, and wish they could have retired earlier. Most research that reports postretirement difficulties and regrets does not control for the loss of income factor, which affects many people and is the source of their unhappiness, rather than the loss of work.[32]

> It has seldom been suggested that people past sixty are glad to quit some of their activities. Handing over is usually described as a loss for which there must be compensation. . . . However, evidence is accumulating that this is not so. . . . Among a population of middle- and working-class people adjustment and satisfaction increase after retirement.[33]

Further, an overwhelming majority of American workers would forgo most of their future pay raises for more time away from work: "A majority of workers would be willing to give up two percent of their current pay for such time, and about one-fourth would give up ten percent or more."[34] The latter figure has doubled in the years between 1965 and 1975.[35]

Thus it appears that there remains in most people a stubborn core of resistance to work, at least as exemplified in the work they are doing—that which Freud called "a natural human aversion to work."[36] And since they must work to get a share of society's resources, they resort to a number of methods to make their work situations livable, if not palatable. Some spend their work time dreaming, fantasizing, and thinking of other things.[37] Others invent games, challenges, or symbolic meanings through which they try to invest their activities with interest.[38] Still others use work as sublimation for other needs and drives.[39] The frequent coffee breaks, personal telephone calls, errands which must be run, joking with one another, and even frequent trips to the toilet are all attempts to get away from the boredom and meaninglessness of much work.

It seems clear that attitudes toward work as a concept and a value, and both expressions about and behavior concerning one's own work, are at considerable variance. Individuals use various methods of overcoming this gap between norms and behaviors—ambivalence, cognitive dissonance, and goal displacement, among others, each of which has been described in detail elsewhere.[40] In summary, however, it can be said that research results concerning work satisfactions differ as they become more specific and focus on respondents' actual jobs rather than on general attitudes.

WORK SATISFACTIONS
AND LIFE SATISFACTIONS

The general relationship between work time and nonwork time was discussed in the section on leisure in Chapter 2. The polar positions might be restated as "leisure as compensation" versus "leisure as spillover." However, few incentive studies even attempt to compare the level of satisfaction found at work with the level of satisfaction arising from outside-work sources. Consequently, when workers report themselves as satisfied or unsatisfied at work, they may be enormously more (or less) satisfied at work than when not working, or only somewhat more or less satisfied, or equally satisfied.

This may have important consequences for the interpretation of research results. If workers who report themselves as "very satisfied" at work mean by this that they are much more satisfied at work than otherwise, or much less satisfied than otherwise, these relationships may easily affect work attitudes. One who is very satisfied at work, but much more satisfied away from work, may relate to the job differently than someone who is not satisfied at work, but much more dissatisfied away from work. This is somewhat akin to the concept of relative deprivation in determining happiness, or the idea of reference groups in determining attitudes. Relative levels of work and nonwork satisfactions are therefore important, although taken into consideration in few studies.

One study that did concentrate on comparisons between work and nonwork situations found that life outside of work was generally perceived as a source of more rewards and less pressure, generating higher satisfaction and being more important.[41] More tangential evidence is found in a study of pervasive human values, in which 38 such values were found to be salient. Work does not even appear on the list.[42] In the kibbutz study discussed earlier, 61 percent of the members were happier during free time than at work; 9 percent of the members were happier at work; 55 percent wanted more free time; and 87 percent wanted Israel's 6-day workweek to be reduced to 5 days. Campbell and associates constructed an index of well-being, and found that the proportion of explained variance (r^2) from nonworking activities was 29; from family life, 28; from standard of living, 23; and from work, 18.[43]

Perhaps the strongest piece of evidence concerning work satisfaction in relation to nonwork satisfaction is the fact that practically no one, in any of the studies, indicated that they would like to work more than they now do for the same or less salary. Even in the kibbutz, which has a strong emphasis on work and pays no salaries, only 2 of 219 respondents expressed the desire to work more. Consequently, it would be wise in conducting incentive research, and in reading such reports, to recognize that satisfactions from work are rarely as great as those from nonwork, except, again, among some professionals, craftspeople, and those in powerful and responsible positions.

COMPONENTS OF WORK SATISFACTION

One of the difficulties in conducting research into work patterns is the complexity of the measurements required.[44] Take satisfaction, for example. Seashore and Taber look for job satisfaction indicators and their correlates, and find this a complex question. They recommend taking into consideration at least the following factors:

antecedents of job satisfaction

macroenvironmental factors

occupational characteristics

organizational environment

the job and job environment

personality characteristics

abilities

transient personality traits

person-environment interactions

objective and subjective work environments

consequences of job satisfaction[45]

Satisfaction at work can be reported, observed, or imputed. Reports, in turn, can be facet-free, as in Herzberg's question asking about satisfaction generally, or facet-specific, asking about the effect of a specified factor on satisfaction. Observed satisfactions involve all the complexities of participant observation, plus the ancient behaviorism/phenomenology debate, since satisfaction cannot be observed directly. The imputation of satisfaction through other indicators, such as productivity, runs all the dangers of lack of validity of which Herzberg's substitution of "motivators" for "satisfiers" is a prime example. For all of these reasons, and others, some researchers have come to the conclusion that "job satisfaction is hardly worth measuring except for individuals or for highly homogeneous sets of persons."[46]

Nevertheless, attempts to measure satisfactions continue, and involve various types of classifications. Kulpinska, for example, distinguishes among autotelic reasons—satisfaction from the work itself; instrumental reasons—a means of acquiring income, power, or prestige; and pressure—direct and social.[47] Locke distinguishes between events (or conditions), consisting of the work, rewards, and context; and agents, consisting of self and others.[48] Obviously, there is no limit to the number of lists that can be made, but from the various studies reviewed in preparation for this book, a fourfold classification of the sources of worker satisfaction or dissatisfaction seems both adequate and useful.

WORKING AS SUCH

An area which is rarely, if ever, taken into account when examining attitudes toward work is the effect of having to work at all. Just as there are workaholics, who do not seem to be able to get enough work to do,[49] and who invent reasons why they must not cease working, so there are the work-inhibited,[50] to whom working may cause real psychic pain. As the British quip puts it: Work is the curse of the drinking man; or, a rough translation of a Hebrew epigram: Work is a pleasure—but I prefer leisure. On a more mundane note, there are mothers of small children, in various countries, who are forced to place their children in the care of others and go to work, on pain of being denied welfare benefits. Not all of them accept this situation as satisfying. Similarly, in addition to the women who enter the labor force gladly, there are many who would have preferred to be house-wives who are forced to do "real" or "market" work by various circum-stances. Many people who would prefer to study, or dabble in the arts, or travel—among other things—are reluctantly forced to go to work by eco-nomic circumstances. Others are forced by social pressures to enter the labor market, even if they could manage otherwise. As Griffiths has observed, in modern western society "everyone must want to work and feel guilty if they can't work. . . . People must work or want to work irrespective of their needs and aspirations."[51]

A great deal has been written about the effect of unemployment, under-employment, and malemployment on the psychic, social, and physical con-ditions of the people or groups involved. The desire to work, when frustrated by various conditions, is said to involve a congeries of ills ranging from changed self-images to sickness and even early death. Work conditions involving stress, or those that are excessively complex or simple, among other factors, are said to result in physical and psychological "dis-ease."[52] It is probably an artifact of widespread socialization toward work as a positive phenomenon that no research seems to have been mounted to study the results of work as a form of social coercion—that is, the possible ills that flow from being forced to work against one's will or inclination. And yet this factor might affect answers to incentive research questions in a manner unrecognized, and therefore not considered.

JOB-RELATED SATISFACTIONS

In addition to feelings about having to work at all, there are attitudes toward the job one holds. The most obvious component concerning one's job is the money involved. Does it pay well, or enough? This question might be answered in absolute terms, that it pays enough to live on, or pays as much as one needs (although not as much as one wants). The answer may be couched in normative terms, that it pays about what the work is worth. Or, the answer may be, and often is, put in relative terms—about what other jobs of this kind pay, or about what other people doing the same work get. Easterlin emphasizes the last category, that feelings of deprivation (and therefore satisfaction) are largely relative.[53] Once the need for money is relatively satisfied, other needs, to use Maslow's formulation, become potent.

One of these is the need for security. Is the job permanent, is there the ever-present fear of being fired, is the job admittedly temporary? Although there are undoubtedly some individuals who prefer transient work, and do not want to be tied down to or by a job, most workers view job security as a highly desirable condition, and unions negotiate over this point and protect members from infractions as strongly as they do where salaries are concerned. Not only is permanence a desired condition in its own right—many social welfare programs specifically exclude transient labor from such things as pension programs, unemployment insurance, illness and maternity programs, and so on. The importance of permanence is emphasized by Rubin, writing of her blue-collar respondents:

> By the time they're thirty, about half are settled into jobs at which they've worked for five years. With luck, they'll stay at them for many more to come. Without it, like their fathers, they'll know the pain of periodic unemployment, the fear of their families doing without. For the other half—those still floating from job to job—the future may be even more problematic. Unprotected by seniority, with work histories that prospective employers are likely to view as chaotic and unstable, they can expect little security from the fluctuations and uncertainties of the labor market.[54]

Some countries recognize the need for job permanance legally protected. In Israel, holding a job for a specified length of time (usually six months or a year) results in legally recognized tenure, and such a tenured employee can only be dismissed for specific causes, involving semilegal procedures with the right of appeal, and is then entitled to one month's gross salary for every year of work.[55]

As one of Rubin's respondents emphasized, what one wants from a job are "good money, good benefits, and seniority."[56] Good benefits include vacations, pension rights, and other fringe benefits, which might include purchasing in a company-owned discount store or subsidized transportation to and from work.

Another job-related satisfier has to do with occupational status and prestige. The desire for a socially acceptable job may be strong enough to be used as a trade-off for salary or permanence. Despite the fact that garbage collectors in some cities are relatively well paid—well paid enough so that there are more applicants than jobs—"garbage collector" is still used as a general description of the lowest level of job types. Hence the sporadic attempts to disguise the nature of the work with honorific titles—sanitary technician, maintenance person, and the like. One of Garson's respondents was speaking to the need for status by saying: "Why should they treat you like dirt just because you work in a factory?"[57] Caplow found that personal service was seen to be inherently degrading, and that working for an individual was less prestigious than working for an organization.[58] The degrees of status attached to a particular job have been investigated many times, both in general and in the area of career and occupational choice. There is little question but that the prestige or status of a certain job plays a part in its classification as a good job or not.

Another factor concerning whether a job is seen as a good job or not has to do with the product. There is evidence that an increasing number of prospective workers, and particularly young ones, are opposed to work that produces items which they consider unnecessary, wasteful, or dangerous. Given a choice of producing toys or weapons, they would opt for toys. Given the same choice between a factory suspected of polluting rivers, shore lines, or the air and one certified as "clean," many would choose the latter.[59]

Hence, when one speaks of having a good job, or being satisfied with one's job, there are a number of factors inherent in the responses which do not have to do with the conditions of the job or the content of the work. In other words, what Strauss's previously quoted respondent was saying, in effect, is that there are levels of goodness regarding jobs.

SATISFACTIONS FROM THE WORK PLACE

Satisfaction or lack of satisfaction with one's job is not the same thing as the satisfactions or their lack which might arise in the work place itself. The effects of physical conditions, such as heat, noise, cleanliness, lighting, restrooms, drinking water sources, and vending machines are clear. In addition, there are those elements which flow from relationships between persons at work—fellow workers, superordinates and subordinates, support and service personnel, and so on. Again, these relationships may not be of great importance in the total life of the worker. Goldthorpe found that only a small number of workers are members of solidary work groups, and there was no indication that the majority were greatly concerned with maintaining close relationships with their workmates, either within or outside the work place.[60] Indeed, as Ingham found, relationships at work may clash with those in the family.[61] Nevertheless, the almost-enforced proximity to other persons may be viewed in varying degrees of pleasantness or its lack. In the kibbutz study, despite the strong emphasis on cooperation and collectivization in the setting, 59 percent of the respondents preferred working completely or almost alone.

The work place may be the forum for an informal organization, with various roles being played out, and one may get satisfaction from being seen as the leader, compromiser, peacemaker, intellectual, or any number of other informal roles.[62] Dissatisfaction, of course, may spring from the same source, that is, from *not* being seen as the leader, or whatever, or from being the rejectee, butt, or scapegoat. In addition, many people try to make otherwise unpleasant or meaningless work livable by making a game of it, or setting themselves challenges, and then get satisfaction or its lack by winning or losing. In some places, there are actual games among the workers, either related to the work or various kinds of lotteries, or—given sufficient free time—poker, chess, backgammon, or the like. There are workers who use free time on the job to make items for themselves or their friends—things which may range from knickknacks to pieces of furniture. The element of free time is important, since most of the people who report that they enjoy themselves in the work place report that their fun comes from daydreaming, the coffee break, or chatting with others.[63] Conversely, there are those who report themselves as unhappy because of free time—when all the work required can be accomplished in two hours of an eight hour day, there are workers who are bored with the empty time. In any case, it is clear that seeing a job as a good job or not and getting satisfactions from the work place are not the same thing, and not even necessarily related.

SATISFACTIONS FROM THE WORK ITSELF

Insofar as satisfactions from the work itself are concerned, the findings are various, but in the same direction. Satisfying work is said to be work which is challenging—but not challenging enough to be frustrating; work which requires all of one's abilities or skills, but no more; work in which one can see the entire product whole, and take pride in it; work which one feels is a contribution to society, and so on. As mentioned in Chapter 5, these various aspects of work are often subsumed under the rubric; self-actualization or self-fulfillment. Self-actualizing work is said to be the best incentive for both satisfaction and production. This stems from Maslow's formulation of human motivations, in which self-actualization is the last, or highest, of human needs. Self-actualization is often defined as using one's powers to the fullest, becoming everything that one is capable of becoming.

The self-actualization theorem can be questioned on three points. For one thing, this becomes a potent motivation only when all the previous normal human needs—physiological, security, love, and self-esteem—have been relatively well satisfied, and these are conditions, as has been shown, that are fulfilled by relatively few jobs. Secondly, as mentioned in the description of the kibbutz study, there is evidence that work patterns determine perceptions of self-fulfillment, and not the reverse.[64] Finally, with all the good intentions in the world, plus effort, plus investment, the great majority of jobs simply cannot be converted into self-fulfilling ones.

One of the objections raised to the idea of full employment or—more specifically—job-creation plans, is that the jobs offered are neither innovative nor personally satisfying.[65] Cass distinguishes between satisfying and fruitful jobs and frustrating and destructive ones,[66] and Marshall goes further, saying, "If you try to define good jobs as we ordinarily do, only about thirty percent of the jobs being created in the private sector can be considered good jobs."[67]

Even a glance at the Dictionary of Occupational Titles is enough to impress one with the number of jobs which are intrinsically devoid of meaning, distasteful, or unesthetic. As one reads the self-accounts of workers as compiled by Terkel,[68] Lasson,[69] Garson,[70] Rubin,[71] and others, it is difficult to understand why anyone would expect workers to get satisfaction from the kinds of work described: stacking ping-pong paddles into piles of fifties; boning tuna fish; putting tags on perfume bottle necks; comparing the code numbers on bottles with those on computer printouts; typing up sextuplicate insurance forms; moving boxes around in a warehouse; or cleaning someone else's house or car.

Take, for example, the young man observed next to the conveyor belt at a certain airport. About once in fifteen minutes a piece of luggage designated for his airline comes along the belt, and he slings it into a metal container. Between suitcases he whistles, smokes, walks around in small circles, leans against the concrete pillar, and stares up at the sky. Even were he to read between suitcases, or do crossword puzzles, or exploit the time in some other way, the question would remain as to what satisfaction one could honestly expect him to get from the actual work itself. And he can be multiplied by innumerable airlines and terminals, and by millions of other people employed in jobs equally devoid of content or meaning. Such workers can play games, set challenges, try to be good workers, enjoy or not enjoy their salaries, surroundings, and fellows, but as for getting satisfaction from the work as such—as they might put it—"No way."

Fein expresses this vividly:

> It is only because *workers choose not to find fulfillment in their work* that they are able to function as healthy human beings. . . . Workers would indeed become mentally ill if they took the behaviorists' proposals to heart. . . . By rejecting involvement in work which cannot be fulfilling, workers save their sanity.[72]

There is also another factor to take into consideration when examining satisfactions or their lack which spring from the actual work being done, and this is the relationship between technology and human labor. Improved technology, which may increase the need for human labor in the short run, almost invariably eliminates jobs in the long run. It also increases the division of labor and simplifies the actual work, often creating—as Durkheim had predicted—alienation and anomie among the workers. However, the most serious effect of technology is the ability to sustain and increase production with fewer workers. It has been estimated, for example, that current production could be maintained with one-half the workers now employed.[73] A serious drive toward higher technology could also reduce work in the service and support sectors—it has been estimated that managers and professionals could, within 5 years, increase their productivity 15 percent through increased use of computers and other automated office tools.[74]

However, western society provides no socially acceptable method of sharing in the fruits of production other than through job-holding. Hence, providing jobs for everyone able and willing to work becomes a goal of overwhelming importance for governments and for public bodies. The problem becomes one of keeping production—which is basically a matter of technology nowadays—and employment in tandem. A number of devices are employed for this purpose. Among these are: reduction in working hours, discussed previously; job sharing, in which two people do one job for half of the salary each; longer vacations; earlier retirement; work creation plans; guaranteed employment programs; training and retraining programs; acceptance of a 5 percent unemployment figure (which in practice may range up to 15 percent)[75] as desirable; and expanding educational subsidies to get people into, or keep people in, educational settings rather than jobs.

The most widespread devices for masking job shortages, however, are featherbedding and goldbricking. In the former, useless jobs are performed in order to stay busy. This is one result of union efforts to protect jobs by insisting that job-reducing machinery be introduced only with guarantees that nobody will thereby lose a job. This results in retaining people in jobs that they know, and everyone else knows, can be performed by a machine— faster, more correctly, cheaper; for 24 hours a day, 365 days a year, with no vacations, sick time, or strikes. Nevertheless, workers must pretend, or pretend to believe, that what they do is important, if not indispensable.

In goldbricking, the work may be important, and may require human labor, but can be done in much less time than that allotted. So workers must conspire with their superordinates, peers, and subordinates to appear busy; or, if not busy, to have no notice taken of it. They must dawdle, gossip, engage in horseplay, take breaks, make personal phone calls, and even leave the work site on personal errands in order to somehow get through the assigned work time. It is made clear to them in a number of ways that filling the time frame is at least as important, if not more important, than what they actually do:

> In industry, a common practice is to pay men [*sic*] by the hour. This indicates that a man's time is what counts rather than how much he accomplishes. Paying for time spent encourages men to put in their times rather than produce

according to abilities. . . . Discharge is based upon factors unrelated to production.[76]

How little importance is attached to what workers actually do during their work time is evidenced by the fact that low production as a cause for discharge or discipline of workers is only fourth on the list of causes, behind misconduct, insubordination, and absenteeism, accounting for only 11 percent of such actions.[77] An earlier study found that nine out of ten workers who lost their jobs did so because of poor health, poor personalities, and poor dispositions; they talked too much, were careless, untidy, intemperate, and unreliable.[78] Further, it is clear that few production workers are free to leave when they have filled their production quotas. Even workers on flexitime must put in a minimum number of hours—not produce a minimum number of units. Insofar as goldbricking is concerned, studies show the phenomenon to be increasing. Hours actually worked relative to hours paid for have declined significantly in the past few decades. In short, unproductive work time has been increasing.[79]

Again, the effect on human satisfactions—let alone on self-image, pride, integrity, and relations with others—has never been empirically examined. However, the feeling of not being needed probably plays at least some part in people's feelings about their jobs.

All of the above should not be taken to mean that there is no work from which people get pleasure, or no work which is self-actualizing. However, from all the studies of work satisfactions, and all the evidence concerning demands for less work time, early retirement, and so on, it is clear that large masses of people—perhaps the majority—do not find the actual work they do a source of satisfaction.

THE QUALITY
OF WORKING LIFE MOVEMENT

As noted previously, concern for workers' satisfactions stems from two sources. One is the assumption that there is a link between satisfaction and productivity—an assumption that will be examined in the next chapter. The second source of concern for workers' satisfactions is a humanitarian concern for workers' happiness as such, often subsumed under the term "quality of working life." Labor unions, governmental bodies, social workers, researchers, and occasional employers have been motivated by this concern, which began in the United States in the 1950s with the work of Herzberg and Davis, and in England at the London Tavistock Institute. There still remains a good deal of confusion concerning the term, and it is used variously. It is found throughout the literature as a virtual synonym for job redesign; for participative decision making; and for various packages of organizational changes. Dyer and Hoffenberg summarize the problem thus:

> The phrase "quality of working life" invokes a sympathetic response among many, but consensus has not yet developed on a definition of the problem that is implied. Thus those who attempt to improve the quality of working life are grappling with an ill-defined problem that occurs in the context of complex systems, and no generally accepted basis exists for the evaluation of their efforts.[80]

The problem is confounded by the fact that many efforts to improve the quality of working life have as their goals both productivity and humanization changes—goals which may be contradictory in some circumstances. Consequently, when management undertakes or approves efforts to improve the quality of working life, workers are often suspicious that the changes are intended to induce them to work harder or are intended to increase productivity, from which others will reap the benefits. In fact, it seems to be generally accepted that "employers are convinced that quality of work life and increased employee satisfaction can help raise the rate of productivity."[81]

Even when the goal is humanization of the work situation, with no specific reference to productivity, there is little consensus as to how to increase worker satisfactions. Herrick and Maccoby address the question of "humanizing work" (their title) in terms of security, equity, individuation, and democracy.[82] As will be noted, these aspects do not relate at all to physical conditions, pace, interpersonal relationships, the product, and— perhaps most notably—to the content of the work itself.

The entire quality of working life movement, insofar as its humanitarian roots and goals are concerned, is relatively new, and hence it is understandable that there have been few attempts to evaluate the success of such efforts. In this vein, Goodman speaks of the lack of follow-up studies. There are many accounts of the planning for, start-up of, and initial success of QWL projects, but few longitudinal studies to find out what happened later. Goodman's contention is that at least 75 percent of such projects were *no longer functioning* 5 years after their inception.[83]

Bar-Gal took a different tack, and studied the kinds of problems that occupational social workers dealt with, among other areas. He found that the tendency was for social workers to deal with that which Herzberg had termed hygiene factors, or dissatisfiers—the conditions of the work, rather than the work itself. Of the former, problems in the area of interpersonal relations—between workers, and between workers and superordinates— were dominant. In other words, occupational social workers seek to reduce dissatisfactions, not to increase satisfactions.[84] Perhaps it is for this reason that one of the few attempts to evaluate attempted changes in the quality of working life found that these resulted in no change at all in job satisfactions.[85]

SUMMARY

Summarizing this chapter on work satisfaction as such, it is clear that a great many people do not really want to work. Having no choice, they not only voice and exhibit resignation, indifference, apathy, and fatalism, they also press for shorter hours, more holidays, and earlier retirement. Indeed, the entire basis of social welfare policy, as discussed in the second chapter, is the fear, or the knowledge, that people will not work if given income from other sources. Hence the determination of welfare payments as a percentage—often a low percentage—of wages.

Insofar as jobs are concerned, relatively few offer what the workers consider good salaries, maximum benefits, and guarantees of permanence, together with high prestige and opportunities for advancement, while providing societally necessary and desirable goods and services without polluting the environment or upsetting the ecology. Further, the coexistence of high unemployment and the permanent shortage of personnel for certain types of jobs, the absenteeism, tardiness, and turnover that these jobs entail, and the need in many countries to import dependent and unsophisticated immigrant labor to support many industries and projects indicate how workers view such jobs.

Insofar as the work place is concerned, perhaps the greatest gains in recent years have been in terms of safety and physical conditions.[86] There is no evidence that the importance of relationships at work has increased, or that work has become more of a central life interest than heretofore. Kaplan even holds that people increasingly tend to identify themselves more in terms of their leisure-time pursuits than in terms of their jobs or occupations.[87]

Where the content of work is concerned, there is little evidence that it is any less boring, meaningless, monotonous, or devoid of content than it has ever been. Consequently, it has been projected that competition for preferred positions will become more and more intense in the future.[88]

Whether workers' satisfaction requires positive reactions to all of the four areas outlined above, or even to one of them, is a question of definition, but it is very questionable whether workers are more satisfied with the work aspects of their lives now than they have been in the recent past, regardless of definition. Whether the immediate future holds more satisfactions than does the present is equally open to serious doubt, and it is within this context that the possible relationship between satisfaction and productivity, discussed in the next chapter, should be viewed.

NOTES

1. P. D. Anthony, *The Ideology of Work* (London: Tavistock, 1977), p. 24.

2. S. Mallet, "The Class Struggle: Death and Transfiguration at Caltex," in E. Shorter (ed.) *Work and Community in the West* (New York: Harper & Row, 1973).

3. H. G. Gutman, *Work, Culture and Society in Industrializing America* (New York: Knopf, 1976), p. 30.

4. For a working paper on union-management cooperation for greater productivity, see S. Z. Mann, "The Politics of Productivity: State and Local Focus." *Public Productivity Review* 4 (1980): 352-367.

5. A. B. Cherns and L. E. Davis, "Assessment of the State of the Art," in L. E. Davis and A. B. Cherns (eds.) *The Quality of Working Life* (New York: Free Press, 1975), p. 34.

6. S. B. Sarason, *Work, Aging and Social Change: Professionals and the One-Life One-Career Imperative* (New York: Free Press, 1977), p. 19.

7. Gorn and Kanungo distinguish between involvement in work in general, and in a particular job. G. J. Gorn and R. N. Kanungo, "Job Involvement and Motivation: Are Intrinsically Motivated Managers More Job Involved?" *Organizational Behavior and Human Performance* 26 (1980): 265-272; similarly, Weiner and Vardi distinguish among attitudes toward the job, the employer, and the career. Y. Weiner and Y. Vardi, "Relationship Between Job Organization and Career Outcomes: An Integrative Approach." *Organizational Behavior and Human Performance* 26 (1980): 81-96.

8. The recently formed Committee for a Shorter Workweek hopes to spread the available work around better, but has no intention of trying to reduce the amount of human labor as such. See W. McGaughey, Jr., *A Shorter Workweek in the 1980's* (White Bear Lake, MN: Thistlerose, 1981).

9. Of the kibbutz respondents, 50 percent saw the proposal for an automated society in which most human labor would be unnecessary as undesirable, and another 20 percent called it catastrophic; see Chapter 5.

10. G. Kateb, *Utopia and Its Enemies* (New York: Schocken, 1972).

11. See "A Personal Note," in D. Macarov, *Work and Welfare: The Unholy Alliance* (Beverly Hills, CA: Sage, 1980).

12. C. K. Brightbill, *Man and Leisure* (Westport, CT: Greenwood, 1961), p. 23.

13. J. Neulinger, "Leisure and Mental Health: A Study in a Program of Leisure Research," in T. B. Johannis, Jr., and C. N. Bull, *The Sociology of Leisure* (Beverly Hills, CA: Sage, 1971), pp. 51-63.

14. B. Gutek, reply to question in discussion of "The Relative Importance of Intrapsychic Determinants of Job Satisfaction," paper delivered at NATO Conference on Changing Patterns in Working Life, Thessaloniki, Greece, 1979; Robinson also discusses the general cultural bias toward expressing contentment, and the positive responses to naive and superficial questions. J. P. Robinson, "Occupational Norms and Differences in Job Satisfaction: A Summary of Survey Research Evidence," in J. P. Robinson, R. Athanasiou, and K. B. Head, *Measures of Occupational Attitudes and Occupational Characteristics* (Ann Arbor: Institute for Social Research, University of Michigan, 1969), pp. 25-78.

15. R. P. Vecchio, "Individual Differences as a Moderator of the Job Quality-Job Satisfaction Relationship: Evidence from a National Sample." *Organizational Behavior and Human Personality* 26 (1980): 305-325.

16. R. Quinn and L. Shepard, *The 1972-1973 Quality of Employment Survey* (Ann Arbor: Institute for Social Research, 1974).

17. J. Taylor and D. G. Bowers, *Survey of Organizations: A Machine-Scored Standardized Questionnaire Instrument* (Ann Arbor: Institute for Social Research, University of Michigan, 1972).

18. L. B. Rubin, *Worlds of Pain: Life in the Working Class Family* (New York: Basic Books, 1976).

19. U.S. Department of Health, Education, and Welfare, *Work in America* (Cambridge: MIT Press, 1973).

20. C. N. Weaver, "Relationships Among Pay, Race, Sex, Occupational Prestige, Supervision, Work Autonomy, and Job Satisfaction in a National Sample." *Personnel Psychology* 30 (1977): 437-445.

21. U.S. Department of Health, Education, and Welfare, *Work in America,* op. cit., p. 16.

22. G. Strauss, "Book Review," of I. Berg, M. Freedman, and M. Freeman, *Managers and Work Reform: A Limited Engagement* (New York: Free Press, 1978); in *American Journal of Sociology* 85 (1980): 1467-1469.

23. M. P. Boisvert, "The Quality of Working Life: An Analysis." *Human Relations* 30 (1977): 155-160.

24. H. J. Weiner and S. H. Akabas, *Work in America: The View from Industrial Social Welfare* (New York: Columbia University School of Social Work, 1974).

25. Ibid.

26. K. Lasson, *The Workers* (New York: Grossman, 1971).

27. Robinson, op. cit., p. 66; this is in line with Fein's comment: "Though not nearly all workers hate their work, very few love it." M. Fein, "Motivation for Work," in R. Dubin (ed.) *Handbook of Work, Organizations and Society* (Chicago: Rand McNally, 1976), p. 492.

28. R. P. Quinn et al., "Evaluating Working Conditions in America." *Monthly Labor Review* 96 (1973): 32-43.

29. *World of Work Report* 6 (1981): 10.

30. B. Walfish, "Job Satisfaction Declines in Major Aspects of Work, Says Michigan Study: All Occupational Groups Included." *World of Work Report* 4 (February 1979): 9.

31. *World of Work Report* 6 (1981): 32.

32. R. Stagner, "The Affluent Society Versus Early Retirement." *Aging and Work* 1 (1978): 25-31; in Barfield and Morgan's study, three-fourths of retired respondents reported being "satisfied" or "very satisfied" with their life since retirement, and sufficient income was found to be the strongest indicator of satisfaction. R. E. Barfield and J. N. Morgan, *Early Retirement: The Decision and the Experience and a Second Look* (Ann Arbor: University of Michigan, 1969).

33. E. Cumming and W. E. Henry, *Growing Old: The Process of Disengagement* (New York: Basic Books, 1966), p. 19; others find "early retirees report greater satisfaction with life in general than do their working counterparts." N. Schmitt, B. W. Coyle, J. Rauschenberger, and J. K. White, "Comparison of Early Retirees and Non-Retirees," *Personnel Psychology* 32 (1979): 327-340.

34. *World of Work Report,* 5 (1980): 72, quoting study for the Department of Labor conducted by F. Best.

35. F. Best, "Preferences on Worklife Scheduling and Work-Leisure Tradeoffs." *Monthly Labor Review* 101 (1978): 31-37.

36. S. Freud, *Civilization and Its Discontents* (New York: Paperback, 1958), pp. 20-21.

37. M. Csikszentimihalyi, *Beyond Boredom and Anxiety* (San Francisco: Jossey-Bass, 1975).

38. One of Garson's respondents tried to see how high she could pile the cat-food component of the tuna fish she was gutting, as a challenge. R. Garson, *All the Livelong Day: The Meaning and Demeaning of Routine Work* (Harmondsworth: Penguin, 1975).

39. K. Menninger, "Work as Sublimation." *Bulletin of the Menninger Clinic* 6 (1942): 170-182.

40. D. Macarov, *Incentives to Work* (San Francisco: Jossey-Bass, 1970).

41. D. Kafry and A. Pines, "The Experience of Tedium in Life and Work." *Human Relations* 33 (1980): 477-503.

42. Y. A. Yadov and A. A. Kissel, "Job Satisfaction: Analysis of Empirical Data and Attempt at Their Theoretical Interpretation," in M. R. Haug and J. Dofny (eds.) *Work and Technology* (Beverly Hills, CA: Sage, 1977), pp. 45-58.

43. A. Campbell, P. E. Converse, and W. L. Rodgers, *The Quality of American Life: Perceptions, Evaluations, and Satisfactions* (New York: Russell Sage, 1976).

44. R. L. Kahn, "The Meaning of Work: Interpretation and Proposals for Measurement," in A. Campbell and P. Converse (eds.) *The Human Meaning of Social Change* (New York: Russell Sage, 1972).

45. S. E. Seashore and T. D. Taber, "Job Satisfaction Indicators and Their Correlates," in A. D. Biderman and T. F. Drury (eds.) *Measuring Work Quality for Social Reporting* (New York: John Wiley, 1976), pp. 89-124.

46. J. P. Campbell and R. D. Pritchard, "Motivational Theory in Industrial and Organizational Psychology," in M. D. Dunnette (ed.) *Handbook of Industrial and Organizational Psychology* (Chicago: Rand McNally, 1976), p. 79.

47. J. Kulpinska, "Workers' Attitudes Towards Work," in Haug and Dofny, op. cit., pp. 35-43.

48. E. A. Locke, "The Nature and Causes of Job Satisfaction," in Dunnette, op. cit., pp. 1297-1349.

49. M. Machlowitz, *Workaholics: Living with Them, Working with Them* (New York: Mentor, 1981).

50. H. A. Robinson and J. E. Finesinger, "The Significance of Work Inhibition for Rehabilitation." *Social Work* 2 (1957): 22.

51. D. Griffiths, *Whither Work* (Bundoora: Preston Institute of Technology Press, 1977), pp. 101-102.

52. D. Coburn, "Job-Worker Incongruence: Consequences for Health." *Journal of Health and Social Behavior* 16 (1975): 198-212; "Work and General Psychological and Physical Well-Being." *International Journal of Health Services* 8 (1978): 415-435; "Job Alienation and Well-Being." *International Journal of Health Services* 9 (1979): 41-59.

53. R. A. Easterlin, "Does Money Buy Happiness?" *Public Interest* 30 (1973): 3-10.

54. Rubin, op. cit.

55. D. Macarov, "Israel's Social Services: Historical Roots and Current Situation," in D. Thursz and J. L. Vigilante (eds.) *Meeting Human Needs: An Overview of Nine Countries* (Beverly Hills, CA: Sage, 1975).

56. Rubin, op. cit., p. 157; others have found similar desires: "Workers primarily want wage increases, greater security, shorter working hours and improved fringe benefits." Fein, op. cit., p. 489; "Workers want steady work, high wages, and good pensions." U. M. Gluskinos and B. J. Kestelman, "Management and Labor Leaders' Perception of Workers' Needs as Compared with Self-Reported Needs." *Personnel Psychology* 24 (1971): 239-246.

57. Garson, op. cit., p. 58.

58. T. Caplow, *The Sociology of Work* (New York: McGraw-Hill, 1954).

59. Parker found that many people employed in banking and insurance had doubts about the social usefulness of their occupations. S. Parker, *The Future of Work and Leisure* (New York: Praeger, 1971), p. 79; see also Macarov, *Work and Welfare . . .*, op. cit., pp. 104, 126-127.

60. J. H. Goldthorpe, D. Lockwood, E. Bechhofer, and J. Platt, *The Affluent Worker: Industrial Attitudes and Behaviour* (Cambridge: Cambridge University Press, 1968).

61. G. K. Ingham, *Size of Industrial Organization and Worker Behaviour* (Cambridge: Cambridge University Press, 1970), pp. 44, 48.

62. G. C. Homans, *The Human Group* (London: Routledge & Kegan Paul, 1951).

63. Csikszentimihalyi, op. cit.

64. D. Macarov, "Reciprocity Between Self-Actualization and Hard Work." *International Journal of Social Economics* 3 (1976): 39-44.

65. Griffiths, op. cit., p. 145.

66. M. Cass, *Development, Employment and the Environment: Is There a Conflict?* Curtin Memorial Lecture delivered at the University of Western Australia, October 11, 1974; quoted by Griffiths, op. cit., p. 26.

67. R. Marshall, "Selective Employment Policies to Achieve Full Employment," in B. D. Dennis (ed.) *Proceedings of the Thirtieth Annual Winter Meeting* (Madison, WI: Industrial Relations Research Association, 1978), p. 7.

68. S. Terkel, *Working* (New York: Random House, 1972).

69. Lasson, op. cit.

70. Garson, op. cit.

71. Rubin, op. cit.

72. Fein, op. cit., p. 493; see also a paper with a revealing title: D. Macarov, "Humanizing the Workplace as Squaring the Circle." Paper presented at the Second World Congress on Social Economics, Jerusalem, August 1981; *International Journal of Manpower* (forthcoming).

73. D. Gerard, "Democracy—A Fiction?" *Social Service Quarterly* 52 (1978): 24-27.

74. *World of Work Report,* 5 (1980): 77.

75. A. Kogut and S. Aron, "Toward Full Employment Policy: An Overview." *Journal of Sociology and Social Welfare* 7 (1980): 85-99.

76. N. R. F. Maier, *Psychology in Industrial Organizations* (Boston: Houghton Mifflin, 1973), p. 154.

77. Berg et al., op. cit., p. 148.

78. K. McFarland, "Why Men and Women Get Fired." *Personnel Journal* 25 (1957): 307.

79. J. W. Kendrick, "Productivity Trends and the Recent Slowdown." in W. E. Fellner (ed.) *Contemporary Economic Problems* (Washington, DC: American Enterprise Institute, 1979), p. 45.

80. J. S. Dyer and M. Hoffenberg, "Evaluating the Quality of Working Life—Some Reflections on Production and Cost and a Method for Problem Definition," in Davis and Cherns, op. cit., pp. 134-149.

81. *World of Work Report,* 6 (1981): 16.

82. N. Q. Herrick and M. Maccoby, "Humanizing Work: A Priority Goal for the 1970s," in Davis and Cherns, op. cit., pp. 63-77.

83. P. S. Goodman, "Quality of Work Life Projects in the 1980s," in *Proceedings of the 1980 Spring Meeting* (Madison, WI: Industrial Relations Research Association, 1980), pp. 487-494.

84. D. Bar-Gal, "Domains of Work and Methods of Work of Occupational Welfare Officers: An Exploratory Study of an Emerging Role." *Journal of Social Service Research,* in press.

85. B. A. Macy, "The Bolivar Quality of Work Life Program: A Longitudinal Behavioral and Performance Assessment," in *Proceedings of the Thirty-Second Annual Meeting* (Madison, WI: Industrial Relations Research Association, 1979), p. 89.

86. B. Strumpel, "Economic Life-Styles, Values, and Subjective Welfare," in B. Strumpel (ed.) *Economic Means for Human Needs: Social Indicators of Well-Being and Discontent* (Ann Arbor: University of Michigan, 1976), p. 22.

87. M. Kaplan, *Leisure in America: A Social Inquiry* (New York: John Wiley, 1960).

88. A. V. Adams, "The American Work Force in the Eighties: New Problems and Policy Interests Require Improved Labor Force Data." *Annals of the American Academy of Political and Social Science* 453 (1981): 123-129.

7

SATISFACTION AND PRODUCTIVITY

Despite the fact that many people get little pleasure from their work, or that levels of work satisfaction are lower than those from nonwork sources, there nevertheless remain differences in the amount of satisfaction that individual workers do achieve, differences from time to time in the same individual's satisfactions, and differences arising from changing situations. Whether these differences are related to productivity makes up the subject matter of this chapter.

The assumption that there is a connection between worker satisfaction and worker productivity, initiated by the Hawthorne studies and supported by Herzberg's semantic switch from satisfiers to motivators, has been the basis of the great majority of incentive studies during the last fifty years. Despite Brayfield and Crockett's finding in 1955 that there may be no such link,[1] researchers and employers have continued to seek ways to make employees more satisfied, secure in the belief that they would then work harder. In some cases the research is directed toward identifying the determinants of worker satisfaction, while in many cases a reason for satisfaction is assumed and the research attempts to institute or increase it.

Research in this area is not rigorous. It has been described as being

> characterized by loose definitions, duplicity, and a sort of swashbuckling, ad hoc correlational approach in which statistical significance replaces social significance. From this morass, support for virtually any position regarding the determinants of satisfaction can be marshalled.[2]

A major problem in such studies is the lack of follow-up over time, leading to the charge that even when incentives seem effective, they may very shortly be seen as "givens," thereby ceasing to influence behavior. As a result of such shortcomings, many researchers suspect that quite radical changes will bring only short-term changes in levels of satisfaction.[3]

Again, as has been pointed out in a number of places, by and large only the successful cases see print—few people or institutions, including researchers, are anxious to advertise their failures.[4] Further, when success is reported, the measure of such success may be increased productivity, without regard to changes in satisfaction levels, or increased reported or assumed satisfactions, without measurement of productivity. It is the rare case that measures both changes in satisfaction and changes in productivity, linking them together by controlling for other possible influences. For example, there are job redesign studies that report gains in both satisfaction and productivity, but fail to take into account that part of the redesign is profit sharing or premium pay for workers, which may be the incentive that is operating on both satisfaction and production, making the remainder of the job redesign features unnecessary.[5]

Even when increases in worker satisfaction lead to increased motivation, there is still the question as to whether this is translated into behavior. We are motivated to do many things that we do not do. On the one hand, there are motivations of roughly equal strength which conflict with one another—to go to work or to take a day off, for example. When both motivations are equally strong, the result is the paralyzing phenomenon of ambivalence. There are also levels of motivation, or stronger and weaker motivations, or—to paraphrase Maslow—potent and prepotent motivations. Then there are those strong, unilaterial, and potent motivations which cannot be effectuated because of circumstances. Just as employment requires opportunity, ability, and motivation, with no two of them being sufficient, so motivation to work hard may be mediated by external factors, such as dearth of materials, or by internal factors, such as fatigue.

Then there is the fact that motivation can only be measured through behavior or self-reports, but not directly. Studies of motivation, then, are really studies of antecedent and subsequent behavior, with the difference attributed—at least in part—to motivation. In any case there is a certain amount of sloppiness in the conceptualization and operationalization of motivational research, with satisfactions, motivations, and behaviors not clearly distinguished.

It is, perhaps, for such reasons that the assistant research director for the AFL-CIO was moved to say:

> Motivation . . . is an abstract concept that has very little relevance, very little pertinence, very little meaning for the industrial world today. . . . Over the years there has developed a considerable body of literature on the subject. A good deal of it masquerades as scientific research, though probably better characterized as pseudo-scientific research. Most of it is unadulterated nonsense that has very little meaning in the real management-labor relationship field.[6]

Consequently, although the majority of researchers dealing with work motivations try to distinguish among satisfactions as such, motivators which lead to satisfactions, satisfactions which are presumed to be motivators, and the behavior which the motivation causes, these distinctions are not easily maintained. Campbell and Pritchard, for example, are very careful in this regard, pointing out that Herzberg's theory is about job satisfaction, not job behavior.[7] Nevertheless, they cite many studies in which behavior is the dependent variable, rather than motivation alone.

The entire relationship between satisfaction and productivity remains cloudy at best. Herzberg did not test for changes in production resulting from greater satisfaction. In his original study he asked people reporting satisfactory experiences if they produced more afterwards (and vice versa), but did not measure their actual output. Since it is difficult to imagine many people reporting a satisfying experience and then denying that it affected them, the reported productivity gains in this study must be taken with a large spoonful of salt. In the replications carried out by others reported in Herzberg's second book, a total of thirty studies are described, including one in Soviet Russia, and in only one of these (simply described as highly intelligent women performing a communications function for a large company) was actual performance measured, by methods not described in a study not named.[8] Thus, Herzberg and many of those who followed him simply assumed that productivity flows from satisfaction, and contented themselves with studying workers' satisfactions.

INDUSTRIAL SETTINGS

There have, nevertheless, been some empirical attempts to relate satisfaction to productivity. Stollberg, writing of the German Democratic Republic, found a correlation between job satisfaction and "socialist relationship to work" (read: hard work) to have a "mean square contingency of .16."[9] Vroom summed up the results of 20 studies in the United States, and found the correlation coefficients to range from .31 to .86.[10] In a study of young Leningrad industrial workers the corresponding coefficient was .14.[11] As a consequence, East Bloc researchers join their western colleagues in concluding that "most contradictory are the indicators of connection between job satisfaction and real productivity of labor,"[12] and, further, "it became clear that job satisfaction cannot by any means always be looked upon as the expression of a positive job attitude."[13]

In fact, studies and surveys of studies are moving to the conclusion that there is no functional, generalizable, replicable relationship between being satisfied at work, being motivated to work harder, and actual hard work.

There have been many reviews of research seeking such linkages. Locke, for example, wrote in 1970, "Investigators have been searching for lawful relationships between job satisfaction and job performance for more than two decades"[14]—to which more than another decade can now be added. Glickman and Brown wrote, in 1974, "The relationship between satisfaction and productivity is more often talked about than demonstrated."[15] In 1975

Locke concluded that job satisfaction exerts little or no causal influence on productivity.[16] Parnes holds that, although in isolated cases improvements in the quality of working life can result in increased productivity, a good deal more rigorous research is necessary before we can surmise an orderly relationship.[17] Strauss holds that not only has the link between being satisfied and working hard not been established, but that in some cases it is the most dissatisfied who work hardest.[18] Lawler and Porter studied 148 middle- and lower-level managers in five organizations in 1967, and found an inverse relationship: "Rather than being a cause of performance, satisfaction is caused by it."[19] Locke also concludes his previously mentioned review by holding that when job satisfaction and productivity *are* related, the evidence favors productivity as a cause of satisfaction, rather than vice versa.[20]

In short, the relationship between worker satisfactions and worker productivity, if there is one, is far from simple. A review of available evidence indicates that there are

> highly complicated relationships among different measures of productivity and satisfaction, and . . . a number of distal or macroscopic forces that influence satisfactions overall. . . . When all is said and the research is done, the relationship between workers' satisfactions and their performance is concomitant in nature: The two are conditioned by the extent to which high productivity is a value in itself and by the extent to which productivity is valued as a means to workers' other aims.[21]

And yet, beliefs die hard:

> If all the research that has been done in this area were to be summarized, no consistent correlation would be found between job satisfaction and job performance. The conditions which determine each are different. In other words, it is possible to have high satisfaction and high performance or high satisfaction and low performance. Conversely, there may be low satisfaction and low performance or low satisfaction and higher performance. *Although no consistent correlation exists,* it would seem *logical,* in the authors' opinion, that if there is a high degree of job satisfaction, it is more likely that high productivity will exist.[22]

It is due to the existence of such confusion and ambivalence that Guion and Landy emphasize that satisfaction, motivation, and production are different concepts and should be studied separately and differently.[23]

There is also another factor which must be taken into consideration when examining the link between satisfaction and productivity. Although, as pointed out previously, definitions of hard work or productivity may contain elements of both quantity and quality, in most of the research discussed so far the settings have been industrial, and there has been an emphasis, albeit not always clear, on quantity. In service occupations, however, quality may be more important.

SERVICE SETTINGS

There are jobs in which relationship is of the essence. To some extent this is true of sales jobs—the relationship created by the salesperson with the customer may account for differences in sales figures which are not attributable to quality, price, or service. Relationships may be even more crucial in an education setting, in which the feelings of teacher and student about one another may affect teaching and learning ability, materials, and methods.[24] In a profession such as social work, however, not only is the relationship between the worker and the client a tool used consciously to achieve certain ends, but the relationship might be the end in itself.[25] Consequently, the distinction between good work and hard work, the various sources of worker satisfaction, and the connection, if any, between work patterns and satisfactions take on a different hue when the research is moved from settings in which workers relate primarily to material objects to settings in which they relate mostly to other people. For this reason, Katz and Danet distinguish among the *manner* in which officials and clients deal with each other, the *procedures* involved, and the *resources* exchanged, that is, the outcome.[26]

In service settings the lack of active satisfactions may affect the manner of service in a way that would have no impact on a perfume bottle, for example, but which would be disastrous if obvious to customers, clients, or other recipients of services. The fatalistic contentment which has been noticed among workers may not affect, or may affect only to a limited degree, their industrial production, but the same attitude displayed in a service-rendering organization might be seen as indifference or even hostility.

For example, to what extent can a social worker who is thoroughly disgruntled with the salary and other conditions of the job, upset by the situation in the work place, and feeling no sense of growth or achievement in the work help a client who is unhappy with his or her job, at work, and with the work itself? Does the bureaucrat perhaps get his or her reputation for not trying to be helpful, or for not working hard, from the fact that there is little satisfaction in the job? Katz and Eisenstadt point out how bureaucrats (in this case, bus drivers) "break role" in order to teach their clients to be customers of the bureaucracy, thus making the bureaucrats' role easier—that is, more satisfying.[27] Katz and Danet document bureaucrats (customs clerks) breaking role in certain categories of cases in order to give vent to their altruistic and humanitarian feelings—again, to achieve satisfaction.[28] Itskhokin holds that a worker who is integrated in his or her role wants to achieve the role's objectives. In the case of a service organization, "a worker integrated with the service object responds to any of the consumer's actual needs for the reward inherent in their gratification."[29]

On the other hand, there is a growing literature about so-called burnout in the service professions—that is to say, apathy, indifference, disgruntlement, and leaving.[30] The effect of these attitudes in the service professions, and especially where the quality of the one-to-one relationship is of the essence, cannot help but be greater than its effect on industrial production. In this vein, Shamir studied the role stress suffered by persons in subordinate service roles (SSRs), and concludes that "measures of job satisfaction, job motivation and role stress should attempt to incorporate relationships with clients in addition to the more conventional aspects and factors measured."[31]

Although the difference between satisfactions in service jobs and industrial jobs may be great, and the effect of that difference important, little attention has so far been given this area. A notable exception is Parker's study of the differences in satisfactions reported by service and business respondents. These findings are worth reporting in some detail.[32]

In response to an open-ended question as to what gave them satisfaction in their work, 69 percent of the service workers in Parker's study mentioned something to do with their clients, compared to 24 percent of the business workers who mentioned something to do with their customers. This is in line with the kibbutz study discussed previously, in which "contact with children and/or pupils" was a source of satisfaction not found in the results of Herzberg-type studies.

Service workers reported feeling more autonomy in their jobs than did the business people and, to a slight extent, that they used their abilities and potentialities more. However, the service people felt more pressured by lack of time to do the kind of job they would have liked to do. This finding is in line with the reports of members of task forces set up in Israel after the Yom Kippur War to deal with returning reservists' problems. They reported that they were able to relate better to clients and to be seen as more positive because their work loads were much less than in their normal settings.[33]

More service workers were found to be involved in their jobs than business workers (67 percent versus 36 percent). When asked about their central life interests, however, the findings of Dubin, in 1962, [34] that workers find their interests outside the work place was reconfirmed as of 1971: "Among business people only eleven percent gave 'work' answers, as compared to twenty-nine percent of service people." That this situation remains relatively stable is attested by the previously quoted Yadov and Kissel study of 1980.[35]

In Parker's study, 57 percent of the business people replied "none" when asked whether they had close friends among the people they worked with, compared with 22 percent in service occupations. Finally, 64 percent of service workers found their jobs encroaching in some degree on their spare time, while only 32 percent of the business people gave the same answer.

Finally, Parker constructed an index of work involvement, and found that

the occupations associated with high work involvement are all service occupations concerned with the problems and development of people; the occupations associated with low work involvement are business ones concerned with impersonal things or with personal relations on a business basis.[36]

SUMMARY

In summary, no generalizable, functional, replicable relationship between workers' satisfactions and their productivity has yet been found. The assumption that satisfied workers work better or harder has found little empirical verification. In those specific instances where there is such a connection, it is liable to be a complex relationship, involving many other variables, and may even be a reverse relationship, with hard work giving rise to feelings of satisfaction. The relationship between satisfactions and work patterns in service occupations might be stronger that that in industrial or business settings, but exhibits itself more in terms of the quality of practitioner-client relationships than in productivity measured quantitatively.

NOTES

1. A. Brayfield and W. Crockett, "Employee Attitudes and Employee Performance." *Psychological Bulletin* 52 (1955): 396-424.

2. R. Katz and J. Van Maanen, "The Loci of Work Satisfaction: Job, Interaction, and Policy." *Human Relations* 30 (1977): 469-486.

3. A. B. Cherns and L. E. Davis, "Assessment of the State of the Art," in L. E. Davis and A. B. Cherns (eds.) *The Quality of Working Life: Problems, Prospects, and the State of the Art* (New York: Free Press, 1975), p. 34.

4. "One wonders how many other failures were never written up for publication." R. A. Katzell, P. Bienstock, and P. H. Faerstein, *A Guide to Worker Productivity Experiments in the United States 1971-1975* (New York: New York University Press, 1977), p. 34; "There is a serious underreporting of failures. Most academic journals do not publish insignificant results, and the failure of an experiment usually implies that there was no significant change in outcomes. Further, most organizations do not want their failures published. . . . Severe underreporting of negative results . . . may lead organizational members to seriously overestimate the probability that a particular strategy will lead to positive outcomes." T. G. Cummings and E. S. Molloy, *Improving Productivity and the Quality of Work Life* (New York: Praeger, 1977), p. 280.

5. It will be recalled that the experimental small work group in the Hawthorne studies increased their income through this structural change—an incentive hardly ever mentioned in discussion.

6. F. Pallara, quoted in J. Gooding, *The Job Revolution* (New York: Collier, 1972), p. 79.

7. J. P. Campbell and R. D. Pritchard, "Motivational Theory in Industrial and Organizational Psychology," in M. D. Dunnette (ed.) *Handbook of Industrial and Organizational Psychology* (Chicago: Rand McNally, 1976), p. 79.

8. F. Herzberg, *Work and the Nature of Man* (Cleveland: World, 1966).

9. R. Stollberg, "Job Satisfaction and the Relationship to Work," in M. R. Haug and J. Dofny (eds.) *Work and Technology* (Beverly Hills, CA: Sage, 1977), pp. 107-121.

10. V. H. Vroom, *Work and Motivation* (New York: John Wiley, 1964).

11. A. G. Zdravomsyslov, V. P. Rozhin, and V. A. Yadov, *Man and His Work* (Moscow: Myse, 1967).

12. V. A. Yadov and A. A. Kissel, "Job Satisfaction: Analysis of Empirical Data and Attempt at their Theoretical Interpretation," in Haug and Dofny, op. cit., pp. 45-58.

13. Stollberg, op. cit.

14. E. A. Locke, "Job Satisfaction and Job Performance: A Theoretical Analogy." *Organizational Behavior and Human Performance* 5 (1970): 484-500.

15. A. S. Glickman and Z. H. Brown, *Changing Schedules of Work: Patterns and Implications* (Kalamazoo: Upjohn, 1974), p. 56.

16. E. A. Locke, "Personnel Attitudes and Motivation." *Annual Review of Psychology* 26 (1975): 457-480.

17. S. Parnes and M. Rosow, *Productivity and the Quality of Working Life* (Scarsdale: Work in America Institute, 1978).

18. G. Strauss, "Job Satisfaction, Motivation, and Job Redesign," *Organizational Behavior: Research and Issues* (Madison, WI: Industrial Relations Research Association, 1974).

19. E. E. Lawler III and L. W. Porter, "The Effect of Performance on Job Satisfaction," in G. A. Yukl and K. N. Wexley (eds.) *Readings in Organizational and Industrial Psychology* (New York: Oxford University Press, 1971), pp. 222-229.

20. Locke, "Personnel Attitudes and Motivation," op. cit.; see also Brayfield and Crockett, op. cit.; and P. C. Smith, L. M. Kendall, and C. L. Hulin, *The Measurement of Satisfactions in Work and Retirement: A Strategy for the Study of Attitudes* (Chicago: Rand McNally, 1969).

21. I. Berg, M. Freedman, and M. Freeman, *Managers and Work Reform: A Limited Engagement* (New York: Free Press, 1978), pp. 37, 290.

22. B. K. Scanlan, "Determinants of Job Satisfaction and Productivity." *Personnel Journal* 55 (1976): 12; quoted in Parnes and Rosow, op. cit.; italics added.

23. R. M. Guion and F. J. Landy, "The Meaning of Work and the Motivation to Work." *Organizational Behavior and Human Performance* 7 (1972): 308-339.

24. See B. C. Reynolds, *Learning and Teaching in the Practice of Social Work* (New York: Holt, Rinehart & Winston, 1942), ch. 22, "Focus on Learners."

25. On the importance of relationship as a goal, see D. Macarov and N. Golan, "Goals in Social Work: A Longitudinal Study." *International Social Work* 16 (1973): 68-74.

26. E. Katz and B. Danet (eds.), *Bureaucracy and the Public: A Reader in Official-Client Relations* (New York: Basic, 1973).

27. E. Katz and S. N. Eisenstadt, "Observations on the Response of Israeli Organizations to New Immigrants." *Administrative Science Quarterly* 5 (1960): 1.

28. E. Katz and B. Danet, "Petitions and Persuasive Appeals: A Study of Official-Client Relations," in Katz and Danet, op. cit., pp. 174-190.

29. A. Itskhokin, "The Dual System." *American Journal of Sociology* 85 (1980): 1317.

30. See, for example, C. Cherviss, *Professional Burnout in Human Service Organizations* (New York: Praeger, 1980); D. H. Fish, *A Study of the Turnover and Separation of Social Workers in Public Welfare Agencies* (Ramat Gan, Israel: Bar-Ilan University School of Social Work, 1976); M. Tamuz, *Work Role Centrality, Role Strain and Organizational Commitment: A Study of Social Workers in Public Welfare* (Ramat Aviv, Israel: Tel Aviv University School of Social Work, 1977).

31. B. Shamir, "Between Service and Servility: Role Conflict in Subordinate Service Roles." *Human Relations* 33 (1980): 741-756.

32. S. Parker, *The Future of Work and Leisure* (New York: Praeger, 1974.

33. D. Macarov, "Use of the Task Force in the Human Services: A Documented Experience." *Administration in Social Work,* in press.

34. R. Dubin, "Industrial Workers' Worlds: A Study of the Central Life Interests of Industrial Workers," in A. M. Rose (ed.) *Human Behavior and Social Processes* (London: Routledge & Kegan Paul, 1962).

35. Yadov and Kissel, op. cit.

36. Parker, op. cit., p. 80.

8

JOB REDESIGN AND PROCESS THEORIES

With increasing evidence that satisfaction and productivity are not easily linked, attention has turned in recent years to other means of increasing worker productivity. Although in many cases it is still assumed that the productivity achieved through these changes is through satisfaction increases, even if not named or measured, in others no assumptions are made and no concern is expressed regarding satisfactions as such. There nevertheless sometimes remains the reverse interpretation—that whatever increases productivity somehow improves the quality of work life. In some instances the latter arises from the looseness of the term "quality of working life,"[1] while in others it is the opposite of the "satisfaction equals productivity" equation, that is, increasing productivity is taken as a sign of improved work life quality.

JOB REDESIGN

Just as "quality of working life" means different things to different people, so the rest of the terminology in this area has not been standardized. Pierce has defined two of the trends subsumed under job redesign, distinguishing between job enlargement, which "refers to horizontal loading/expansion of jobs . . . an increase in the number and variety of activities," and job enrichment, which "represents vertical loading/expansion . . . an increase in employee's planning, organizing, directing and controlling their own jobs."[2]

Job enlargement is a reversal of Adam Smith's and Frederick Taylor's thrust toward division of labor into ever-smaller units, and specialization on simpler and simpler tasks. The assumption is that the result is not only Durkheim's predicted alienation and anomie (which might or might not affect productivity), but monotony, boredom, and lack of interest, which can have results ranging from low productivity through lack of precision to outright sabotage. Consequently, efforts to improve this situation include training and retraining workers to perform more tasks or activities than before, either at the work that they are doing or in order for them to move around from task to task. At the other end of the "variety" range is the creation of autonomous work groups, or designing the work in "modules," in which the workers themselves decide which parts they want to do.

Job enlargement is thus bounded by simplification and specialization on the one side and variety and generalized skills on the other. The point at which satisfaction, or productivity, or both, are maximized probably varies from person to person.

Job enrichment is referred to under many different terms—democracy, participation, autonomy, and others. The major thrust is that workers do not simply take orders, but participate in decision making on many levels—how to do their own jobs, how the work should be designed and structured, time schedules, and up to company policy, including payment plans. There are, however, a number of problems and difficulties regarding worker participation in decision making as a means of creating either satisfaction or higher productivity.

For one thing, there is danger of establishing that which Verba refers to as pseudo-democracy[3]—giving people the illusion that they can decide things that have been pre- or other-determined. This is often referred to as "giving people the feeling that they are deciding." Pseudo-democracy arises when the limits of decision making are not made clear, and decisions must therefore be reversed because they have exceeded the limits; because the cards are stacked by having certain members convinced in advance of the decision desired by management; by supporting those people who lean toward management's views, in a number of subtle and not-so-subtle ways; and so on.[4] The danger of pseudo-democracy is not only that the decisions made may not reflect the real feelings of the workers, but that once it has become clear how they have been manipulated, or how their decisions are disregarded in practice, workers not only become disinclined to participate in the exercise in the future, but they become cynical about all participative devices, and about all decisions so made.

Moreover, despite generally accepted views to the contrary, there are many employees who do not want to take on the additional effort and thought required. Their attitude is, "I'm paid to do my job—not management's. If they want me to make decisions, let them pay me for it." Others do not want the responsibility—"Just tell me what to do and I'll do it. If it's wrong, that's your problem." Still others see participation as a proposed substitute for important gains—more money and shorter hours. Then there are those who feel that they are asked to participate in small decisions, almost as a sop, while the important decisions are made "upstairs." Finally, there are those who reject what Locke calls "job involvement" (as distinct from job satisfaction)[5]—they do not take their work seriously and have no important personal values at stake in the job. Consequently, when human relations factors are commingled with other factors, such as decision making, it is quite likely that any increase in production arises because of better decisions, brought about by better inputs, better information, and the application of practical knowledge, rather than through the satisfaction of having participated in a decision. Anderson points out that "the notion, often expressed, that one enjoys his work to the degree that he is free to make all the decisions about it, is a folk idea which is true only if abundantly qualified." An empirical study of workers in the Tartar Republic established a correlation of .25 between workers' participation in production management and productivity of labor at their work places,[7] and Aitkin and Hage found that participation in agency decision making was strongly related to *alienation* from work.[8] Raskin, discussing workers' participation on the governing bodies of their enterprises concludes:

> My observation . . . makes me doubt . . . that board representation actually does give the worker a feeling of intimate participation in top-level policy. . . . Indeed, few workers have either a desire for such participation or a belief that they have much to contribute in this type of managerial decision.[9]

In reviewing the empirical evidence regarding participation in decision making, Neider holds that much of the literature has been criticized as being little more than a hodgepodge of inconsistencies in empirical findings,[10] and, in any case, "participation alone will *not* lead to increases in effort or productivity."[11]

In this vein, Hackman and Oldham hold that autonomy must be part of a mix of a number of changes. Testing a "Motivation Potential Score," they postulate the need for skill variety, task identity, task significance, autonomy, and feedback.[12] Consequently, many efforts directed at job redesign include a number of elements in their planning. Cummings and Molloy examine 78 experiments, in which the major changes are identified as:[13]

autonomous work groups;

job restructuring;

participative management;

organization-wide change;

organizational behavior modification;

flexible working hours; and

the Scanlon Plan, which is a particular type of job redesign.

The lack of correlation between attitudes and productivity is easily seen in the results of these studies, because in some of them productivity increased but attitudes did not change; in others, attitudes changed but productivity did not increase; in still others, both productivity and attitudes changed; and, inevitably, there were some studies in which neither changed.

The major finding of this very thorough review of attempts to increase productivity and satisfactions is that almost anything done in these directions will have some success:

autonomous work groups—"Existing evidence supports the positive effects attributed to autonomous work groups."

job restructuring—"Job restructuring produces improvements in performance and quality of work life."

participative management—"Is an effective strategy for improving productivity and the quality of work life."

organization-wide change—"Is a powerful strategy for improving performance and the quality of work life."

organizational behavior modification—"Improvements in the area of costs, withdrawal, productivity, and quality."

flexible working hours—"An increase in productivity, more favorable attitudes, reduction of absenteeism and turnover."

the Scanlon Plan—"Efficacious in improving performance and . . . there are some grounds for accepting the claims made about its positive effects on quality of work life."

This record of unmitigated successes regarding the methods used (although not every case was successful in every aspect) has echoes of the first reactions to the Hawthorne experiments—no matter what is done, the situation improves. This may bespeak a number of possibilities. One, that the satisfaction and production level of workers is so low that almost any intervention results in an increase, or, second, that some unrecognized factor is at work which is not related to the actual content of the interventions. Again, it might be that the number of undocumented failures using these methods so far outweigh the successes that what is actually being reported is based on absence of control groups. Finally, there is the possibility that these experiments, or their reports, are so flawed as to be unreliable.

In any case, one can echo Sarason's previous comment by asking why, if things are so good, are they so bad? Productivity in American industry has been slowing in recent years, and the amount of satisfaction expressed by workers has been declining. Katzell and associates also reviewed worker productivity experiments, concentrating on the 103 that were published between 1971 and 1975. They classified the major thrust of the experiments as follows:

selection and placement

job development and promotion

appraisal and feedback

training and instruction

management by objectives

goal setting

financial compensation

job design

group design

supervisory methods

organizational structure

physical working conditions

work schedule

sociotechnical system[14]

They found that although 85 percent of the experiments reported favorable effects, their limitations raise questions about the validity and/or generalizability of their findings. These experiments lacked control groups, used nonequivalent comparison groups, contained peculiarities of both measurement and program, problems concerning the sample groups, and statistical inadequacies. In fact, of the studies reporting improvements, 80 percent were methodologically flawed, while 20 percent of those reporting no improvement were so flawed.

When interventions other than attempts to increase satisfactions are examined, very few of them are or can be quantified and measured. Of the 103 experiments described by Katzell and his associates, in almost no case is the incentive measured in such a way that the effect of increased or decreased amounts can be evaluated. In regard to participative decision making for example, the change is described: "Some decision-making power was shifted from the laundry foreman to a committee of laundry employees."[15] In another case, "representatives from each work group formed a coordinating task force to discuss and recommend operating improvement."[16] Many of the reports were more precise, but even in the case of the original experiments, in contradistinction to the abstracts, few were measurable in the sense that increases or decreases could be built into replications. In Orpen's study, "the results did *not* indicate significant outcomes for enrichment on the work outcomes of performance and productivity. . . . Enrichment improved attitudes but had little effect on productivity, whether assessed by ratings or output."[17]

There is also the problem of identifying the variable actually responsible for production increases when these occur. When a number of changes are made simultaneously—size of the work group, amount of participation, and method of payment, for example—the operative variable is obscured. It is far from clear, even in successful cases, how much of the reported increase results from more effort on the part of workers and how much from improved communications, better decisions, and more efficient methods alone. Fein, for example, holds that the percentage of workers who would benefit from work fulfillment programs amounts to only about 15 percent to 20 percent of the blue-collar workers.[18]

The entire record of the job redesign effort to date has been surveyed by some experts and found wanting. Continuing to refer to it as quality of working life, van Assen and Wester say: "If one takes a closer look at the results and the impact of this 20-year history of Q.W.L. projects, the picture is rather dismal."[19] They attribute this failure to the fact that, in their view, work design is a preventive rather than ameliorative process, and factories, organizations, and the like must be designed with the principles they enumerate in mind. Specifically, first there is product design, then determination of the technology and, in particular, the manufacturing process to be used, then the structure or design of the work organization. Job content is the last link in the chain of decisions, and thus is heavily curtailed insofar as alternatives are possible.

Berg and associates, however, report on a case in which the principles of job redesign were applied during the construction and manning of a new industrial plant. The initial results were described as "positive developments," but—as happens in so many cases—there followed "dubious and negative" results. The latter were blamed, in part, upon the supervisors, who saw their authority, power, and position threatened by the changes.[20] Perhaps this is why Berg and associates found that

> whatever the short term gains, interventions focusing on worker participation and work design only rarely lead to sustained experimental efforts. . . . Virtually none of many celebrated and well-documented work redesign efforts since the 1950s has been revisited by the investigators who initially reported on their great benefits. It is likely that a majority of even the most promising experiments died in their infancy.[21]

Doubts have also been expressed concerning the Scanlon Plan, which is often cited as the very prototype and model of a comprehensive, multifaceted job redesign program. A major feature of such programs is the sharing of savings made through productivity with the workers involved. None of the studies published indicates what happens when for some reason—increase in the cost of energy or raw materials, for example—no savings result despite productivity increases. Drucker says:

> It may be highly desirable that workers have a financial stake in the business. But wherever tried—and we have been trying worker ownership for well over a century—it has worked only as long as the enterprise is doing well. It works

only in highly profitable businesses. And so do all the variants of workers' participation in profits, such as the American Scanlon Plan of profit and productivity bonus. As soon as business profits drop, worker ownership no longer resolves the conflict between wage as living and wage as cost.[22]

Another problem in evaluating the efficacy of job redesign plans in terms of worker productivity, rather than in enterprise production, is the fact that individual records are rarely kept, and never published. Consequently, it is not possible to know how many or which workers increased their work as a result of a particular change or a combination of changes. That some workers increased their efforts greatly, others somewhat, still others not at all, and some even decreased their efforts, cannot be determined from the reports of job redesign that are available.

Finally, there is the view that if job redesign efforts have not given rise to any general theories or constructs concerning increasing production, let alone productivity, it is not because these efforts have failed, but because they have not yet been tried on a sufficiently broad scale. Parnes, for example, holds that no comprehensive program incorporating most or all of the various theories of increased satisfaction, motivation, and production has really been undertaken.[23]

PROCESS THEORIES

One method of attempting to explain individual behavior in organizations is termed motivation theory, which can be subdivided into content and process elements. Content theory consists of job related rewards, and attempts to relate behavior to variables such as promotion, security, recognition, achievement, and similar items, of which Herzberg's work was a beginning effort. Campbell and Pritchard say that empirical taxonomic work in this area is "amazingly sparse."[24] Process theory, on the other hand, tries to define the major variables necessary for explaining choice, effort, and persistence, such as incentives, drives, reinforcement, and expectancy. Measures to influence motivation which are based on these theories are generally more subtle, sophisticated, and complex than those derived from content theories. For example, whereas content theory might seek to determine how much of a salary raise is required to make an individual work harder, process theories would want to know why the worker made that decision, if it matched his or her expectations, seemed equitable, provided reinforcement, and so on. These variables are sometimes referred to as "moderators," and sometimes as individual differences. Thus Pierce says that individual differences moderate the nature of the job design-employee response relationship.[25]

Campbell and Pritchard, in a comprehensive overview of the history, progress, current situation, and problems of motivation theory research, hold that the dominant theme in motivational explanations of human behavior in organizations is the expectancy-instrumentality-valence theory (VIE).[26] Expectancy is defined as the perceived relationship between a given degree of effort expenditure and a given level of performance. In other words, will more effort produce more units? Instrumentality refers to the perceived contingency that one outcome has for another. If more units are produced, will it result in more money? Valence refers to the perceived positive or negative value ascribed by the individual to the possible outcomes of action on the job. Is the money important enough to demand, or be worth, the effort?

Each of these components has been subjected to both theoretical and experimental research, involving a large number of subconcepts, such as the amount of information required to arrive at expectancy or instrumentality, to what extent outcomes are external or internal, and so on. Campbell and Pritchard sum up their survey of the empirical research based on process theories—or, more precisely, VIE theories of motivation—by saying: "In sum, the available data do not portray the VIE model as a very powerful explainer of behavior."[27]

There are, of course, other theories concerning the motivations of workers. Equity theory involves a comparison with other people, times, or situations, resulting in greater or lesser motivation. Most research on equity theory has been in terms of money payments. Subconcepts studied include self-esteem, intimacy of relationship with the other being compared, the element of job security, and others.

Goal setting is another field of motivational research. Although there is little attention paid to how or why certain goals are chosen, there is considerable research on the effects of difficult versus easy, or long-term versus short-term, goals. Unfortunately, most of this research has been in simulated situations, and its application to the real world is not yet known. In addition, the question of how one gets a worker to accept someone else's idea as to what should be his or her goal is not clearly answered.

Other theories concerning work motivation include McClelland's nAch[28] (variously referred to as need achievement, achievement need, and need for achievement), although—as will be discussed later—the relationship between working hard and achieving may be seen as nonexistent to some, tenuous to others, and synonymous only in the case of workaholics. Other motivational theories include attribution theory, social facilitation theory, social exchange, reciprocity, nonmonetary reward contingencies, and several others.

All of these theories can be and have been criticized, both positively and negatively, in total or in detail.[29] Three important factors seem to mark them all, however:

First, although the majority of researchers dealing with work motivations try to distinguish among satisfactions as such, motivators which lead to satisfactions, satisfactions which are presumed to be motivators, and the behavior as such, these distinctions are not easily maintained in the real world, in research studies, and in the reports of studies by others. Although many researchers and interpreters of research read Herzberg-type studies as dealing with job behavior or productivity, these studies—as Campbell and Pritchard are careful to point out—deal with expressed satisfaction, not observed or measured behavior. Nevertheless, even in Campbell and Pritchard's overview of content and process theories, there is often confusion among satisfaction, motivation, and behavior.

Second, although researchers may eschew the satisfaction-equals-motivation theorem, the so-called content variables—salary increases, promotions, seniority—are clearly designed to offer the workers satisfaction. The process variables, too—VIE, equity, goal setting, and the like—are only operational because they are designed to result in satisfactions such as fulfilling expectations, achieving equity, and reaching goals. Thus they are, in the final analysis, methods of achieving different satisfactions through different routes, and the questions that pertain to a generalizable satisfaction-productivity link apply equally to them.

Finally, there is the question of lack of individuation of the results. Most process studies, like content, job redesign, and other studies, deal with overall changes in the work situation, and total changes in production or productivity. It is not possible to discern which, or how many, workers responded in great measure, which in some measure, and which not at all or negatively. Positive results—or their lack—could conceivably be the result of large changes on the part of a small group. Granted, the total increase in production might be all that management wants, but research designed to determine why some people work harder than others, or designed to induce people to work harder, cannot afford to neglect the individual, small group, or even large group variable. Consequently, the next two chapters deal with this subject.

NOTES

1. For example, Glaser says: "What is meant by the 'quality of worklife' (QWL)? Basically it is a process by which all members of the organization . . . have some say about the design of their jobs in particular and the work environment in general." E. M. Glaser, "Productivity Gains Through Worklife Improvement." *Personnel* 57 (1980): 71-77. This definition will come as a surprise to the occupational welfare officers studied by Bar-Gal, who hardly dealt with the

question of participation in decision making. D. Bar-Gal, "Domains of Work and Methods of Work of Occupational Welfare Officers: An Exploratory Study of an Emerging Role." *Journal of Social Service Research,* in press.

2. J. L. Pierce, "Job Design in Perspective." *Personnel Administrator* 25 (1980): 67-75.

3. S. Verba, *Small Groups and Political Behavior* (Princeton, NJ: Princeton University Press, 1961).

4. Bolweg quotes an Australian experience in participation, consisting of three people from management and three from the shop-floor: "Game, set and match to the Company." J. F. Bolweg, "The Quality of Working Life: An Industrial Relations Perspective," in *Proceedings of the Thirty-Third Annual Meeting* (Madison, WI: Industrial Relations Research Association, 1980), pp. 174-184.

5. E. A. Locke, "The Nature and Causes of Job Satisfaction," in M. D. Dunnette (ed.) *Handbook of Industrial and Organizational Psychology* (Chicago: Rand McNally, 1976), p. 1301.

6. N. Anderson, *Dimensions of Work: The Sociology of a Work Culture* (New York: McKay, 1964), p. 77.

7. A. Tikhonov, *The Content and Organization of Work as Specific Factors in the Process of Formulation of Attitudes to Work,* quoted in V. A. Yadov and A. A. Kissel, "Job Satisfaction: Analysis of Empirical Data and Attempt at Their Theoretical Interpretation," in M. R. Haug and J. Dofny (eds.) *Work and Technology* (Beverly Hills, CA: Sage, 1977), pp. 45-58.

8. M. Aitkin and J. Hage, "Organizational Alienation: A Comparative Analysis." *American Sociological Review* 31 (1966): 497-507.

9. A. H. Raskin, "Toward a More Participative Work Force," in C. S. Sheppard and D. C. Carroll (eds.) *Working in the Twenty-First Century* (New York: John Wiley, 1980), pp. 90-105.

10. L. L. Neider, "An Experimental Field Investigation Utilizing an Expectancy Theory View of Participation." *Organizational Behavior and Human Performance* 26 (1980): 425-448.

11. Ibid., p. 426.

12. J. R. Hackman and G. R. Oldham, "Motivation Through the Design of Work: Test of a Theory." *Organizational Behavior and Human Performance* 16 (1976): 250-279.

13. T. G. Cummings and E. S. Molloy, *Improving Productivity and the Quality of Work Life* (New York: Praeger, 1977).

14. R. A. Katzell, P. Bienstock, and P. H. Faerstein, *A Guide to Worker Productivity Experiments in the United States 1971-1975* (New York: New York University Press, 1977).

15. Ibid., p. 58.

16. Ibid., p. 100.

17. C. Orpen, "The Effects of Job Enrichment on Employee Satisfaction, Motivation, Involvement, and Performance: A Field Experiment." *Human Relations* 32 (1979): 189-217.

18. M. Fein, "Motivation to Work," in R. Dubin (ed.) *Handbook of Work, Organization, and Society* (Chicago: Rand McNally, 1976), pp. 465-530.

19. A. van Assen and P. Wester, "Designing Meaningful Jobs: A Comparative Analysis of Organizational Design Practices," in K. D. Duncan, M. M. Gruneberg, and D. Wallis (eds.) *Changes in Working Life* (New York: John Wiley, 1980), pp. 237-252.

20. I. Berg, M. Freedman, and M. Freeman, *Managers and Work Reform: A Limited Engagement* (New York: Free Press, 1978), pp. 162-163.

21. Ibid., p. 164; Pierce completely agrees. Pierce, op. cit., p. 73.

22. P. F. Drucker, *Management: Tasks, Responsibilities, Practices.* (New York: Harper & Row, 1973), p. 191.

23. S. Parnes and M. Rosow, *Productivity and the Quality of Working Life* (Scarsdale: Work in America Institute, 1978).

24. J. P. Campbell and R. D. Pritchard, "Motivation Theory in Industrial and Organiza-

tional Psychology" in M. D. Dunnette (ed.) *Handbook of Industrial and Organizational Psychology* (Chicago: Rand McNally, 1976), pp. 63-130.

25. J. L. Pierce, "Job Design in Perspective." *Personnel Administrator* 25 (1980): 67-75.

26. Campbell and Pritchard, op. cit., p. 79.

27. Ibid., p. 92.

28. D. C. McClelland, *The Achieving Society* (New York: Free Press, 1961).

29. White says that nineteen years of theory building and empirical research have not provided much hope for finding generalizable individual difference moderators, and calls for the search to be abandoned. J. K. White, "Individual Differences and the Job Quality-Worker Response Relationship: Review, Integration and Comment." *Academy of Management Review* 3 (1978): 267-280.

9

WORK PERSONALITIES

Throughout the search for determinants of human productivity there runs general acknowledgment that personality differences might account for much of the variation between findings of different studies, or for the area of behavior not accounted for by the variables examined. On the other hand, there seems to be general—almost stubborn—reluctance to take such factors into account, or to investigate them.

Hulin and Blood discuss the relationship between job size and satisfaction, commenting that the relationship cannot be assumed in general but is dependent to a great extent on the backgrounds of workers in the sample.[1] Berg and associates say, regarding satisfactions at work, that they are not linked to worker experience in a general way, but they *are* relative to a great variety of particular worker experiences and traits.[2] Lawler and Suttle mention a relatively permanent characteristic of the individual's personality that reflects the generalized perception of competence across all task situations.[3] Campbell and Pritchard note the absence of relevance, in the VIE model, for particular people in a particular situation.[4] Ingham holds that workers bring different predispositions to their work and thus respond differently to very similar tasks.[5] Goldthorpe and associates also call attention to the variety of meanings that work may come to have for different employees.[6] Ward and Wall recognize that a person is sometimes seen to be a hard worker "by disposition," as it were.[7] Ingham also notes that most studies ignore individual variations—in need for work-centered relationships, for example—and consequently calls for work orientations to be viewed as the independent, rather than the dependent, variables.[8] Munts and Garfinkel make the same point in terms of the value placed on work: "Different people put differing values on work as opposed to other activities."[9] Others hold that there is enough consistency in human behavior to make predictions based on a person's past performance: "Overall, it is fair to say that when an individual enters the formal work organization, not only has his personality been determined, but so, too, have many of his attitudes and much of his behavior."[10] Strauss arrives at the same conclusion, although limiting it to one aspect of work:

> It does seem reasonably clear that because of their personality differences people do vary substantially in their needs for challenge and autonomy [at

work]. . . . Personality differences, in turn, may be caused by variations in culture and family child-rearing practices (and possibly even genetic factors).[11]

Seashore, in discussing the components of job satisfaction, attributes 30 percent of the total to "stable demographic and personality characteristics," but in another context dismisses these same stable attitudes and states as "uninteresting" from the point of view of research.[12] Campbell and Pritchard sum up this lacuna, saying:

> There is really no reason why we should not carefully review the past history of individuals, attempt to document the outcomes that controlled their behavior, and use this information in conjunction with individual judgements about future preferences to account for effort or choice behavior.[13]

Of the few studies which have investigated differences in individuals as moderating their responses to work or to incentives, three predominate. One of the earliest was an attempt to isolate differences between lower- and middle-class respondents, and this study used urban and rural backgrounds of workers as a surrogate for class differences—a method which has been criticized. Later studies identified class differences through other factors. The second area has been around respondents' reported adherence to the Protestant Work Ethic; and the third has to do with differences arising from the so-called higher order need strength. The latter derives from Maslow's postulation of the needs for affection, self-esteem, and self-actualization as being of a higher order than the physiological needs or the need for security.[14] It is clear that the last two areas do not investigate the history of the worker, and thus are more properly subsumed under process theories.

Although there have been few empirical studies of the differences in workers' individual reactions to work incentives or situations as such, there have been some which examined or postulated various aspects of basic approaches to work. Salvendy holds that the pace at which people work is highly individualized, and can hardly be changed by either external or internal efforts. He holds that each person has a basic work pace which is individual to him or to her: "Instruction, guidance, and better testing will carry the worker only so far, and then the individual work pace takes over."[15] Shipley makes somewhat the same point insofar as the hours of work are concerned. Some people, by nature, as it were, can take shift work, split shifts, night work, and flexible hours to a much greater extent than others can.[16] Zaleznik speaks of the style of one's working behavior—working alone may be quite characteristic of the lifestyle of some workers, that is, part of their "character armoring," while it would be distasteful to others.[17] While Hale is more hyperbolic about that which he calls "individual rhythm," he makes the same point concerning individual differences:

Many people find themselves in careers that are rhythmically aligned ideally for them. Their basic rhythms seem to have the same intensity, tempo and harmony as have their jobs. . . . There are . . . many people whose own life/work conditions are out of sync . . . the intensity from work to life is many degrees apart.[18]

Yadov and Kissel, writing in a Russian context, emphasize the importance of individual personalities, saying, *inter alia,* "The source of motivation is often not the need itself . . . but a disposition . . . fixed in the structure of the personality."[19] Similarly, Stollberg—writing in East Germany—castigates the West for knowing "no model of a worker personality centred on real personality development."[20] Neither the former nor the latter, however, base their empirical work on the postulation of personality patterns concerning work.

Despite these allusions to personality differences and stable patterns concerning work that abound in the literature, there is very little definition, and less empirical examination, of the phenomenon. Only Neff, among western writers and researchers on work, seems to have come to the formulated conclusion that work attitudes and patterns are more or less stable components of the personality, fashioned by all the socializing influences to which other aspects of the personality are exposed, and that differential reactions to offered incentives and various work patterns may stem from such basic personality differences:

Adult work appears to be the outcome of a long process of individual development, starting in childhood and passing through many vicissitudes and stages, setbacks and advances. . . . [Work personality] is a semiautonomous area of the general personality. . . . Work behavior engages the affects, requires a prolonged period of social learning, is governed by more or less enduring habits of response, is formed by events of which the adult person may be largely unaware.[21]

Having been said, the fact seems obvious. Everyone knows people who work hard at everything they do, people who rarely work hard at anything, and people at various points along the continuum. The range of possible lifetime work patterns is from that of "workaholics," for whom work is in the nature of an addiction,[22] through those people who have achieved "fatalistic contentment" at work,[23] through those who have what Freud called a "natural aversion to work,"[24] to the patterns of those who believe, with Sumner, that work kills.[25]

DIFFERENCES IN WORK PATTERNS

The differences in stable work patterns may be categorized as follows:

WORKAHOLICS

The term is said to have been invented by Oates in 1971.[26] He defined workaholics (himself included) as those who have an "addiction to work, the compulsion, or the uncontrollable need to work incessantly." Overbeck says that "a workaholic is one who suffers from an inability or unwillingness to break away from his compulsion to work."[27] To some, the workaholic is seen in negative terms, or even as emotionally ill: "Anxious, guilt-ridden, insecure or self-righteous about . . . work."[28] Others view the phenomenon favorably: "Those whose work and pleasures are one."[29]

Machlowitz's definition is perhaps the most objective. She defines the workaholic as one whose work "always exceeds the prescriptions and expectations of those with whom or for whom the workaholic works."[30] Indeed, Machlowitz did not confine herself to description, but from her study derived four types of workaholics: the dedicated, the integrated, the diffuse, and the intense.

OVERWORKERS

This is the term used for one of the extreme groups in the kibbutz study. Although the kibbutz study did not ask about workaholics, the definitional difference is clear. Overworkers are not necessarily compulsive and driven. They do not work extra hours or look for more work to do. They may enjoy their leisure as much or more than their work. But they work hard and well—harder and better than average—when they do work.

AVERAGE WORKERS

These are the workers toward the middle of the continuum. They work "by the book," but do not exert themselves unduly. These are the people who, as noted previously, use about 44 percent of their potential in their jobs. Their patterns may vary somewhat at various times, in different tasks, or in response to some incentives, but not enough—on a sustained basis—to move them out of the average worker category.

UNDERWORKERS

These are, obviously, the opposite of overworkers. In the kibbutz study they were at the lower end of the continuum. These are somewhat analogous to the unemployed that the British term "somewhat unenthusiastic," although the term is used here for those who are working. They work, but are easily distracted, exert themselves but little, and, if there are quotas to be met, either barely make the quota or consistently fall short.

THE WORK-INHIBITED

This is the term used for those who would rather not work, and exhibit it in their behavior. They differ from the underworkers in trying not to undertake work, whereas underworkers try to reduce their work, or not finish it. These are analogous to the British "voluntarily unemployed," or, more popularly, the lazy bums. Robinson and Finesinger diagnose work inhibition as a blockage attributable to psychological factors.[31] Whereas workaholics may evoke either favorable or unfavorable reactions, the work-inhibited are almost always scorned, with the possible exception of the adage, usually delivered wryly, that all progress is attributable to lazy people, as they always seek easier ways to do things.

One important factor stands out from these various methods of labeling workers and work patterns—that they are seen as stable, perhaps lifelong, constellations. Or, in other words, work patterns are not seen as readily manipulable, changing with externally offered or motivated incentives. On the contrary, the reaction to incentives is conditioned by the work personality of the individual. As Hoppock put it, summing up the results of one of the few longitudinal studies done: "The person who dislikes his job needs to change his job more than he needs to change himself."[32]

To the extent that work patterns are deep, relatively immutable, behavioral traits, perhaps the best that conventional work incentives can do is to improve the work patterns of poor workers, to a degree, for a time, and to make good workers work even harder, also for a time. However, whether lazy persons can be made into workaholics, or the reverse, or even if basically poor workers can be transformed into good workers through the introduction of profit sharing, participation, seeing the job whole, different supervisory styles, or through other changes in the conditions and/or the content of the job remains highly doubtful. In any case, basic, enduring changes in work patterns that might be read as having changed an underworker to an overworker or a workaholic do not appear in the literature, nor do they seem to have been demonstrated through experience or experiment. One possible, although tangential, experience is that of McClelland, who demonstrated that achievement motivation could be developed in adults,[33] but the congruence between hard work and achievement motivation is not great, especially since the latter was measured by entrepreneurial behavior, which may even be the antithesis of attempting to succeed through working hard.

DETERMINANTS OF WORK PERSONALITIES

Studying the factors that affect human development, or even attitudinal development, is an extremely complex undertaking,[34] and there is no reason to believe that the development of work personalities and attitudes is any less so. Indeed, the conclusion may be reached that the determinants of different patterns of work are as unknown and as apparently unknowable as are the determinants of musical talent or mathematical ability. However, following the ancient maxim, "It may not be given you to complete the task; but neither are you free to desist,"[35] it seems incumbent upon persons engaged in labor relations research, or any of its ramifications, to at least take into consideration the possibility of the existence of work personalities, and to examine their possible determinants.

There seem to be three major assumptions concerning the development of personalities and personality patterns: the Freudian, the Ericksonian, and the Rankian. The assumptions of the Freudian school have been termed "originology," and explained as "the assumption that the *real* developmental experiences occur in childhood, that the essential patterns are fixed at this time, with the rest of life being a repetition of the early patterns."[36] This seems to be the view taken by McClelland in his original studies of need for achievement, as he used Thematic Apperception Tests to throw light on his subjects' early childhood experiences and the child-care patterns to which they were exposed. In the strictly orthodox interpretation of this view, work personalities, like other aspects of the personality, are laid down in early childhood and are subject to change only through use of deliberate psychoanalytical techniques.

Another school of thought, epitomized by Erikson, would argue that although the personality tends to be persistent and controlling, it continues to develop and change throughout life. Along this line, Neugarten argues that "while there is continuity of personality, there is at least as much change as there is stability."[37] Maddi goes further and argues for radical changes in personality following the childhood years.[38] Brim and Wheeler argue that there is continual change after childhood years, brought about by changes in conditions. They define personality, however, in terms of role behavior exclusively, which may limit the application of their findings.[39] In this connection it is interesting that Strauss distinguishes between personality changes and changes in self-identity.[40]

Finally, there is the behavioral modification school, stemming from Rank, which would argue that behavior can be changed through deliberate conditioning, regardless of changes or lack of changes in personality. McClelland, in his later experiments to inculcate achievement need in adults, exemplifies this school of thought.[41] In fact, it is the behaviorist approach which implicitly underlies the bulk of incentive studies and programs, which address work patterns purely on the behavioral level.

Those attempts to change work patterns that focus on motivation are closer to the neo-Freudian school in attempting to change cognition and perception, in hopes that from these changes there will result changes in work behavior. However, to the writer's knowledge, there have been no attempts to increase productivity through efforts to change personalities, unless society's ceaseless attempts at socialization toward work, through all of the organs of mass persuasion, education, religion, and so on, are seen as indirect attempts to influence early childhood development through parental behavior and child-care patterns.

On the other hand, we simply do not know whether the work aspects of personality are as persistent and controlling as are other aspects, or are a more shallow area. Nor do we know whether the work aspects are embedded in other aspects, or whether they can be isolated, as Adorno isolated authoritarianism and McClelland isolated achievement need.

In view of such questions, it is both unfortunate and limiting that, as compared to the thousands of studies that have been done on work incentives as such, very little empirical work has been done on individual differences in work patterns, on individual variations in responses to presumed incentives, and on the possible determinants of such differences. A large-scale Russian study, for example, that looked at young workers in Leningrad factories, examined socioeconomic factors, technological factors, the workers' needs, interests, ideals, strivings, inclinations, nervous systems, and much more, but specifically disavowed interest in personality or its development: "As far as the basic personality characteristics of the worker . . . is concerned, we have formulated no hypotheses whatever."[42]

The research that has been done or that has been proposed can be divided between that which can be termed correlational, that is, seeking to link certain personality attributes to work patterns; and causational, looking for the reasons for the differences in work patterns. Correlational studies include those which examine relationships between authoritarianism,[43] anxiety, achievement need, and so forth, and work patterns. It is in this vein that Menninger says that hard work can be a form of sublimation.[44] Although not mentioned by Menninger, hard work can also be a form of substitution, flight, displacement, and alienation. In any case, correlational studies examine the here-and-now relationships of attributes and work patterns.

Causational studies look to the developmental history of individuals to determine at what point, for what reason, and in what way they moved toward becoming over- or underworkers, or any other category. Both Ingham and Goldthorpe emphasize the importance of this line of inquiry. The former holds that an attempt should be made to trace and specify "the *sources* of differences in orientation" to work, in factors outside the work situation.[45] The latter calls for tracing workers' views of work back to typical life situations and experiences.[46]

Correlational studies are important in their own right, and have many implications and applications for theory and practice. However, once personality attributes related to work patterns are identified, the question as to the genesis of these attributes, and whether there are work attitudes or patterns which are themselves separate, free-standing parts of the personality, almost inevitably arises, and requires further inquiry into the development of these attributes. The second possibility, then, and one that has been almost totally neglected, is to search for the beginnings of habitual work attitudes and patterns in the developmental history of individual workers. This approach, in effect, is intended to "leapfrog" over correlations and focus immediately on possible causes.

The area of attitudes toward work as part of normal personality development is almost *tabula rasa* insofar as the literature is concerned, and completely so as regards empirical studies. There have been a few speculative articles concerning the development of, or influences on, work personalities, some tangential investigations which can logically be applied to work patterns, but very few actual studies. Of the latter, Dalton's study stands out as an example of the direction in which such research could have gone—but did not.

In Whyte's study of 300 factory workers, all but 9 adhered to the work-group-determined norm. Although in most studies 291 of 300 workers responding in the same way would constitute the bulk and the totality of the report, Dalton—Whyte's associate—decided not to neglect the negative cases, and studied their characteristics in an effort to determine why they did not react like all the others. Although a sample of 9 is obviously too small to arrive at definitive results, he nevertheless determined that all 9 came from rural or small-town backgrounds, and that all of them were Protestants and had somewhat similar fathers.[47] Unfortunately, the clues contained in these findings were not picked up by others, and in studies of the effects of various incentives, differential reactions and negative cases remain neglected.

Even on a speculative basis, the literature reveals almost complete disregard for differences in work patterns as arising from developmental factors. One will look in vain, for example, for the subject "laziness" in the indexes of books on sociology, psychology, child development, personality, and certainly on labor relations and patterns. Only in rather philosophical musings is the subject mentioned, and even then under the heading of idleness, which is not the same thing as laziness, and which is much more socially acceptable, although still subject to disapproval. Burton, for example, in his *Anatomy of Melancholy,* says:

> Opposite to exercise is idleness (the badge of gentry) or want of exercise, the bane of body and mind, the nurse of naughtiness, stepmother of discipline, the chief cause of this and many other maladies, the devil's cushion . . . his pillow and chief reposal.[48]

Interestingly, however, the remedy Burton proposes for idleness is not work, which he does not value highly, but rather study, which he does value:

There is none so general, so aptly to be applied to all sorts of men, so fit and proper to expel idleness and melancholy, as that of study. . . . Study is the delight of old age, the support of youth, the ornament of prosperity, the solace and refuge of adversity, the comfort of domestic life.[49]

Bertrand Russell, too, spoke of idleness rather than of laziness, and it is symptomatic of attitudes toward work that the very mention of "In Defense of Idleness" evokes a smile on the face of the speaker, the listener, or both.

This lack of serious, sustained attention to the causes, consequences, dynamics, and uses of laziness leads one to feel like McGland:

He had read most of the literature on the psychopathology of sloth . . . without being convinced that anybody really knew very much about it.[50]

THE FACTORIES STUDIES

Since the kibbutz study described previously confirmed the lack of a relationship between satisfactions and hard work, and perusal of the literature indicated that, together with other possible factors, basic personality patterns played their part in determining work patterns, a series of exploratory studies was undertaken to seek hypotheses and to test methodology.

In seeking a setting for such studies, three criteria were seen as important: that workers be doing substantially the same work and receiving the same salary, with no premiums or bonuses paid for additional productivity; that workers be identifiable as overworkers or underworkers; and, obviously, that the workers be available for interview.

The necessary setting was found in 2 large-scale Israeli industries, in which workers were routinely rated by their foremen 4 times a year as to their work (not their production) records. The first study was done in 1979, with 75 usable respondents; the second was done in 1980, with 120 respondents. It should be emphasized that the basic thrust of these studies concerned developmental and demographic factors that bear on work reputations, and no attempt was made to correlate work patterns with personality traits, such as rigidity, or with transient attitudes, such as anger. Consequently, most questions (aside from demographic ones) dealt with the past history of the individual.

Three aspects of the methodology used deserve mention, and these have to do with the definition of hard work, the use of supervisor ratings, and recollections as data.

HARD WORK VIS-À-VIS GOOD WORK

Just as in the kibbutz study there was a question of the relative weight given by peers to hard work, good work, and responsibility, so these factories included in their rating scales elements of each. One factory used nine elements, each of which was further subdivided into four to twelve specific items. Total scores were then summarized on a scale of one (for negative) to five (for positive). The major elements used by this factory in evaluating workers were:

expertise

discipline

quality of work and precision

relationships with other workers

productivity

responsibility and trustworthiness

attitude regarding materials and equipment

safety-mindedness

identification with the work and the firm

Another, equally large Israeli industry uses a form with 22 items, rated on a 7-point scale, but with a further rating by the foremen as to how important each of those items is for the particular task being undertaken. That scale includes:

knowledge necessary to fulfill the task

quality of work

amount of work

dedication to task

attendance

diligence

discipline

intelligence and understanding

initiative

orderliness

care of equipment and supplies

obedience to safety regulations

attitude to others

cooperation with superiors

independence

leadership ability

analytic ability

ability to plan

organizing ability

decision-making ability

supervisory ability

administrative ability

Ratings based on these scales were used by the supervisors in identifying the overworkers and underworkers for this study. However, in exploring workers' subjective feelings about themselves, their fathers, their first jobs, and so on, they were asked to give their definitions of hard work, and to relate to them in answering subsequent questions.

Examination of these self-anchoring definitions indicated that workers, too, defined hard work as containing several elements. When all the responses were tallied, over 50 percent contained physical effort, in one way or another. Long hours or overtime were defined as hard work in 27 percent of the total responses, while investing oneself or intellectual effort were each given about 15 percent. When individuals' responses were used for the basis of calculations, 36 percent mentioned physical effort and 18 percent gave long hours, while investment of self and intellectual effort were given 10 percent each. In short, workers tend to define hard work mostly in terms of physical energy expended and hours worked.

SUPERVISOR RATINGS

The categorization as overworkers or underworkers in the factories studies was done on the basis of supervisor ratings. In spite of the use of the rating scales outlined above, some problems remained. Despite efforts to objectivize ratings through use of subareas and ranges of answers, there remained a subjective element, arising from the definition of hard work used by each foreman. What one considered very hard, another might have considered reasonably hard, or even not hard at all. This danger, it was hoped, would be minimized by using at least ten foremen, so that their differences would cancel each other out, at least to some extent.

A further limitation in reputational techniques as used in the factories studies is the paucity of lower-range ratings. Few foremen are prepared to admit that they tolerate poor workers on their staffs or teams, and the comparisons thus tend to be between better and worse workers, rather than between good and bad workers. In Israel, this limitation is mitigated somewhat by the difficulty of dismissing workers who have achieved tenure—as discussed previously—even for poor work or not working hard.

Just as in the kibbutz study workers were asked to rate themselves and such ratings were subsequently used to compare with their peer ratings, so in the factories studies self-ratings were sought for comparison with supervisor ratings. Whereas 67 percent of the respondents in the factories studies were rated as above average by their supervisors, 76 percent so rated themselves. Conversely, while supervisors called 33 percent below average, only 24 percent described themselves thus. Consequently, the same tendency to rate oneself as a better worker than others do operated in these factories. Whether these are simply socially acceptable answers, or whether workers really do think they work harder than others think they do, is not revealed in the data.

USE OF RECOLLECTIONS AS DATA

Just as operationalizing the independent variable—over- or under-workers—contains difficulties, so does the other end of the spectrum: operationalizing identification of developmental factors. McClelland observed the patterns of parents as their children attempted to achieve, asked retrospective questions, and used projective techniques, Thematic Apperception Tests, which consisted of showing respondents pictures, asking them to respond with stories, and categorizing the stories according to the amount of nAch present.[51]

Insofar as there are TATs standardized to indicate differential patterns of child care, as viewed retrospectively, this would probably be the most reliable method of determining past child-care patterns. However, the use of TATs is culture-bound, time-consuming, and expensive. Hence, the methodology that will probably remain predominant is that of retrospective questions asked of respondents.

While Kelman has outlined some of the problems inherent in any type of survey or question-and-answer research,[52] the use of restrospective questions involves the specific question of the accuracy of recollections of childhood. This may be doubly confounding when the events being recalled are subjective, such as images of fathers, rather than objective, such as place of birth. When examined empirically, however, there is considerable evidence that childhood events are recalled with considerable accuracy.[53] Robbins even holds that children's memories are more accurate than those of their parents—that is, people remember their own childhoods more accurately than they remember their children's growing up.[54] Robins did a longitudinal study of deviants and concluded, methodologically speaking, that "a general population should . . . provide more than 84 percent reasonably accurate interviews about adulthood, and the 80 percent reasonably accurate interviews about childhood obtained in this study."[55]

Zaleznik and associates even hold that selective memory is a desirable trait for such research, since the event is important only insofar as it is perceived as important by the child: "Parents' behavior affects a child's development only to the extent and in the form in which the child perceives it. This perception is a function of the real event and the intra-psychic experience of which it is a part of the expectations a child develops in the life cycle."[56] Consequently, it seems that retrospective answers concerning developmental factors should be given a great deal of credence in the kind of research being proposed and discussed.

Developmental Aspects Investigated

The absence of a body of knowledge, or previous studies, concerning the development of work personalities—or personality differences concerning work—made necessary an exploratory, hypothesis-seeking, study. In seeking promising areas for exploration, assumptions were drawn from a number of tangential fields and studies. These included demographic variables—country of origin, age, education, position in family, and religiosity; and developmental factors—parents' economic situation, child-care patterns, school experiences, the influence of role models, and previous work experiences.

The Sample

The total sample in both factories numbered 195 workers. Although both men and women were included in the sample, the latter made up less than 10 percent of the total. All of the workers were doing substantially the same type of hand labor, and none of them were paid on a piecework or productivity basis.

The Findings

Since these studies were hypothesis-seeking in nature, their major value was in indicating which areas of development seem worth pursuing further. Hence, the actual findings will be mentioned at the appropriate places below.

FACTORS AFFECTING THE DEVELOPMENT OF WORK PERSONALITIES

DEMOGRAPHIC VARIABLES

Country of Origin

Almost no one believes that the propensity to work hard is genetically determined (despite Strauss's previously quoted comment that this is possible). Hence, it must be a result of socialization processes, which, in turn, may differ from culture to culture. Andras speaks of differences in child-rearing practices over time,[57] but this could as readily apply to different countries or cultures. Strauss also emphasizes this when he says that personality patterns concerning aspects of work may be caused by variations in cultures and (thereby) in family child-rearing practices.[58] De Vos, discussing achievement motivation and its relation to hard work, points out that in cultures in which status is ascribed, rather than achieved—as in Japan—

hard work cannot be ascribed to motivation to achieve.[59] Indeed, Japanese society has been said to rest on duties, rather than rights, and consequently the behavior of the traditional Japanese worker is quite different from that of his or her western counterpart. On the other end of the spectrum, an African respondent is reported to have said that if an Israeli-style kibbutz were established in Africa—that is, a work situation with no foremen or bosses— most of the members would spend their days sleeping.[60] Israeli society also ascribes different work habits to people from different cultures. An impressionistic, anecdotal report on factory workers in a small development town in Israel reports that immigrants from Russia work very hard, as though determined to equal or surpass their conditions in Russia. Moroccans in the same factory are said to work hard when they work, but to take time off without warning, for family celebrations which may occur often, and continue for more than a week. The immigrants from India were described as being more concerned with theological and philosophical matters than with mundane affairs like work, and—in the words of the report—came to work whenever the spirit moved them.[61]

These impressions give some credence to the notion that national/cultural characteristics have a bearing on adult work patterns. Israel, with relatively large groups of immigrants from over a hundred countries, is fertile ground for testing some of these views empirically, but unfortunately there have been only a few studies, and these are not always comparable due to differences in samples and methodology. The general tenor of these studies, however, contradicts the popular impression that some of these groups (read: westerners) work harder than do others (read: North Africans and Middle-Easterners).

These conclusions are borne out by the findings of both the kibbutz and factories studies. In the former, 54 percent of the respondents were born in Europe and 37 percent in Israel. In the latter, 58 percent were born in North Africa or the Middle East, and 23 percent in Israel. Comparisons between overworkers and underworkers showed no significant differences on the basis of place of birth, whether these were examined in gross categories of Israelis versus westerners versus easterners, or in detail concerning groups of countries, or even individual countries. Of course, representation of some countries was too small to signify, or was absent altogether. There were no Japanese, no Africans, and only a few Indians. Thus, it is possible that the emphasis placed upon working hard is substantially the same in the countries examined but may be quite different in other countries or cultures.

In any case, the area of national/cultural differences deserves more study than it has yet received from incentive researchers. If work patterns are truly related to child-care methods, and if the latter differ from culture to culture, then there should be some evidence of this in workers' origins. This is not, of course, a simple matter to investigate. The behavior of one who arrived in a new country at age twenty might differ considerably from that of one who arrived as an infant. Even in these cases, the extent to which the family retained its previous patterns in the new country would have to be taken into account. The influence of American culture on the Amish, for example, is negligible as compared to its impact on some other groups. In addition, there are many intervening variables between cultural origins and current work behavior which make research in this area complicated.

Perhaps the most comprehensive cross-cultural study dealing with work organizations and work behavior is that of Hofstede. Using data from two surveys within the HERMES corporation in 1968 and again in 1972, consisting of over 116,000 questionnaires from 40 countries, he has categorized countries along 4 axes: power distance, uncertainty avoidance, individualism, and masculinity. Within these clusters, he outlines the differences in organizational structures and climates which exist, and the consequences for worker behavior. For example, Hofstede finds that when organizational development techniques are used which require feedback from others, insecurity is the result in Latin countries, frustration (for the initiator) and insecurity and guilt on the part of the worker in Japan, competition among the French, irrelevance for Germans, and acceptance for Americans and British.[62]

Consequently, in settings in which workers represent different cultural groups, or even subcultures, such as Scots, Welsh, and Irish in the United Kingdom, or Mohicans, Chicanos, WASPs, and "rednecks" in the United States, or even the so-called culture of poverty, workers' reactions to similar incentives may differ radically, on this basis alone.

Age

Although age is not a differential developmental factor—everyone inevitably aging, at the same chronological rate—there is room to wonder whether work personalities change as a result of age per se. Although there are findings concerning the relationship between age and satisfactions at work, there is less concerning productivity. Insofar as satisfactions are concerned, there seems to be general agreement in the literature that older workers express more satisfaction. When specific components of satisfaction are examined, however, security, relationships, comfort, and being of service increase with age, while the importance of intrinsic aspects of work, developing one's abilities, advancement opportunities, and pleasure decrease.[63]

Insofar as productivity is concerned, Cherrington found the 17-26 age group to value hard work and craftsmanship less than the over-26 groups.[64] Levinson, discussing the mode and content of *creative* people, uses age 35 as the turning point in this respect.[65] In the two factories studies, and in some small-scale follow-up studies done by students as exercises, there was an unmistakable trend toward a connection between increasing age and hard work. In almost every case, workers over 35 years of age were better workers than those under 35.

Wright and Hamilton propose three possible reasons for changes in satisfaction (but not productivity) with age: that young workers subscribe to a different set of values; that the surrender process described previously takes place, and they learn to be satisfied with less; and that older workers, through the natural working of the system, simply have better jobs. Their data support this last hypothesis.[66] Hofstede offers substantially the same reasons, but adds *Zeitgeist*—drastic systemwide changes in conditions which cause everyone's values to shift.[67]

In other words, changes in work patterns related to age may represent changes as age increases; or changes in those needs which are related to age—marriage, children, financial need, and so on. On the other hand, it is also possible that people who are younger now were subjected to different influences during their childhood than were older people—influences which lead them to take work less seriously.[68] There is a good deal of evidence in the literature that young people in the work place today relate differently to work than did young people in the past. Younger workers seem to demand different things from their work and their work places; in Yankelovich's terms, they are a "new breed" of workers.[69] Andras also raises the possibility that work patterns have changed over the last twenty years or so, with changes in child-rearing practices.[70] Whether the permissiveness said to be related to the Spock generation has resulted in lesser efforts to work hard will not be known until the results of longitudinal research are available in the future.

Amount of Education

The relationship between education and work patterns is a complex one, involving both the demands and the rewards of various jobs on the one hand and the amount, type, and content of the educational experience on the other. Miner found that most people have more intelligence than they need for the jobs they are doing,[71] and O'Toole holds that it is the people who are over-educated for their tasks who are responsible for the defects, failures, accidents, and errors in the work place, rather than the uneducated workers.[72] Argyris found that lower-skilled employees tended to express a desire to experience routine and sameness.[73]

Insofar as amount of education alone is concerned, there seems to be no logical reason to believe that this is correlated with hard work or its lack, except that the more educated may be expected to perceive, or to be offered, opportunities for advancement or methods of achieving their goals other than through hard work. Although in the kibbutz study many differences between members were correlated with amount of education, neither in that study nor in the continuing studies was this a factor in distinguishing between work patterns. It should be noted, however, that very few of the respondents in any of these studies were educated beyond high school, and many did not finish high school, so that differences which otherwise may have arisen did not show up.

Position in Family

Among all those who have studied and written about normal development, only Alfred Adler seems to have addressed the phenomenon of laziness directly. In Adler's psychology, the difference between the only child, the oldest child, middle children, and the youngest child accounts for many differences in their childhood experiences, and therefore in their adult personalities. Some of the findings concerning the effect of birth order are noncomparable, while others are contradictory. For example, Rosen holds that first-borns are more competitive than the later born,[74] while Dubno and Freedman hold that they are more conforming.[75] Singer holds that first-borns pay more attention to parental expectations, and see themselves as having values similar to those of their parents.[76] Others have found evidence that first-borns receive greater pressure for more mature behavior from parents than do the later borns.[77] Only children, on the other hand, are said to be disadvantaged in that they are not pushed to more mature behavior by the presence of younger siblings, as are first-borns.[78] In any case, the influence of birth order is not simple. A great deal depends upon the number of children in the family, the time between births, sex, and other factors. Toman has examined a great number of these permutations in detail, as family constellations.[79]

Insofar as work patterns are concerned, Ansbacher interprets Adler to mean that laziness is a functional defense against feelings of inferiority or lack of self-confidence.[80] Such lack of self-confidence may arise from birth order. According to Ansbacher, the oldest child places much emphasis on rules, and feels that not only should the rules be obeyed, but that they should not change. Hence, one might expect oldest children to accept hard work as an important rule of life that should be obeyed; and one would not expect them to be active among the young workers who demand meaning and relevance from work.

The second child is said to be imbued with a striving which is unconquerable until the goal has been reached or retreat results in the beginnings of neuroses. A youngest child may suffer from inferiority feelings which, as pointed out previously, may use laziness as a mask. The only child is often born in a timid and pessimistic atmosphere, where economic anxieties predominate.

As is evident, the effect of birth order on adult work patterns has hardly been conceptualized, let alone tested. Strumpfer unsuccessfully sought correlations between birth order and achievement needs,[81] but, as will be discussed later, there is good reason to question whether hard work is an indication of need to achieve, in the sense used by McClelland.

In the factories studies, and in two of the small follow-up studies, it was clear that middle children predominated over both first and last children as overworkers (there were only 8 only children in the 195 respondents—a number too small to be comparable). Again, it must be emphasized that family constellations are influenced by a great many factors. However, it is interesting that the middle child "behaves as if he were in a race, is under full steam all the time, and trains continually to surpass his older brother and conquer him."[82] If working hard is synonomous with being in a race and trying to surpass others, then the results of the studies mentioned above are consonant with Adler's expectations for the middle child. In other words, all other things being equal (which they never are), there is a better chance of a middle child being an overworker than of an oldest or youngest child. In any case, both the theory and these rather tentative findings indicate that it is worthwhile to include position in family—and a good deal of information about that position, including sex of siblings, spacing, and so on—in research designed to identify developmental factors in current working patterns.

Religiosity

As noted in Chapter 2, work as a religious duty became codified with the advent of Protestantism and Luther's contention that one served God by working in one's vocation. The influence of this doctrine spread throughout the western world, and was not confined to Protestant sects. In fact, it is often referred to, in America, as the American work ethic, or as the western work ethic, or simply as the work ethic. Even divested of its religious origins or connotations, the work ethic holds that work is a value in and of itself, without regard for its material or psychic rewards.[83]

It is not surprising, then, that conventional wisdom, which holds that work is a moral imperative or a religious injunction, and which is reinforced by countless admonitions to work or to work hard, expects to find a relationship between religiosity and work patterns. There is a widespread feeling that work and religious consciousness are related.

There are a number of possible ways to probe the correlation between religiosity and work patterns, and three are suggested here. One possibility is to examine the amount or extent, and perhaps the content, of religious education or training undergone by the respondent. This might include attendance at religious, as opposed to secular, schools; religious education in addition to secular education, via Sunday schools, afternoon schools, or the like; religious instruction on the part of a priest, preacher, or rabbi; and/or preparation for and participation in religious rites of passage.

A second area is the area of present practice or religious identification. This could be probed both in terms of attendance at services and participation in other practices, and in terms of the extent to which the respondent considers himself or herself a religious person.

Finally, it is possible to probe attitudes toward work, leisure, and the proper vocation of people through direct and indirect questions. Rotenberg used this last method in his research, using the Shortened Protestant Ethic Scale, and found that Americans adhere more closely to the ethic than do Jewish Israelis. He also found differences on this score between Moslem and Christian Arabs.[84] Schechter, however, found no difference between Jewish groups from various countries and cultures insofar as reported adherence to the Protestant Ethic is concerned.[85] Mirels and Garrett found that Protestant Ethic scores were positively correlated with occupational choice for jobs demanding a concrete pragmatic approach and negatively correlated with jobs requiring emotional sensitivity and human values.[86] Stone, however, holds that adherence to the Protestant Ethic is not an important mediating difference concerning how satisfaction with the work itself will be influenced by changes in job scope.[87]

Of the respondents in the factories studies, 38 percent went to religious schools when they were young; 44 percent described their schooling as having been in "traditional" (not Orthodox) schools; and 18 percent went to secular schools. However, only 23 percent call themselves Orthodox today; 59 percent consider themselves traditional; and 17 percent are secular. In addition to probing these two areas, respondents were queried concerning their adherence to the Protestant Ethic, using the shortened version mentioned above.

It should be understood that all of the respondents were Jewish, and consequently only differences in degrees of religiosity, but not differences in religions, could be examined. In no case were significant correlations found between religious education and work patterns, present religious identification and work patterns, or adherence to the Protestant Ethic and work patterns.

Nevertheless, and especially in view of Dalton's previously mentioned finding that all of the rate-busters were Protestants, possible linkages between religious factors and work patterns deserve further study.

HISTORICAL VARIABLES

Parents' Economic Situation

Although conventional wisdom holds that children from poor families necessarily learn to work hard, there is a good deal of evidence that poverty is a deterrent to hard work, ambition, and the desire to achieve. Rosen and D'Andrade found that nAchievement scores for middle-class adolescents were significantly higher than for their lower-class counterparts.[88] Arnold and Rosenbaum emphasize that the typical poor child does not receive overt motivation to study from his parents or peers, and is therefore not usually well motivated toward achievement.[89] Robinson states that "working class parents foster attitudes in their children which make them dependent, indifferent, and apathetic."[90] Hulin and Blood add another dimension to this discussion, insofar as work is concerned, holding that the lower-class city dweller in America is less likely to be sympathetic to middle-class values such as hard work.[91] Zaleznik goes further, holding that social class origin affects not only an individual's values but also identification with a role model.[92] Insofar as the parents are role models, social class has been found to interact with parent-child relationships.[93]

Consequently, respondents in this study were asked if, during their childhood, their parents had been rich, financially comfortable, just managing, having difficulty, poor, or very poor. In the total results of all the studies under review, there is a strong indication that it is the children of rich, well-to-do, or economically managing parents who work hard, whereas the underworkers tend to come from poorer families.

These findings bear out the contention of those researchers who feel that lower-class families do not inculcate in their children the middle-class value of hard work as a means to success. Despite the popular notion that adversity results in hard work, the findings of these studies indicate the reverse—that poverty creates the attitude that it does not pay to work hard. This is understandable in light of the facts concerning poverty: Most of the poor people in the western industrialized countries are not those who have not worked, or not worked hard, but the aged, the young, and the disadvantaged,[94] who are poor despite their hard work or that of their parents. Wealth, or nonpoverty, is seen more as a result of luck, inheritance, connections, or abilities other than those of work—such as education, cleverness, or ambition—or as a result of the social system as such.

Again, it is obvious that familial reactions to the same economic circumstances may vary, with consequent variations in attitudes toward work and in the inculcation of those attitudes. As a factor influencing adult work patterns, however, parental economic circumstances should not be neglected.

Child-Care Patterns

Even among those who believe that personality changes throughout life there is agreement that parental handling during childhood has an important effect on later development. In studying achievement motivation, McClelland roots this in parental handling.[95] Zaleznik emphasizes parent-child relationships in terms of affection and discipline in connection with work patterns.[96] Green speaks of parents as projecting their own ambitions into the careers of their children, and this may be analogous to projecting their own superego as regards work onto their children.[97] Two aspects of parental handling were probed in these studies: the kind of discipline generally used, and parental encouragement to do well in school.

Discipline

The effect of parental handling on adult behavior has been subjected to a great deal of research in various areas, but not insofar as work patterns are concerned. The closest analogy to studies of child-care patterns vis-à-vis work patterns is the work done by McClelland and those who followed his methodology.[98] McClelland, however, studied the need for achievement and, as noted above, there are many people who do not see hard work as the vehicle for achieving their goals. Indeed, McClelland's research linked child-care patterns to entrepreneurial behavior—that is, the initiative, desire, and courage to strike out on one's own, which is not the same thing as working hard at one's job. In fact, later studies contrasted entrepreneurial to bureaucratic behavior,[99] and it is the latter which is characterized by acting according to rules laid down by others—a situation much closer to that requiring hard work. Consequently, although the importance of child-care patterns in determining adult patterns is emphasized by McClelland's research, the findings concerning entrepreneurial behavior should not be seen as necessarily presaging the same findings regarding hard work.

Further, there are connections between parents' economic situation and child-care patterns. Many writers emphasize the different methods of discipline, rewards and punishment, and socialization generally in lower-class and middle-class families.[100] The factories studies attempted to probe the area of parental handling through questions related to methods of discipline, ranging from spanking through withholding of rewards, verbal reprimands, expressions of unhappiness, and indifference. As a general trend among the responses, it was the overworkers who reported more severe punishments than did the underworkers. The former reported spanking more often, habitually or occasionally, while the latter reported verbal reprimands and expressions of unhappiness.

Again, the caution must be issued that the studies mentioned were exploratory and highly tentative. Nevertheless, or perhaps for this reason, no correlation was found between parents' economic situation (or social class) and method of discipline. Yet the overworkers' backgrounds contained more severe punishment on the part of parents than did that of underworkers.

Educational Experiences

The amount of education achieved by an individual is only one, and perhaps among the least important, aspect of the effect of education on working patterns. During the many years spent in school—often up to twelve years, and in some cases even more—attitudes, reactions, and habits are developed which might very well carry over into working life. Indeed, given the people who go to work immediately after leaving school, it would be surprising if they did not.

In looking at the content of educational experiences, three possible areas present themselves. One is the amount of effort expended; a second is the amount of success achieved; and the third is the relationship between these two factors.

The amount of effort expended in school is important insofar as it might set a pattern which becomes habitual and is continued in the work place. As Wheelis puts it, action which defines people, which describes their character, is action which has been repeated over and over and so has come in time to be a coherent and relatively independent mode of behavior.[101] So it might be that people who try hard to achieve in school throughout their educational careers develop patterns of working hard. This factor, however, like all the others, is complex. It involves parental pressure or support, natural ability, the presence of reinforcements, and the element of challenge, among others. Generally speaking, however, the school setting has some close similarities with the work place. For one thing, regardless of parental interest and supervision or their lack, there is almost always pressure from the teacher to invest oneself in the learning experience. Just as the work foreman pressures for more, harder, or more productive work, in one way or another, so the teacher expresses pleasure or displeasure, or issues rewards and punishment, for effort expended. As the threat of less salary or dismissal is in the background at the work place, so the threat of poor grades, extra homework, nonpromotion, or expulsion operates in the classroom.

Of course, it is possible that classroom patterns are already laid down by preschool experiences. However, in the view of those who do not accept the establishment of immutable personality patterns by age five or six, the school experience can be a strong determinant of later patterns.[102] Consequently, inquiry into the amount of effort habitually exerted in school seems a reasonable area of exploration. In the factories studies, there was a clear, statistically significant difference between the workers who said that they tried hard all of the time in school, most of the time, or usually and those who said they tried hard only sometimes, rarely, or never. The overworkers were those who worked hard; the underworkers did not exert much effort in school.

These findings did not indicate, of course, whether the tendency to work hard at school was already present, or whether the results of the school experience itself determined and fixed these patterns. In other words, efforts at school could conceivably have paid off, thereby indicating the effort was worthwhile. Conversely, underwork could have resulted from effort which did not pay off, indicating that effort is not worthwhile. Indeed, underwork could result from lack of effort at school which nevertheless resulted in positive rewards, indicating that it is not necessary to work hard. Thus, the causation of the correlation between school effort and adult work patterns remains to be explored.

Educational Achievements

Any assumption that those persons who achieved good marks in school are, or become, hard workers in adult life is extremely tenuous. A congeries of factors must be taken into account, including natural ability, subject matter, school level, modes of teaching, and many outside factors. Only to the extent that good marks are considered to be solely, or mostly, the result of effort expended could a correlation be thought to exist. Indeed, in accordance with the views quoted above, that many people are overeducated for their jobs, one could even surmise that school achievements, whether measured in amount of education or level of grades, would be inversely related to hard work. This, of course, would ultimately depend on the level and attainments of the education as related to the educational requirements of the job. In any case, for what it may mean, no trend as regards educational attainments was discernible in the studies of overworkers and underworkers discussed here.

School Effort and School Achievement

Reinforcement theory and, to some extent, expectancy theory would lead one to believe that effort rewarded leads to continuing effort, while unrewarded effort leads one to cease trying. Consequently, it is the congruence between effort and attainments that might be important as a determinant of working patterns. Hence, in order to examine the possibility that aberrant subgroups or individuals varied widely enough to affect the totals, a correlation between each individual's reported school efforts and results was sought. For overworkers, a correlation of .25 was found; for underworkers, .63. In other words, underworkers' efforts and results were more closely correlated than were those of overworkers: For overworkers, trying hard and achieving good marks, or not trying hard and not receiving good marks, was less related than it was for underworkers. Conversely, underworkers saw more relationship between effort, or its lack, and results than did overworkers. Insofar as these data are concerned, the assumption that effort which achieves results inspires a continuing pattern of effort is not supported, at least insofar as these respondents' reported school experiences are concerned.

Parents' Interest in Studies

Another possible determinant of both efforts and attainments in school is that of parental pressure and interest. To what extent did this aspect of parental handling (mentioned briefly above) affect the creation of work patterns? Did parents who worried about their childrens' progress in school, who were interested in their studies and encouraged them, shape patterns that continued to express themselves in work? Like the other factors, this is a complex area, involving the parents as role models, positive/negative/ambivalent feelings on the part of the children, natural abilities, and much more. Nevertheless, parental pressure and behavior in regard to school behavior as an analogue for later work patterns arises from McClelland's findings regarding achievement need.

In the studies mentioned herein, respondents were asked to what extent each of their parents was interested in, and encouraged achievement in, their school progress. In both the case of the father and the mother, interest in school progress was correlated with underworking. That is, the underworkers reported their parents as more interested and more encouraging concerning studies than did the overworkers. The overworkers, conversely, reported to a greater extent that their parents left their school progress to the other parent, to teachers, or were simply too busy to be interested.

This finding, tentative as it is, is a reversal of what logic and common-sense would indicate. One possible interpretation, therefore, is that the underworkers, even as children, needed to be encouraged and urged to work, while their counterparts—the overworkers to be—did not. If so, the interest and encouragement for the large part did not achieve its goal, as the underworkers remained underworkers despite such support.

Another possibility is that school work and real work are simply too different—that patterns built up regarding the former are not transferable to the latter. Still another possibility is that, once freed of parental constraints and restraints which are operative throughout the school years, there is a reaction to pressures to study that exhibits itself in negative behavior at work. Finally, it is possible that the small sample and exploratory nature of the research quoted resulted in an artifact that will disappear in replications.

Role Models

Kelman, in discussing methods of opinion change, points out that identification with a role model is an important influence in the determination of opinions (which in his usage is almost synonymous with attitudes).[103] Conventional wisdom also assigns an important place to role models in the formation of behavioral habits. Consequently, it is not surprising that there are some references in the literature to the importance of role models in the determination of working patterns. Both Deutscher[104] and Zaleznik mention the father as a role model in this connection, while the latter also mentions teachers as having an influence, at least insofar as career choice is concerned.[105] Whyte, in describing the effective leadership of Jack Carter, attributes his style to role models, including a teacher and some fellow workers.[106] Levinson also emphasizes the need to ask who a person's heroes or models are or were.[107]

It is interesting that in the references to parents as role models, as found in the literature, the influence of the mother is hardly considered.[108] It is not clear whether this stems from conscious or unconscious sexism, an assumption that mothers do not or did not work, a sample of male workers only, with the accompanying assumption that only the image of the father as a worker is important, or some other reason.[109]

There are some difficult methodological problems involved in studying the impact of role models, while distinguishing between overworkers and underworkers. Unless one specifically probes the direction of the influence—toward more or toward less work—it is difficult to know whether either sample would have been better or worse workers without such influence. In other words, to the extent that both overworkers and underworkers reported that they were influenced by teachers, for example, it would be appealing, but unsound, to think that they were influenced in the direction of their present designations.

Insofar as the father as the role model is concerned, this is potentially confounded by the variety of relationships that might have existed between the youngster and his father. For example, the father might have been seen as a hard worker, while lack of positive identification with him might have resulted in a rejection of this model. Goodwin found that sons of nonworking parents had as strong commitments to work as did the sons of working parents.[110] Consequently, one of the complexities in this area is whether the father was voluntarily unemployed or wanted work but could not find it.

In the factories studies overworkers were significantly more influenced by a variety of possible role models than were underworkers; mothers as role models appeared to be the major influence among all workers; and the influence of teachers was significantly greater for overworkers than for underworkers. In view of the complexities mentioned above, correlations were sought between the image of the father as a good, average, or poor worker—as reported in response to one question—and the amount of influence exerted by the father, as asked in another. Of those reporting congruence between the image of the father as a good worker and heavy influence of this image on present patterns, 70 percent were overworkers, while 69 percent of those reporting an image of the father as a poor worker and heavy influence on present work patterns were underworkers.

Thus, both from the responses obtained in the factories studies and from hints in the literature, it would seem that the influence of role models is an important, although perhaps difficult, area for further exploration.

Previous Work Experiences

Among those who feel that the work personality is malleable, or, at least, not laid down for all time by childhood experiences, there is emphasis on previous experiences as culminating in present patterns. Kohn and Schooler hold that current work patterns are the result of cumulative work experiences in the past.[111] Presumably, satisfying and rewarding past patterns tend to be repeated. Kahn says that habits of work learned long ago to ensure job security or to satisfy an exacting supervisor become functionally autonomous, coming to be preferred for themselves.[112] Some put the case more generally: "The individual's identity is shaped by the kind of work he does."[113] Others are more specific. Mortimer and Lorence say:

> While it is often assumed that occupations "mold" the personality . . . this "occupational socialization hypothesis" has rarely been examined empirically. In contrast, the alternative "occupational selection hypothesis," that persons choose their work on the basis of already formed psychological characteristics, has been thoroughly investigated and confirmed by sociologists . . . and psychologists.[114]

It is far from clear, unfortunately, to what extent stable personality patterns affect first and subsequent job experiences, thus reinforcing themselves. Pragmatically, most employers tend to believe that past patterns are more or less controlling, as given the choice of employing someone whose reputation in the past job was as a non-hard worker, as opposed to someone known to have worked hard, few employers would inquire as to the reasons for the non-hard work in the past on the assumption that the proferred job would make a change for the better in the worker's pattern.

On the other hand, the factories studies indicated a convergence on the norm: When workers were asked to rate themselves in their first jobs and— later on the questionnaire—to rate themselves on their present jobs, those who said they were hard workers previously reported themselves as working less hard currently, while those who described themselves as underworkers in the past reported themselves as working harder now.

The area of changing patterns from job to job is an important one, for in it may be contained the key to whether work patterns are relatively stable habits to which one tends to revert, or whether changes in conditions, incentives, and other factors—both internal and external—create real changes, at least for as long as they are in effect.

OTHER FINDINGS

Despite the fact that the factories studies mentioned here were exploratory in nature, with small samples, some of the other findings may prove of interest. When asked their opinions as to why some people work harder than others, 37 percent felt this was part of the general nature or personality of the worker, 25 percent felt that work habits were determined by work conditions, 16 percent attributed it to home training, and 13 percent answered "patriotism."

When asked about the reasons for their own work patterns, 26 percent said they worked in accordance with the demands of the job, 23 percent gave money or advancement as their reason, 19 percent attributed it to their own nature, and 18 percent said they enjoyed their work.

SUMMARY

It seems clear that people react in a variety of ways to the same work situation, and to those changes which are intended to be incentives for harder work. At least part of these differential reactions arise from relatively stable attitudes and behaviors which have been summarized as the "work personality." It is not clear to what extent the work personality overlaps with other aspects of the individual's personality, or to what extent it is freestanding and identifiable. Nor is it clear when, why, and in what form differences in work personality begin to appear. Much less research has been done on the determinants and the influences of work personalities than on other areas of work incentives, despite the acknowledgment by many researchers that this may be an influential area.[115]

Misgav, for example, says:

> Much research indicates that biographical factors and personality factors relate to work satisfaction . . . and it is necessary to relate to them in understanding research on work satisfactions.[116]

Campbell and Pritchard sum up the situation, saying, "So far . . . questions concerning the job outcome population have suffered from considerable benign neglect."[118]

One reason for this neglect might be the lack of clearly visible "action implications" in such research. Much of the current incentive research is either sponsored by, or requires the cooperation of, employers. Their interest, understandably, is in research that they can apply in increasing satisfactions, productivity, or both. The determinants of stable work personalities seem too vague, too distant, and too inflexible—or too little subject to manipulation—for their identification to be useful. This is a familiar argument concerning basic as opposed to applied research, but without resorting to the classic response that nothing is more useful than a good theory, it is possible to point out several possible applications.

From a cluster of variables which might be found to correlate with specific work patterns—say, high effort and middle children from poor backgrounds for whom hard-working fathers were role models, or any other combination—it might be possible to identify workers or potential workers who would be happier, or more productive, or both, in some tasks rather than others. Conversely, there are certainly tasks which require precision rather than effort. This might make it possible to follow Glaser's suggestion that "personnel should be selected who can be motivated to strive for excellence in job performance."[118] There are also jobs which require neither great precision nor much effort, such as the aforementioned job of picking an occasional suitcase from a conveyor belt and putting it into a bin. Validated replicated studies of developmental factors might make it possible to suit the worker better to the job, thus creating more satisfaction among workers and more efficiency in the use of human resources.

Further, combining findings from research into developmental factors with conventional incentive research might indicate for whom more or less participation in decision making would be effective; for whom more challenge, or responsibility, or equity, or the like, might be important; for whom not; and even for whom it might be a negative experience.

Even if there were no such immediate applications of the possible findings, research along the lines indicated would nevertheless be important. When McClelland investigated the need for achievement and found this to be primarily a result of child-care patterns, the field was not abandoned because of the seeming impossibility of changing child-care behavior. Rather, McClelland and associates began investigating the possibility of simulating such patterns, or circumventing their effects. The result was the experiment in inculcating the need for achievement in adults which—in the case of Indian businessmen—was reported as successful. In the same manner, until it is known which developmental factors are important, how they interact with each other, and how they affect other variables, it is impossible to try to change them, counteract them, or strengthen them.

Nor is it necessarily true that developmental factors cannot be changed. Child-care patterns do change. Sometimes this is in reaction to other societal changes, but the changes brought about among large sections of American parents by one book, written by Dr. Benjamin Spock, should not be underestimated. Similarly, changes in child-feeding habits in many parts of the developing world—bitterly opposed by many nutritionists—were brought about by advertising on the part of baby food manufacturers. School curricula are often changed by legislative directive. Textbooks and popular books both reflect and influence public mores, as Rodgers has pointed out regarding work in American publications from 1850 to 1920.[119] Movies, television, and—perhaps most important—television series offer role models that affect the young. The rest of the mass media also have their effect—how many American adults still feel guilty about leaving food on their plates because of the "starving Armenians," or still admire "plucky little Finland" as the only nation that paid its World War I war debt to America?

These are all manipulable influences—some easier and some harder—no less than conventional incentives to work. But until a great deal more research is done in this area, the extent to which work patterns are determined by personality development, and to what extent reactions to various incentives are different on the same basis, must remain mostly a matter for speculation.

NOTES

1. C. L. Hulin and M. R. Blood, "Job Enlargement, Individual Differences, and Worker Responses." *Psychological Bulletin* 69 (1968): 41-55.

2. I. Berg, M. Freedman, and M. Freeman, *Managers and Work Reform: A Limited Engagement* (New York: Free Press, 1978), p. 41; italics in original.

3. E. E. Lawler and J. L. Suttle, "Expectancy Theory and Job Behavior," *Organizational Behavior and Human Performance* 9 (1973): 482-503.

4. J. P. Campbell and R. D. Pritchard, "Motivation Theory in Industrial and Organizational Psychology," in M. D. Dunnette (ed.) *Handbook of Industrial and Organizational Psychology* (Chicago: Rand McNally, 1976), p. 79.

5. G. K. Ingham, *Size of Industrial Organization and Worker Behaviour* (Cambridge: University Press, 1970), p. 48.

6. J. H. Goldthorpe, D. Lockwood, E. Bechhofer, and J. Platt, *The Affluent Worker: Industrial Attitudes and Behaviour* (Cambridge: University Press), 1968.

7. P. Ward and T. Wall, *Work and Well-Being* (Harmondsworth: Penguin, 1975), p. 20.

8. Ingham, op. cit., p. 43.

9. R. Munts and I. Garfinkel, *The Work Disincentive Effects of Unemployment Insurance* (Kalamazoo: Upjohn, 1974), p. 56.

10. B. M. Bass and G. V. Barrett, *Man, Work, and Organizations: An Introduction to Industrial and Organizational Psychology* (Boston: Allyn & Bacon, 1972), p. 70.

11. G. Strauss, "Workers: Attitudes and Adjustments," in J. M. Rosow (ed.) *The Worker and the Job: Coping with Change* (Englewood Cliffs, NJ: Prentice-Hall, 1974), p. 80.

12. S. E. Seashore and T. D. Taber, "Job Satisfaction Indicators and Their Correlates," in A. D. Biderman and T. F. Drury (eds.) *Measuring Work Quality for Social Reporting* (New York: John Wiley, 1976), pp. 109, 113.

13. Campbell and Pritchard, op. cit., p. 122.

14. For a review of such studies, see D. J. Cherrington and J. L. England, "The Desire for an Enriched Job as a Moderator of the Enrichment-Satisfaction Relationship." *Organizational Behavior and Human Performance* 25 (1980): 139-159.

15. G. Salvendy, "Can the Slow Worker Go Faster?" *Industry Week* 168 (March 1971): 43.

16. P. Shipley, "Technological Change, Work Scheduling, and Individual Well-Being," in K. D. Duncan, M. M. Gruneberg, and D. Wallis (eds.) *Changes in Working Life* (Chichester: Wiley, 1980), pp. 39-53.

17. A. Zaleznik, G. W. Dalton, and L. B. Barnes, *Orientation and Conflict in Career* (Boston: Harvard University, 1970), p. 212.

18. W. Hale, Jr., "Sensing the Rhythm." *Infection Control and Urological Care* 4 (1979): 19-20.

19. V. A. Yadov and A. A. Kissel, "Job Satisfaction: Analysis of Empirical Data and Attempt at Their Theoretical Interpretation," in M. R. Haug and J. Dofny (eds.) *Work and Technology* (Beverly Hills, CA: Sage, 1977), p. 50.

20. R. Stollberg, "Job Satisfaction and Relationship to Work," in Haug and Dofny, op. cit., p. 117.

21. W. S. Neff, *Work and Human Behavior* (New York: Atherton, 1968), p. 84.

22. M. M. Machlowitz, *Workaholics: Living with Them, Working with Them* (New York: Mentor, 1981).

23. J. P. Robinson, "Occupational Norms and Differences in Job Satisfaction: A Summary of Survey Research Evidence," in J. P. Robinson, R. Athanasiou, and K. B. Head, *Measures of Occupational Attitudes and Occupational Characteristics* (Ann Abor: Institute for Social Research, University of Michigan, 1969), p. 66.

24. S. Freud, *Civilization and Its Discontents* (New York: Paperback, 1958), pp. 20-21.

25. W. G. Sumner, *Social Darwinism* (Englewood Cliffs, NJ: Prentice-Hall, 1963), p. 1.

26. W. F. Oates, *Confessions of a Workaholic* (New York: Abingdon, 1971).

27. T. J. Overbeck, *The Workaholic* (Chicago: Loyola University, 1977), p. 16.

28. C. Curtis, "They Can't be Workaholics—They're Having Too Much Fun." *New York Times* (March 30, 1975), p. 30; see also "Letters to the Editor—Workaholics," *New York Times* (October 24, 1976).

29. Winston Churchill, quoted in G. C. Taylor, "Executive Stress," in A. A. McLean (ed.) *To Work Is Human* (New York: Macmillan, 1967).

30. Machlowitz, op. cit., p. 3.

31. H. A. Robinson and J. E. Finesinger, "The Significance of Work Inhibition for Rehabilitation." *Social Work* 2 (1957): 22.

32. R. Hoppock, "A Twenty-Seven Year Follow-Up on Job Satisfaction of Employed Adults." *Personnel and Guidance Journal* 38 (1960): 485-492.

33. D. C. McClelland, *Motivating Economic Achievement* (New York: Free Press, 1975), ch. 2, "Can Adults Acquire a Strong Need to Achieve?"

34. McKeachie says: "Despite heroic efforts to determine basic dimensions of personality, personality researchers seem in little agreement about what these dimensions are." W. J. McKeachie, "Motivation, Teaching Methods and College Learning," in D. C. McClelland and R. S. Steele (eds.) *Human Motivation: A Book of Readings* (Morristown, NJ: General Learning Press, 1973), pp. 447-473.

35. S. Raskin, *Ethics of the Fathers* (New York: Bloch, 1959).

36. Zaleznik et al., op. cit.; Heckhausen holds that the future achievement behavior of the adult can be predicted by age ten. H. Heckhausen, *The Anatomy of Achievement Motivation* (New York: Academic, 1967), p. 147.

37. B. Neugarten, "A Developmental View of Adult Personality," in J. E. Birran (ed.) *Relations of Development and Aging* (Springfield, IL: Charles C Thomas, 1964).

38. S. R. Maddi, *Personality Theories* (Homewood, IL: Dorsey, 1968).

39. O. G. Brim, Jr., and S. Wheeler, *Socialization After Childhood* (New York: John Wiley, 1966).

40. A. Strauss, "Transformations of Identity," in A. M. Rose (ed.) *Human Behavior and Social Processes* (Boston: Houghton Mifflin, 1962).

41. McClelland, op. cit.

42. A. G. Zdravomyslov, V. P. Rozhin, and V. A. Iadov, *Man and His Work* (White Plains, NY: International Arts and Sciences Press, 1967); translated by S. P. Dunn.

43. Lauterbach raises the question as to whether certain kinds of jobs or occupations attract people with different degrees of authoritarianism. "In many cases, the relation between the type of activity or position and the degree of authoritarian attitude would be very illuminating to explore." A. Lauterbach, *Men, Motives and Money: Psychological Frontiers of Economics*

(Ithaca, NY: Cornell, 1959), pp. 25-26; Faunce and Dubin discuss the "fit" between personality attributes and job requirements, and find the compensatory model more supported than the spillover model, but call for more research in the area. W. A. Faunce and R. Dubin, "Individual Investment in Working and Living," in L. E. Davis and A. B. Cherns (eds.) *The Quality of Working Life: Problems, Prospects, and the State of the Art* (New York: Free Press, 1975), pp. 299-316.

44. K. Menninger, "Work as Sublimation." *Bulletin of the Menninger Clinic* 6 (1942): 170-182.

45. Ingham, op. cit.

46. Goldthorpe et al., op. cit., p. 185.

47. W. F. Whyte, *Money and Motivation* (New York: Harper & Row, 1955).

48. R. Burton, *The Anatomy of Melancholy* (London: Chatto and Windus, 1907).

49. Ibid.

50. P. DeVries, *Reuben, Reuben* (New York: Bantam, 1965), p. 169.

51. D. McClelland, *The Achieving Society* (New York: Free Press, 1961).

52. H. C. Kelman, *A Time to Speak: On Human Values and Social Research* (San Francisco: Jossey-Bass, 1968).

53. S. Waldfogel, "The Frequency and Affective Character of Childhood Memories." *Psychological Monographs* 62 (1948); G. J. Dudycha and M. M. Dudycha, "Some Factors and Characteristics in Childhood Memories." *Child Development* (1933-1934): 265-278; M. L. Kohen and J. A. Clausen, "Parental Authority Behavior and Schizophrenia." *American Journal of Orthopsychiatry* 26 (1956): 297-313.

54. L. Robbins, "The Accuracy of Parental Recall of Aspects of Child Development and Child Rearing Practices." *Journal of Abnormal and Social Psychology* 66 (1963): 265-276.

55. L. N. Robins, *Deviant Children Grow Up* (Baltimore: Williams and Wilkins, 1966), p. 285.

56. Zaleznik et al., op. cit.

57. R. K. Andras, "Introductory Speech," in *Work in a Changing Industrial Society* (Paris: Organisation for Economic Co-operation and Development, 1975), p. 13.

58. G. Strauss, op. cit.

59. G. A. De Vos, *Socialization for Achievement: Essays on the Cultural Psychology of the Japanese* (Berkeley: University of California Press, 1973).

60. M. E. Kreinin, *Israel and Africa: A Study in Technical Cooperation* (New York: Praeger, 1964).

61. D. Ben Menachem, "A Proposed Programme for the Social Absorption of Immigrants from Russia, India, and North Africa in Dimona." *Adult Education in Israel* 24 (1974): 8 (Hebrew).

62. G. Hofstede, *Culture's Consequences: International Differences in Work-Related Values* (Beverly Hills, CA: Sage, 1980).

63. Ibid., p. 362.

64. See *World of Work Report*, 4 (January 1979): 8.

65. H. Levinson, *The Great Jackass Fallacy* (Boston: Harvard, 1973).

66. J. D. Wright and R. F. Hamilton, "Work Satisfaction and Age: Some Evidence for the 'Job Change' Hypothesis." *Social Forces* 56 (1978): 1140-1158.

67. Hofstede, op. cit.

68. U. Bronfenbrenner, "The Changing American Child—A Speculative Analysis," in R. C. Coser (ed.) *Life Cycle and Achievement in America* (New York: Harper & Row, 1969), pp. 1-20.

69. D. Yankelovich, "Work, Values, and the New Breed," in C. Kerr and J. M. Rosow (eds.) *Work in America: The Decade Ahead* (New York: Van Nostrand Reinhold, 1979).

70. Andras, op. cit.

71. Quoted in M. K. Freedman, "The World of Work," in *Young People and the World of Work* (New York: National Federation of Settlements and Neighborhood Centers, 1963), p. 13.

72. J. O'Toole, *Work, Learning and the American Future* (San Francisco: Jossey-Bass, 1977), p. 28.

73. C. Argyris, "The Individual and the Organization: An Empirical Test." *Administrative Science Quarterly* 4 (1959): 145-167.

74. B. C. Rosen, "Family Structure and Achievement Motivation." *American Sociological Review* 28 (1961): 574-585.

75. P. Dubno and R. D. Freedman, "Birth Order, Educational Achievement and Managerial Attainment." *Personnel Psychology* 24 (1971): 63-70.

76. E. Singer, "Adult Orientation of First and Later Children." *Sociometry* 34 (1971): 328-345.

77. T. Falbo, "The Only Child: A Review." *Journal of Individual Psychology* 33 (1977): 47-61.

78. Ibid.

79. W. Toman, *Family Constellation* (New York: Springer, 1976).

80. H. L. Ansbacher and R. R. Ansbacher (eds.), *The Individual Psychology of Alfred Adler* (New York: Harper & Row, 1956), p. 391.

81. D. J. Strumpfer, "Failure to Find Relationships Between Family Constellations and Achievement Motivation." *Journal of Psychology* 85 (1973): 29-36.

82. Ansbacher and Ansbacher, op. cit.

83. For discussion of work as a societal value and as a religious obligation, see D. Macarov, *Incentives to Work* (San Francisco: Jossey-Bass, 1970), ch. 4, "Incentives to Work"; *The Design of Social Welfare* (New York: Holt, Rinehart & Winston, 1978), ch. 10, "Work and Welfare: The Influence of the Protestant Ethic"; and Macarov, *Work and Welfare: The Unholy Alliance*, op. cit., ch. 7, "Work as Normalcy: Everybody Does It So It Must Be the Right Thing To Do," and ch. 8, "Work as Morality: The Opium of the Classes."

84. M. Rotenberg, *Damnation and Deviance: The Protestant Ethic and the Spirit of Failure* (New York: Free Press, 1978).

85. G. Schechter, "Influence of the Protestant Ethic on Patterns of Achievement and Loneliness within Different Ethnic Groups in Israel." MA thesis, Hebrew University, Jerusalem (Hebrew).

86. H. L. Mirels and J. B. Garrett, "The Protestant Ethic as a Personality Variable." *Journal of Consulting and Clinical Psychology* 36 (1971): 40-44.

87. E. F. Stone, "The Moderating Effect of Work Related Values on Job Score-Job Satisfaction Relationship." *Organizational Behavior and Human Performance* 15 (1976): 147-167.

88. B. C. Rosen and R. D'Andrade, "The Psycho-Social Origins of Achievement Motivation." *Sociometry* 22 (1959): 185-218; also in U. Bronfenbrenner (ed.), *Influences on Human Development* (Hinsdale, IL: Dryden, 1972), pp. 566-580.

89. M. G. Arnold and G. Rosenbaum, *The Crime of Poverty* (Skokie, IL: National Textbook, 1973), p. 31.

90. J. P. Robinson, "Occupational Norms . . . ," op. cit.; Hess makes the same point. R. D. Hess, "The Transmission of Cognitive Strategies in Poor Families: The Socialization of Apathy and Underachievement," in V. L. Allen (ed.) *Psychological Factors in Poverty* (Chicago: Markham, 1970), pp. 73-92.

91. Hulin and Blood, op. cit.

92. Zaleznik et al., op. cit.

93. M. L. Kohn, "Social Class and Parent-Child Relationships: An Interpretation," in R. L. Coser (ed.) *Life Cycle and Achievement in America* (New York: Harper & Row, 1969), pp. 21-42.

94. Macarov, *Work and Welfare . . .* , op. cit., pp. 77-78.

95. D. C. McClelland, "Sources of *n* Achievement," in McClelland and Steele, op. cit., pp. 319-377; see also D. R. Miller and G. E. Swanson, "Child Training in Entrepreneurial and Bureaucratic Families," in E. Katz and B. Danet (eds.) *Bureaucracy and the Public* (New York: Basic Books, 1973), pp. 108-121.

96. Zaleznik et al., op. cit.

97. A. Green, "The Middle Class Male Child and Neurosis." *American Sociological Review* 11 (1946): quoted in T. Caplow, *The Sociology of Work* (New York: McGraw Hill, 1954), p. 273.

98. McClelland, op. cit.

99. Miller and Swanson, op. cit.

100. F. L. Strodtbeck, "Family Interaction, Values, and Achievement," in D. C. McClelland, A. L. Baldwin, U. Bronfenbrenner, and F. L. Strodtbeck, *Talent and Society: New Perspectives in the Identification of Talent* (Princeton: Van Nostrand, 1958), pp. 135-194.

101. A. Wheelis, *How People Change* (New York: Harper & Row, 1973), p. 11.

102. Early education has been held to have a strong predictive value for alcoholism and crime, so its predictive value for work patterns should not be underestimated; see W. McCord and J. McCord, *Origins of Alcoholism* (London: Tavistock, 1960).

103. H. C. Kelman, "Processes of Opinion Change," in W. G. Bennis, K. D. Benne, and R. Chin (eds.) *The Planning of Change* (New York: Holt, Rinehart & Winston, 1964).

104. M. Duetscher, "Adult Work and Developmental Models." *American Journal of Orthopsychiatry* 38 (1968): 882-892.

105. Zaleznik et al., op. cit.

106. W. F. Whyte, *Organisational Behaviour: Theory and Application* (Homewood, IL: Dorsey, 1969).

107. Levinson, op. cit., p. 40.

108. Levinson is an exception in emphasizing both parents: "A critically important aspect . . . derives from the values of the parents. If a person can recall not so much what his parents did but how in behaviour they emphasized certain values, he will probably then be able to discern more clearly . . . ideal elements in those values." Levinson, op. cit., p. 40.

109. See, for example, W. G. Dyer, "Family Reactions to the Father's Job," in A. B. Shostak and W. Gomberg (eds.) *Blue-Collar World: Studies of the American Worker* (Englewood Cliffs, NJ: Prentice-Hall, 1964), pp. 86-91.

110. L. Goodwin, *Do the Poor Want to Work?: A Social-Psychological Study of Work Orientations* (Washington, DC: Brookings, 1972); B. T. Tooney, "Work Ethic and Work Incentives: Values and Income Maintenance Reform." *Journal of Sociology and Social Welfare* 7 (1980): 148.

111. M. L. Kohn and C. Schooler, "Occupational Experience and Psychological Functioning: An Assessment of Reciprocal Effects." *American Sociological Review* 38 (1973): 97-118.

112. R. L. Kahn, "Value, Expectancy, and Mythology," in G. G. Somers (ed.) *The Development and Use of Manpower* (Washington, DC: Industrial Relations Research Association, 1967).

113. J. M. Jerzier and L. J. Berkes, "Leader Behavior in a Police Command Bureaucracy: A Closer Look at the Quasi-Military Model." *Administrative Science Quarterly* 24 (1979): 1-23; Sarason puts it simply: "The experience of work shapes the shaper." S. B. Sarason, *Work, Aging and Social Change: Professionals and the One Life-One Career Imperative* (New York: Free Press, 1977), p. 21.

114. J. T. Mortimer and J. Lorence, "Work Experience and Occupational Value Socialization: A Longitudinal Study." *American Journal of Sociology* 84 (1979): 1361-1385.

115. "Characteristics of workers must be taken into account if change programs are to be successful." T. G. Cummings and E. S. Molloy, *Improving Productivity and the Quality of Work Life* (New York: Praeger, 1977), p. 278.

116. M. Misgav, *The Relationship Between Job Satisfaction Factors and Job Behavior* (Ramat Gan, Israel: Bar-Ilan University, Department of Psychology, n.d.), (Hebrew).

117. Campbell and Pritchard, op. cit., p. 103.

118. E. M. Glaser, "Productivity Gains through Worklife Improvement." *Personnel* 52 (1980): 71-77.

119. D. T. Rodgers, *The Work Ethic in Industrial America 1850-1920* (Chicago: University of Chicago Press, 1974).

10

MONEY, MANAGEMENT, MORAL VALUES, AND MACRO-EVENTS

In addition to the possible sources of worker productivity discussed so far, there remain other credible areas to be examined. Some of these, such as money, are so obvious that they are often taken for granted; others, such as world events, are so subtle or far removed that they are overlooked.

MONEY

That people work for money seems so obvious that it is often not even taken into consideration. Money as a surrogate for the things it can buy is so important in people's lives that despite all the other meanings that work might have for some people—structure, status, self-esteem, and so on—if money were to be removed as an incentive, it is extremely doubtful that there would remain more than a handful of workers in any given society. Even in the kibbutz the work is seen as making possible the maintenance of the members. Indeed, as pointed out in Chapter 2, the wage-stop which runs through all social welfare programs is based squarely on the assumption that, given money from other sources, most people would stop working.

Although the use of money as a motivator has been said to be coeval with the existence of money itself,[1] its use in motivational research was emphasized by Taylor, who felt this was practically the only thing the worker wanted from the job. The Hawthorne studies, as has been pointed out, in essence denigrated money as an incentive, although both the experimental group, the short-lived control group, and the rest of the workers were paid on a group-productivity basis. Herzberg was ambivalent as to the role money played in his experimental settings; job redesign and restructuring studies often include changes in payment without clear specification of the timing, the amount, or the results;[2] and money as important has been consistently downgraded by most social scientists.[3]

And yet, when four sources of motivation are studied, namely, money, goal setting, participation, and job enrichment, money as a motivator resulted in the largest median improvement, and the highest proportion of studies showing improvement.[4] Further, whether one studies satisfactions or productivity, the connection with money is clear. Comparing satisfactions as reported by workers at various income levels, the relationship is unidirectional: The lower the income the less the satisfactions.[5] Assemblers and machinists gave pay as the only reason for staying on the job from three to seven times more often than did craftsmen and setters, process workers, and white-collar workers.[6] Of course, this relationship may be mediated by the fact that lower-paying jobs are more uncomfortable, have lower status, and generally contain more dissatisfiers and fewer satisfiers than do better-paying jobs. Yet money, as Easterlin has pointed out, continues to play an important part in determining the amount of satisfaction.[7] Robinson, in reviewing the survey research literature, says:

> A good deal of evidence we have reviewed so far pinpoints wages as a major, if not the major, determinant of job *satisfaction*. Nor is this concern confined to the lower-income occupations. The available evidence essentially agrees that wage complaints are common to all occupations.[8]

Thurow, seeking higher *productivity,* links it directly with "those things that are good for the individual—higher income."[9] A Bureau of Labor Statistics report examines the relationship between real compensation per hour and output per person per hour, over a 32-year period, and finds the correlation so close that it has been termed a "rather startling" relationship.[10]

Strumpel found a strong connection between satisfaction with income and general sense of well-being,[11] and Katona found that this did not weaken as more income is acquired, until the very highest levels of the income distribution are reached.[12] Others have studied the widespread impression that the affluent, or certainly the very wealthy, tailor their work patterns according to the income tax bracket in which it would put them. Barlow and associates studied just that, and came to the conclusion that the disincentive effects of the progressive income tax are indeed minor.[13]

On the other hand, there is considerable evidence that only when the basic physiological needs are met, to use Maslow's terminology, do higher needs become potent. That is, until the worker is making enough money to manage, considerations other than income are relatively unimportant. Although Huizinga found that both the lower and the higher occupational levels are affected by the so-called higher needs, "the lower needs become stronger—and hence, apparently, are fulfilled to a lesser extent—the lower in the occupational hierarchy we go."[14]

Consequently, although other needs may arise and affect work patterns, when money is paid on a differential basis for hard work and/or productivity, it is a potent incentive. Even in Whyte's factory study, which indicated the influence of small group pressure in holding quotas down,[15] the quotas were set by consensus which took financial need into consideration. In the criticisms of the Hawthorne studies, it will be remembered, the small group was paid on the basis of productivity. Further, although some of the group's need for money was satisfied to the point that they preferred talking and horsing around to more income, the replacement of two members brought into the group an older woman whose need for money was occasioned by her sick mother. She became the "straw boss," setting the pace and urging the others on. Smith experimented with money as an incentive, and varying times in which to complete the task. He found that money was a potent incentive when offered, and that, given the same money for different time periods, people were anxious to finish quickly to have time for other things.[16] All of which adds up to the conventional wisdom that people work mainly for money, but would prefer to do other things.

It would be a mistake, however, to assume that money always and in all ways controls the worker's behavior. Adam Smith's "economic man" exists only as an abstraction, and its reification may have done incalculable damage to individuals and to society. As Bensusan-Butt says:

> That men are usually greedy for ever more material goods when they can be obtained without excessive toil is a vague generalisation of the truth of which no expert investigations are required to persuade any one. . . . The belief that extreme poverty involves deep suffering of kinds that vanish at higher income levels is a truth readily acceptable and a sufficient basis for making its relief a duty to others . . . [but] incidental consequences of the theory of Economic Man have been that it is taken to sanctify the imitative material greed conventional in many advanced economies, and to justify . . . an almost paranoid obsession with the distribution of income and the proper progressivity of the tax system.[17]

In summary, it might be said that although money is a very complex subject within the context of incentive research, changing its meaning for workers at various times and under different circumstances, it remains a necessary condition for all work, and a sufficient one for those on the lowest economic levels, or those whose basic needs have not been or are not being met.

MANAGEMENT

Whereas money has been described as the oldest incentive to work insofar as individuals are concerned, changing the way group leaders or supervisors do their jobs has been described as the oldest strategy for changing what goes on in work groups.[18] Herzberg's declaration that a supervisor is successful to the point that he (or she) concentrates on the workers' needs, rather than on production, may be a statement of the extreme position in this regard.[19]

Drucker points out that many of the traditional functions of the supervisor have been taken over by others: personnel people and quality control people; maintenance people and schedulers; coordinators and planners. "As a result, the supervisor has been left with the sole function of maintaining discipline, that is, with the function of being feared."[20] Drucker's proposal is to change the role to that of "assistant"—one who assists the workers by being sure they know their work and have the tools.[21]

It is almost as difficult to factor out the influence of changed supervisory behavior on productivity as it is to isolate the influence of money, because many of the change strategies include—deliberately, as a side effect, or instrumentally—a changed role, stance, or attitude on the part of the supervisor. Autonomous work groups, job redesign, goal setting and feedback—all involve changed supervisory practices. Katzell and associates did locate reports of thirteen experiments in changing supervisory methods in an attempt to increase productivity.[22] Of these, six were flawed by having statistical significance not reported or doubtful, or were questionable because of major limitations of the experiment. Of the remaining seven, two (factory workers and office workers) improved in quantity of production alone; three (factory workers, university workers, and hospital workers) improved in quality of work alone; one (laundry workers) improved in quantity, production costs, and absenteeism; and one (hospital workers) improved in quality of work, absenteeism, and attitudes. Robinson and associates also list a number of experiments probing supervisory styles, but their studies deal exclusively with satisfactions, and not with productivity.[23] Moore, however, found that productivity increased when supervisors used public praise and private reprimand, to a much greater extent than the reverse.[24]

Most of the modern literature on supervision stems from the experiments of Lewin, Lippitt, and White on democratic, autocratic, and laissez-faire atmospheres in groups.[25] The general assumption, sometimes validated by experiment,[26] is that democratic supervision results in higher productivity (although sometimes the assumption is, via satisfaction). However, Gellerman points out that at least three factors affect this situation: the extent to which the job requires teamwork; the consistency of the supervisor's behavior; and the personality of the workers.[27]

The importance of managerial discipline in acquiring worker productivity is emphasized by the findings of Franke and Kaul, mentioned previously, regarding the Hawthorne studies.[28] Despite what they regard as the mythology arising from those studies, their reanalysis indicated that no less than 79 percent of productivity increases came about because of supervisory discipline. It will be remembered that the supervisor cautioned, threatened, and disciplined all the group members, eventually removing two of them from the group. It is possible that the climate and attitudes regarding work in general and the role of the supervisor in particular have changed since those days, and that workers today would not respond to discipline in the same way.[29] Still, one is left wondering if the factor of close supervision and demands for hard work might not be a rather neglected source of harder work.

There is, however, another aspect of management that affects worker productivity and, incidentally, supervision, and that has to do with the demands of the job. When people who have indicated that they could work harder than they do are queried as to why they do not work harder, a very common answer is simply that the job does not require it. Given the increases in productivity brought about by changes in methods, machines, and materials mentioned previously, and the various ways in which this increased productivity is dealt with, including nonwork time during work hours, it is no secret that giving people jobs, and having them put in their hours, is at least as important as the products or services which they produce. Consequently, many workers—supported by their unions—tend to see increased individual productivity as harder work at disliked jobs, the setting of higher norms that will then become the standard, and the elimination of jobs. The latter may be seen as eliminating opportunities for others, for possible job changes for self, or for possible advancement and/or income.

One possible source of increasing per-person productivity, then, in settings that can make it possible, might be a return to a type of piecework, in which the worker has a certain amount of work to be done, and can leave when that quota is filled, without loss of income, regardless of the amount of time it takes. The "joker" in this proposal is that although the worker might be very happy to put in hitherto unexpended effort to get the job done quickly, and society might even gain from the things that would be done in the additional time free from work, the employing organization, paying the same salary for the decreased worktime, would gain nothing from the increased per-person productivity and would probably be disinclined to participate in such a system, despite worker happiness and societal gains.

MORAL VALUES

There is another source of work incentives—and even differential work patterns—that is rarely taken into consideration, and that is work as a moral responsibility. It is true, as has been mentioned previously, that work as an idea, a concept, an ideology, has been invested with moral, including religious, values. But when individual reactions to work situations are examined, this factor is not often taken into consideration. And yet there are societies which emphasize this aspect at all times, and others in which it becomes important at certain times.

The emphasis placed upon work as a value in the Soviet bloc is not only societal, but there are attempts to imbue each worker with the belief, or knowledge, that his or her work is important in itself. Consequently, although the Soviet Union did not begin with complete equality of income for all citizens (or workers), there was an attempt to limit the amount of inequality between jobs and between workers, so that work would be performed for its own sake, and not as an attempt to gain more income. This framework has become considerably distorted, particularly when fringe benefits are taken into consideration.[30]

The idea of moral incentives was taken over by the Castro revolution in Cuba, however. Bernardo has shown how in 1966 the proponents of "moral incentives," led by Che Guevara, triumphed over the more liberal economic planners who wished to emulate the Yugoslav and pre-1968 Czechoslovakian methods of development.[31] Essentially, moral incentives meant that the worker was to be motivated entirely by his commitment to the society and his fellow citizens and remuneration in the form of money and other "material rewards" was to be phased out of Cuban society.

The efficacy of purely moral incentives had already begun to be questioned in 1971, when Bernardo did his study, and there has probably been further deterioration in these ideals today, but the general objective remains highly influential in Cuba.

The People's Republic of China has also put heavy emphasis on moral incentives to work. Although they originally adopted the Soviet 8-grade scale for manual labor in industry, there are nevertheless inequalities, often expressed in fringe benefits. Thus, top officials of the army and the party are chauffeur-driven in Red Flag cars (the largest automobile made in China). The next echelon drive their own Red Flags; below them are officials in chauffeur-driven Shanghais (the somewhat lighter and smaller Chinese-built cars); followed by officials driving their own Shanghais. The prosperous worker, however, has a motor-powered bicycle; the middle-class worker, a regular bicycle; and the equivalent of the masses—walk. Hard work is rewarded with "points" rather than money, and with enough points one can acquire a bicycle, a television set, or even a larger apartment.

In the Chinese agricultural commune—of which there are tens of thousands—the underlying principle is not that of the Israeli kibbutz—from each according to his ability, to each according to his need—but a more capitalist version: From each according to his ability, to each according to his work. Again, points are awarded hard workers. In both industry and in the communes, there is a great deal of social pressure exerted against those who do not work hard, emanating from the "cadre," at work and at home.

Consequently, in both Cuba and in China—and to some extent within the Soviet bloc—there still remains a heavy component of moral incentives in daily work patterns.

MACRO-EVENTS

Finally, insofar as incentives to work are concerned, there are those societywide events that Hofstede refers to as *Zeitgeist*.[32] One of the most obvious of these is war, or the threat of war. In every country that depends upon its own production in great part for war material, the surge of patriotism that war brings is like no other spur. As Manchester says:

> The production miracle was accomplished by thousands of hard-driving executives and millions of workers, some skilled veterans and some young women fresh from the kitchen or the bargain counter. . . . If the passage of a quarter-century has rendered obsolete the weapons which came off World War II assembly lines, it cannot touch the exploits of those who toiled there, competing with equally determined workers in Krupp, Fiat, and Mitsubishi factories.[33]

During World War II there developed in many defense industries, as well as in other places, a workers' "social system" whose sanctions against absenteeism were far more effective than those of managers.[34]

There are other societywide phenomena which affect work patterns, and one of these is the threat or actuality of a recession or a depression. The fear of loss of a job which is coupled with the knowledge that there is no other job available seems to be a potent incentive. In Franke and Kaul's study of the Hawthorne data, they found that 14 percent of the increase in productivity could be traced to the fact that there was a depression on.[35] This was the second largest factor in the productivity increase. Others have also described what it meant to have a job during the Great Depression, and what it meant to have no job.[36]

Finally, there are events which are macro in the context of the individual, although they affect him or her alone. Some of the respondents in the factories studies volunteered that they started trying to work hard only when they got married, or had a child. Others respond to different changes in their life situations. It is a common phenomenon, in many countries, that new immigrants, and even foreign laborers, work hard. The hard work of the new immigrants to the United States is proverbial, and has formed the basis of many stories and novels. The mass immigration into Israel, immediately after the establishment of that state, was marked by the immigrants' determination to get ahead economically. The same phenomenon is noted in Australia today, and among the Russian Jews arriving in the United States and in

Israel. This drive to "make it" by working hard often extends to the second generation, in a variation of Hansen's law,[37] while the third generation, even if they have not succeeded economically, tends to adjust to the norm for the host population.

In summary of this chapter, it can be said that money, supervision, the inculcation of work as a moral value, and events in the life of the country and the individual also affect work patterns.

NOTES

1. E. A. Locke, D. B. Feren, V. M. McCaleb, K. N. Shaw, and A. T. Denny, "The Relative Effectiveness of Four Methods of Motivating Employee Performance," in K. D. Duncan, M. M. Gruneberg, and D. Wallis (eds.) *Changes in Working Life* (Chichester: Wiley, 1980), pp. 363-388.

2. T. G. Cummings and E. S. Molloy, *Improving Productivity and the Quality of Work Life* (New York: Praeger, 1977), pp. 5-6.

3. Locke et al., op. cit., p. 363.

4. Ibid., p. 375.

5. H. P. Brown, *The Inequality of Pay* (Oxford: University Press, 1977); D. Macarov, *Incentives to Work* (San Francisco: Jossey-Bass, 1970).

6. J. H. Goldthorpe, D. Lockwood, F. Bechhofer, and J. Platt, *The Affluent Worker in the Class Structure* (Cambridge: Cambridge University Press, 1969), p. 57.

7. R. A. Easterlin, "Does Money Buy Happiness?" *Public Interest* 30 (1973): 3-10.

8. J. P. Robinson, "Occupational Norms and Differences in Job Satisfaction: A Summary of Survey Research Evidence," in J. P. Robinson, R. Athanasiou, and K. B. Head, *Measures of Occupational Attitudes and Occupational Characteristics* (Ann Arbor: University of Michigan, 1969), p. 54.

9. *World of Work Report,* 6 (April 1981): 32.

10. Ibid.

11. B. Strumpel, "Economic Life-Styles, Values, and Subjective Welfare," in B. Strumpel (ed.) *Economic Means for Human Needs: Social Indicators of Well-Being and Discontent* (Ann Arbor: University of Michigan, 1976), pp. 19-65.

12. G. Katona, *The Mass Consumption Society* (New York: McGraw-Hill, 1964).

13. R. Barlow, H. E. Brazer, and J. N. Morgan, *Economic Behavior of the Affluent* (Washington, DC: Brookings, 1966), p. 130.

14. G. Huizinga, *Maslow's Need Hierarchy in the Work Situation* (Gronigen: Wolters-Noordhof, 1970), p. 195.

15. W. F. Whyte, *Money and Motivation* (New York: Harper & Row, 1955).

16. C. P. Smith, "The Influence of Testing Conditions and Need for Achievement Score and Their Relationship to Performance Scores," in J. W. Atkinson and N. T. Feather (eds.) *A Theory of Achievement Motivation* (New York: John Wiley, 1966).

17. D. M. Bensusan-Butt, *On Economic Man* (Canberra: Australian National University Press, 1978), pp. 172-173.

18. R. A. Katzell, P. Bienstock, and P. H. Faerstein, *A Guide to Worker Productivity Experiments in the United States 1971-75* (New York: New York University Press, 1977), p. 27.

19. F. Herzberg, B. Mausner, and B. B. Snyderman, *The Motivation to Work* (New York: John Wiley, 1959), p. 10.

20. P. F. Drucker, *Management: Tasks, Responsibilities, Practices* (New York: Harper & Row, 1974), p. 280.

21. Ibid., p. 261.

22. Katzell et al., op. cit.

23. Robinson et al., op. cit.

24. H. Moore, *Psychology for Business and Industry* (New York: McGraw-Hill, 1942).

25. K. Lewin, R. Lippitt, and R. K. White. "Patterns of Aggressive Behavior in Experimentally Created 'Social Climates.'" *Journal of Social Psychology* 10 (1939): 87.

26. See, for example, R. Likert, *New Patterns of Management* (New York: McGraw-Hill, 1961).

27. S. W. Gellerman, *The Management of Human Relations*. (New York: Holt, Rinehart & Winston, 1966), pp. 34-38.

28. R. H. Franke and J. D. Kaul, "The Hawthorne Experiments: First Statistical Interpretation." *American Sociological Review* 43 (1978): 623-643.

29. For a "different" view of the supervisor's role, see H. Mintzberg, *The Nature of Managerial Work* (New York: Harper & Row, 1973).

30. For more detail on the Russian situation, see Brown, op. cit.

31. R. M. Bernardo, *The Theory of Moral Incentives in Cuba* (University: University of Alabama Press, 1971).

32. G. Hofstede, *Culture's Consequences: International Differences in Work-Related Values* (Beverly Hills, CA: Sage, 1980), p. 344.

33. W. Manchester, *The Glory and the Dream* (Boston: Little, Brown, 1973), p. 296.

34. I. Berg, M. Freedman, and M. Freeman, *Managers and Work Reform: A Limited Engagement* (New York: Free Press, 1978), p. 28.

35. Franke and Kaul, op. cit.

36. C. Bird, *The Invisible Scar* (New York: Pocket Books, 1966).

37. Hansen's Law holds, generally, that what the grandparent (immigrant) generation wanted to forget, the grandchildren generation wanted to remember. M. L. Hansen, "The Third Generation in America," in H. D. Stein and R. A. Cloward (eds.) *Social Perspectives on Behavior* (New York: Free Press, 1958), pp. 139-144.

II

INCENTIVE RESEARCH:
SUMMARY, ETHICS, AND APPLICATION

In the preceding chapters an attempt has been made to outline the extent and the depth to which work permeates every aspect of modern society. An important element in the work world—and therefore in society itself—has been the constant search for greater productivity. At one time this was an attempt to ease the life of the worker; it then became a desire to increase production; and today it continues for both these reasons, although they often become intermingled.

In the course of this look at history, the scientific management school, the human relations school, and the structuralist approach were described. Deeper examination of the Hawthorne studies, however, raised the question as to whether the reported increases in productivity were the result of better human relations, or of supervisory discipline, the worsening depression, and rest periods. Consequently, a study done in an Israeli kibbutz was described—a study which found Herzberg's distinction between satisfiers and dissatisfiers to exist in a moneyless setting; which found no difference between overworkers and underworkers based on the amount of satisfaction; and which raised questions concerning the relationship between self-actualization and hard work.

Before examining the possible connection between satisfactions and work patterns, a look at the literature concerning work satisfactions as such indicated that few people get more satisfactions from their work than from their nonwork activities, and those that do are high in the hierarchy or in the free professions. When attitudes concerning the necessity to work, the job, the work place, and the work itself are concerned, most people accept the fact that they have to work and try to make the best of it, but given the opportunity, they opt for shorter hours, longer vacations, more holidays, and less work during work time.

The connection between work satisfactions and work patterns was next examined. Although there are undoubtedly instances in which satisfactions at work result in harder work, there are also many in which it does not. In fact, a reverse connection has even been identified. Consequently, this study, like so many before it, has found no generalizable, functional, replicable link between work satisfactions and hard work. There is some evidence, however, that insofar as direct service jobs are concerned, the quality of the service may be affected by the feelings of the worker.

Turning from satisfactions as such, the area subsumed under "job redesign" was examined, followed by the so-called process theories. In regard to the former, there are again instances of success, but there are so many idiosyncratic features in such reports that even careful reviews are unable to identify specific elements that usually lead to greater productivity. Indeed, in at least one review everything that was tried led to increased productivity, the implications of which were discussed. Insofar as process theories are concerned, their major weakness is that they do not identify the respondents who responded to the changes, and so it is impossible to know whether the results were based upon changes within a small group, or individuals, or the entire sample, and the range of changes over individuals. Insofar as both of these areas are concerned, it has been charged, in effect, not that they have failed, but that—taking all of the possible variables into account—they have never been properly tried.

The next possible source for worker productivity—basic, stable, personality patterns—was examined in terms of country of origin, age, education, position in family, religiosity, parents' economic circumstances, child-care patterns—including discipline and parents' interest in school progress—educational experiences and achievements, role models, and previous working patterns. Although the importance of personality differences is often mentioned as an intervening variable in other incentive studies, it is rarely taken seriously into account, or investigated; while the developmental factors that make for stable working patterns have never been investigated as such.

Finally, the subjects of money, management, moral values, and macro-events were examined for their impact upon working patterns.

In summary, it is apparent that the factors that influence work patterns are so numerous, so complex, and so interrelated that it is no wonder that no general theory, or even constructs, have so far emerged from the wealth of material which exists. In short, despite at least fifty years of unremitting search for the factors that make for greater worker productivity, it can be said with great seriousness by acknowledged experts that "in terms of desired job outcomes, or rewards, we still have very fragmentary knowledge about why people work."[1]

And yet there is little question but that the desire to increase workers' satisfactions as such, and the desire to achieve greater worker productivity, will lead to continuing research on the subject. It is probable that such research will continue to concentrate on the here-and-now changes in situations, rather than on the historical and developmental aspects, although in the long run the latter may prove more controlling and more important. But the shop-floor factors are more easily subject to manipulation, and it is around the issue of manipulation of workers that the question of ethics revolves.

In the eyes of most workers, incentive research is not very different from Taylor's speedup—the ultimate goal is to induce people to work harder. Even when the ostensible and stated goal of the research or the change is simply to increase workers' satisfactions, there is still widespread suspicion that the goal is actually to increase productivity. Even proponents of the quality of working life movement have difficulty disassociating better quality of life from higher or better production.[2]

This suspicion is not confined to the workers themselves. When the Human Factors Panel of the NATO Scientific Affairs Committee sponsored a conference on "Changes in the Nature and Quality of Working Life" at Thessaloniki, Greece, in 1979, the original plan called for the conference sessions to take place on the university campus, but the students at the university, viewing the conference as planning to exploit workers, necessitated a change in venue.

Indeed, most incentive research is undertaken with the avowed purpose of increasing productivity, although not always at the expense of the worker. As such, this research complements one of the main streams of societal values mentioned previously—the pursuit of productivity. Consequently, it is quite possible that even the results of research into developmental factors leading to differential work personalities could be used exploitatively. That is, instead of being used to fit workers to jobs, it can be used simply to exclude from employment—or good jobs—persons whose developmental histories indicate that they are not likely to be, or to become, hard workers. Thus, to sexism, racism, and discrimination against the aged, there might be added discrimination against the potentially lazy.

There is, however, another possibility concerning uses to which knowledge of developmental factors concerning working patterns could be put. It has been pointed out and explicated elsewhere that the amount of human labor needed, and consequently the number of jobs available, might be severely curtailed in the future, either through increasing automation—microprocessors and robots, for example—or through changes in energy sources or amounts. Job sharing, reduction in working time, make-work and featherbedding, and measures to hide unemployment, such as training and retraining courses, may reach the end of their usefulness when the amount of *human* labor necessary is so small that it will occupy a minority of the population for very limited periods.[3]

This drastic change in the human condition will not only require a restructuring of the economy, social welfare, and the society as a whole; it will also necessitate a new set of values concerning the meaning of life and the things that are important and valuable for a person to do.[4] Whether the basic value of a particular society will be, or will include, education, religion, the arts, warm human relationships, good parenting, volunteering, or other aspects of life is subject to conjecture, but if work is no longer available or required, then the heavy emphasis formerly placed upon work as a measure of worth, the only acceptable means of support, inherently ennobling, and as the obligation of a normal person, a good neighbor, a good citizen, and a moral or religious person will have to be changed.

Socialization for work in a workless society can only lead to frustration, mental (and perhaps physical) illness, and social unrest. To the extent that human labor becomes less important, and the opportunity to work becomes less available, resocialization of individuals during their developmental period to other values and activities will be necessary. Knowledge concerning the factors that shape and influence work personalities thus becomes a matter of the highest societal importance for those who view the future as a continuation of the past, that is, persisting reduction in the hours, days, and years of work required of human beings, to the point that it becomes inconsequential. In this view, identification of developmental factors leading to work patterns is for purposes the opposite of exploitation—to help people become socialized to living with very little or no work in their lives, experiencing this situation as an opportunity, rather than a deprivation, a blessing, rather than a curse.

Fortunately or unfortunately, the uses to which new bits of knowledge will be put are not under the control of the researcher, and it is undoubtedly true that information uncovered in the pursuit of desirable goals has been and can be put to infamous uses. As an overarching value, however, just as we generally believe it is better to be healthy than ill, to be free rather than enslaved, so we can only believe that it is better to have knowledge than to be ignorant. Whether uncovering the roots of hard work will lead to nourishing them or stamping them out, they must first be uncovered.

NOTES

1. L. E. Davis and A. B. Cherns (eds.), *The Quality of Working Life: Problems, Prospects and the State of the Art* (New York: Free Press, 1975), p. 120.

2. Seashore, for example, proposes that quality of working life be defined by "effectiveness in work roles." S. E. Seashore, "Defining and Measuring the Quality of Working Life," in Davis and Cherns, op. cit., pp. 105-118.

3. D. Macarov, *Work and Welfare: The Unholy Alliance* (Beverly Hills, CA: Sage, 1980).

4. For some possible scenarios, see V. C. Ferkiss, "Technological Man," in J. A. Inciardi and H. A. Siegel (eds.) *Emerging Social Issues: A Sociological Perspective* (New York: Praeger, 1975); A. Mitchell, "Human Needs and the Changing Goals of Life and Work," in F. Best (ed.) *The Future of Work* (Englewood Cliffs, NJ: Prentice-Hall, 1973).

APPENDIX

Responses to the Kibbutz Questionnaire (N = 219)

Question Number	Question Content	No.	%	Net %[a]
1	*Respondent's Number*			
2	*Branch*			
	Not known, no answer	1	.5	.5
	Factory	24	11.0	11.0
	Building	2	.9	.9
	Landscape gardening	2	.9	.9
	Fruit stand	2	.9	.9
	Education and child care	39	17.8	17.8
	Bookkeeping	4	1.8	1.8
	Hothouses	11	5.0	5.0
	Sport and cultural center	2	.9	.9
	Clinic and health care	4	1.8	1.8
	Studying	3	1.4	1.4
	Movement work	7	3.2	3.2
	Metal shop, garage, electrician	6	2.7	2.7
	Secretariat	5	2.3	2.3
	Technical secretariat	3	1.4	1.4
	Clothes storeroom	9	4.1	4.1
	Household supplies storeroom	3	1.4	1.4
	Trucking cooperative	3	1.4	1.4
	Laundry	1	.5	.5
	Beekeeping	2	.9	.9
	Sewing room	6	2.7	2.7
	Woodworking shop	2	.9	.9
	Hairdresser	1	.5	.5
	Library	2	.9	.9
	Outside work	17	7.8	7.8
	Fruit trees (other than citrus)	12	5.5	5.5
	Field crops	11	5.0	5.0
	Citrus trees	7	3.2	3.2
	Sheep	1	.5	.5
	Ceramics	2	.9	.9
	Sanitation	3	1.4	1.4
	Kitchen	11	5.0	5.0
	Dining room	4	1.8	1.8
	Poultry	4	1.8	1.8
	Work assigner	2	.9	.9
	Care of invalid	1	.5	.5

Question Number	Question Content	No.	%	Net %[a]
3	*Sex*			
	Male	112	51.1	51.1
	Female	107	48.9	48.9
4	*Age*			
	18-30	74	33.8	33.8
	31-50	79	36.1	36.1
	50+	66	30.1	30.1
5	*Marital status*			
	Single	33	15.1	15.1
	Married	171	78.1	78.1
	Widowed	4	1.8	1.8
	Divorced	11	5.0	5.0
6	*Children in the kibbutz*			
	No answer, single	39	17.8	
	Yes	164	74.9	91.1
	No	16	7.3	8.9
7	*Family (brothers, sisters, parents) in kibbutz*			
	No answer	1	.5	
	Yes	84	38.4	38.5
	No	134	61.2	61.5
8	*Education*			
	Did not finish elementary school	15	6.8	6.8
	Finished elementary school	43	19.6	19.6
	Began, did not finish high school	50	22.8	22.8
	Finished high school	89	40.6	40.6
	Began, did not finish university	19	8.7	8.7
	B.A.	1	.5	.5
	M.A.	2	.9	.9
9	*Vocational training courses*			
	No answer	6	2.7	
	Courses connected with present work	86	39.3	40.4
	Courses connected with other work	38	17.4	17.8
	Both of the above	33	15.1	15.5
	None	56	25.6	26.3
10	*Physical limitations (including age)*			
	No answer	1	.5	
	None	149	68.0	68.3
	Some	52	23.7	23.9
	Great	17	7.8	7.8
11	*Service in underground*			
	No answer	1	.5	
	No	150	68.5	68.8
	Yes	68	31.1	31.2

Question Number	Question Content	No.	%	Net %[a]
11a	*Service in Zahal (Israeli army)*			
	No answer	2	.9	
	Did not serve	97	44.3	44.7
	Private to corporal	67	30.6	30.9
	Sergeant to sergeant major	36	16.4	16.6
	Lieutenant to captain	11	5.0	5.1
	Above captain	6	2.7	2.8
11b	*Discharge date from Zahal*			
	No answer	14	6.4	
	Did not serve	97	44.3	47.3
	Still serving	2	.9	1.0
	After 1967	38	17.4	17.1
	1961-1966	35	16.0	17.4
	1956-1960	11	5.0	5.4
	1955 and before	22	10.0	10.7
12	*Service in foreign army*			
	No answer	1	.5	
	Did not serve	187	85.4	85.8
	Served	31	14.2	14.2
13	*Birthplace*			
	No answer	1	.5	
	Same kibbutz	40	18.3	18.3
	Another kibbutz	8	3.7	3.7
	Israel, but not in kibbutz	33	15.1	15.1
	Europe	118	53.9	54.1
	Middle East/North Africa	14	6.4	6.4
	North America	2	.9	.9
	Latin America	3	1.4	1.4
14	*Years in kibbutz*			
	Born in kibbutz	40	18.3	18.3
	1-5	13	5.9	5.9
	6-15	25	11.4	11.4
	16-18	27	12.3	12.3
	19-22	13	5.9	5.9
	23-29	38	17.4	17.4
	30+	63	28.8	28.8
15	*Past and present positions*			
	No answer	1	.5	
	No positions	57	26.0	26.1
	Secretary, treasurer, work coordinator, member secretariat	43	19.6	19.7
	Committee member, branch coordinator, committee chairman, work assigner	118	53.9	54.1
16	*Time in present branch*			
	No answer	4	1.8	
	Less than month	10	4.6	4.7

Question Number	Question Content	No.	%	Net %[a]
	Month to six months	26	11.9	12.1
	Seven to twelve months	13	5.9	6.0
	Year to two years	27	12.3	12.6
	Permanent in branch	139	63.5	64.7
17	*Time in previous branch*			
	No answer	5	2.3	
	Less than year	52	23.7	24.3
	Year to two years	19	8.7	8.9
	Permanent in branch	34	15.5	15.9
	No previous branch	109	49.8	50.9
	The work in my branch			
18	No answer	11	5.0	
	Requires more ability than I possess	40	18.3	19.2
	Requires less ability than I possess	33	15.1	15.9
	Matches my ability	135	61.6	64.9
19	No answer	15	6.8	
	Is completely routine	37	16.9	18.1
	Is somewhat routine	70	32.0	34.3
	Is not at all routine	97	44.3	47.5
20	No answer	13	5.9	
	Offers me sufficient scope to make decisions	118	53.9	57.3
	Offers me limited scope to make decisions	76	34.7	36.9
	Does not offer me scope to make decisions	12	5.5	5.8
21	No answer	14	6.4	
	Is unpleasant	25	11.4	12.2
	Is rather pleasant	131	59.8	63.9
	Is very pleasant	49	22.4	23.9
22	No answer	13	5.9	
	Requires very high intelligence	5	2.3	2.4
	Requires high intelligence	41	18.7	19.9
	Requires normal intelligence	130	59.4	63.1
	Requires minimum intelligence	30	13.7	14.6
23	No answer	11	5.0	
	Is usually done by women	69	31.5	33.2
	Is usually done by men	68	31.1	32.7
	Is usually done by both men and women	71	32.4	34.1
24	No answer	10	4.6	
	Requires no physical effort	15	6.8	7.2
	Requires a little physical effort	24	11.0	11.5
	Requires some physical effort	123	56.2	58.9
	Requires great physical effort	47	21.5	22.5
25	No answer	14	6.4	
	Requires more skill than I have	69	31.5	33.7
	Matches my skill	114	52.1	55.6
	Requires less skill than I have	22	10.0	10.7

Question Number	Question Content	No.	%	Net %[a]
26	No answer	19	8.7	
	The pace is too fast	34	15.5	17.0
	The pace is reasonable	149	68.0	74.5
	The pace is too slow	17	7.8	8.5
27	No answer	13	5.9	
	I see the work as women's work	69	31.5	33.5
	I see the work as man's work	67	30.6	32.5
	The division is irrelevant	70	32.0	34.0
28	No answer	26	11.9	
	I am on good relations with everyone in the branch	103	47.0	53.4
	I am on good relations with most people in the branch	74	33.8	38.3
	I am on good relations with only a few people in the branch	14	6.4	7.3
	I am on good relations with no one in the branch	2	.9	1.0
29	No answer	11	5.0	
	I work alone	43	19.6	20.7
	I work alone most of the time	41	18.7	19.7
	I work with less than 10 others	90	41.1	43.3
	I work with between 11 and 25 others	31	14.2	14.9
	I work with more than 25 others	3	1.4	1.4
30	No answer	28	12.8	
	No possibility for individual participation in decisions	19	8.7	9.9
	Limited possibility for individual participation in decisions	68	31.1	35.6
	Good possibility for individual participation in decisions	73	33.3	38.2
	Very good possibility for individual participation in decisions	31	14.2	16.2
31	No answer, or works alone	60	27.4	
	Strong group pressure to work hard	28	12.8	17.6
	Some group pressure to work hard	32	14.6	20.1
	No group pressure to work hard	94	42.9	59.1
	Group pressure not to work hard	5	2.3	3.1
32	No answer	27	12.3	
	Excellent physical conditions at work	11	5.0	5.7
	Pretty good physical conditions at work	30	13.7	15.6
	Average physical conditions at work	113	51.6	58.9
	Poor physical conditions at work	30	13.7	15.6
	Very poor physical conditions at work	8	3.7	4.2
33	No answer	27	12.3	
	Good possibilities of being sent on a course	107	48.9	55.7
	Little possibilities of being sent on a course	35	16.0	18.2
	No possibilities of being sent on a course	50	22.8	26.0
34	No answer, or works alone	92	42.0	
	Branch coordinator is good as an expert	63	28.8	49.6

Question Number	Question Content	No.	%	Net %[a]
	Branch coordinator is average as an expert	55	25.1	43.3
	Branch coordinator is poor as an expert	9	4.1	7.1
35	No answer, or works alone	94	42.9	
	Branch coordinator is good as a team leader	55	25.1	44.0
	Branch coordinator is average as a team leader	53	24.2	42.4
	Branch coordinator is poor as a team leader	17	7.8	13.6
36	No answer, or works alone	96	42.9	
	Branch coordinator gives instructions very well	32	14.6	25.6
	Branch coordinator gives instructions well enough	77	35.2	61.6
	Branch coordinator gives instructions badly	16	7.3	12.8
37	No answer, or works alone	97	44.3	
	Branch coordinator always comments on good work	20	9.1	16.4
	Branch coordinator sometimes comments on good work	59	26.9	48.4
	Branch coordinator never comments on good work	43	19.6	35.2
38	No answer, or works alone	94	42.9	
	Branch coordinator and I are on very good terms	32	14.6	25.6
	Branch coordinator and I are on good terms	86	39.3	68.8
	Branch coordinator and I are not on good terms	6	2.7	4.8
	Branch coordinator and I are on bad terms	1	.5	.8
39	No answer, or works alone	98	44.7	
	Branch coordinator treats everyone equally	84	38.4	69.4
	Branch coordinator does not treat everyone equally	37	16.9	30.6
40	No answer, or works alone	104	47.5	
	I would be a better branch coordinator than the present one	7	3.2	6.1
	I would be as good a branch coordinator as the present one	23	12.8	24.3
	I would not be as good a branch coordinator as the present one	80	36.5	69.6
41	No answer	79	36.1	
	I prefer a branch coordinator who excels as an expert	40	18.3	28.6
	I prefer a branch coordinator who excels as a team leader	43	19.6	30.7
	I prefer a branch coordinator who excels as a work organizer	57	26.0	40.7
42	No answer	12	5.5	
	Generally speaking, I am seen as a very good worker	58	26.5	28.0
	Generally speaking, I am seen as a good worker	120	54.8	58.0
	Generally speaking, I am seen as an average worker	28	12.8	13.5
	Generally speaking, I am seen as a poor worker	1	.5	.5
43	*Compared to other workers in the same branch, I see myself as*			
	No answer	23	12.8	
	A very good worker	47	21.5	24.6
	A good worker	106	48.4	55.5

Question Number	Question Content	No.	%	Net %[a]
	Slightly better than an average worker	17	7.8	8.9
	An average worker	21	9.6	11.0
44	*My status, in the eyes of other is*			
	No answer	9	4.1	
	Very low	1	.5	.5
	Somewhat low	7	3.2	3.3
	Average	57	26.0	27.1
	Good	129	58.9	61.4
	Very good	16	7.2	7.6
45	*Generally speaking, I am*			
	No answer	2	.9	
	Very satisfied with my life	52	23.7	24.0
	Reasonably satisfied with my life	137	62.6	63.1
	Neither satisfied nor dissatisfied	9	4.1	4.1
	Somewhat dissatisfied with my life	17	7.8	7.8
	Very dissatisfied with my life	2	.9	.9
46	*Generally speaking, I am on good terms with*			
	No answer	3	1.4	
	Everyone in the kibbutz	75	34.2	34.7
	Everyone in the kibbutz, with a few exceptions	99	45.2	45.8
	More than half the members of the kibbutz	18	8.2	8.3
	About half the members of the kibbutz	12	5.5	5.6
	Less than half the members of the kibbutz	12	5.5	5.6
47	*My opinion*			
	No answer	8	3.7	
	Is taken very seriously	4	1.8	1.9
	Is taken seriously	43	19.6	20.4
	Is taken as seriously as that of anyone else	135	61.6	64.0
	Is not taken as seriously as it should be	11	5.0	5.2
	Is not taken very seriously	13	5.9	6.2
	Is not considered at all	5	2.3	2.4
48	*Opportunities for individuals to participate in decisions which affect the entire kibbutz are*			
	No answer	5	2.3	
	Very good	22	10.0	10.3
	Good	60	27.4	28.0
	Reasonably good	96	43.8	44.9
	Bad	31	14.2	14.5
	Very bad	5	2.3	2.3
49	*I have asked to be transferred to another branch*			
	No answer	12	5.5	
	Yes	42	19.2	20.3
	No	165	75.3	79.7
50	*My family in the kibbutz*			
	No answer, or no family in the kibbutz	27	12.3	

Question Number	Question Content	No.	%	Net %[a]
	Is satisfied that I am working in the present branch	116	53.0	60.4
	Does not care which branch I work in	49	22.4	25.5
	Would prefer that I work in another branch	27	12.3	14.1
51	*I prefer*			
	No answer	18	8.2	
	To work in one branch permanently	180	82.2	89.6
	To work in one branch permanently with occasional periods in another branch	19	8.7	9.5
	To change branches at least once a year	2	.9	1.0
52	*Regarding changing work places daily*			
	No answer	8	3.7	
	I support	5	2.3	2.4
	I oppose	206	94.1	97.6
53	*Generally speaking, members of this kibbutz are regarded*			
	No answer	2	.9	
	Equally	15	6.8	6.9
	Equally, but with some exceptions	75	34.2	34.6
	Rather unequally	94	42.9	43.3
	Very unequally	33	15.1	15.2
54	*Generally, I would say that members of this kibbutz are*			
	No answer	11	5.0	
	Very friendly	3	1.4	1.4
	Friendly	103	47.0	49.5
	Indifferent	82	37.4	39.4
	Unfriendly	18	8.2	8.7
	Very unfriendly	2	.9	1.0
55	*I was placed in the present branch by*			
	No answer	5	2.3	
	Request, election, personal desire	99	45.2	46.3
	Training and experience	37	16.9	17.3
	Solution to personal problem	29	13.2	13.6
	Assigned by work assigner	41	18.7	19.2
	Rotation	8	3.7	3.7
56	*Generally speaking, I would like*			
	No answer	6	2.7	
	Much more free time	25	11.4	11.7
	A bit more free time	92	42.0	43.2
	Free time as at present	94	42.9	44.1
	A bit more work time	2	.9	.9
57	*I work more than the normal amount of time in my branch*			
	No answer	14	6.4	
	Always	15	6.8	7.3

Question Number	Question Content	No.	%	Net %[a]
	Usually	41	18.7	20.0
	Sometimes	118	53.9	57.6
	Never	31	14.2	15.1
58	*During my free time, I am*			
	No answer	37	16.9	
	Happier than during work time	111	50.7	61.0
	Less happy than during work time	17	7.8	9.3
	As happy as during work time	54	24.7	29.7
59	*If it would not hurt the economic situation of the country, I would*			
	No answer	3	1.4	
	Favor a five-day workweek	188	85.8	87.0
	Oppose a five-day workweek	28	12.8	13.0
60	*If the kibbutz succeeds economically, the additional income should be used to*			
	Start new programs	177	30.0	30.0
	Improve housing	155	26.1	26.1
	Give longer vacations	85	14.3	14.3
	Shorten hours of work	83	13.9	13.9
	Liquidate difficult and unpleasant branches	63	10.6	10.6
	Make other changes	32[b]	5.3	5.3
61	*If automation makes most present work unnecessary, I would view that as*			
	No answer	4	1.8	
	Ideal	12	5.5	5.6
	Desirable	51	23.3	23.7
	Undesirable	108	49.3	50.2
	Catastrophic	44	20.1	20.5
62	*Prestige in this kibbutz is based mainly upon*			
	Responsibility	118	19.3	19.3
	Verbal ability	97	15.9	15.9
	Sociability	93	15.2	15.2
	Intelligence	91	14.9	14.9
	Education	84	13.8	13.8
	Hard work	35	5.7	5.7
	Factors outside the kibbutz	33	5.4	5.4
	Prestige of the parents	32	5.2	5.2
	Ideological position	20	3.3	3.3
	Other factors	7[b]	1.1	1.1
63	*I think the ideal age for retirement is*			
	No answer	10	4.6	
	50	2	.9	1.0
	55	5	2.3	2.4
	60	22	10.0	10.5
	65	59	26.9	28.2

Question Number	Question Content	No.	%	Net %[a]
	70	14	6.4	6.7
	75	19	8.7	9.1
	Other, or conditional	88	40.2	42.1
64	*Satisfactions from work*			
	Pleasant work	127	20.1	20.1
	Relationships with others	116	18.4	18.4
	Creativity	114	18.1	18.1
	Seeing results	93	14.7	14.7
	Profitability of the work	79	12.5	12.5
	Use of initiative	54	8.6	8.6
	Working with others	23	3.6	3.6
	Use of skills	20	3.1	3.1
	Other	6	.9	.9

65   *Feelings about remaining in the kibbutz*

Positive
The idea of leaving the kibbutz has never entered my mind.
If I were to leave this kibbutz, it would only be to live in another kibbutz.
I once thought about leaving the kibbutz, but I no longer do.
If circumstances forced me to leave the kibbutz, I cannot imagine myself
    becoming reconciled with it.
I cannot imagine myself living outside of the kibbutz.
I have never seriously thought of leaving the kibbutz.

Negative
I will almost certainly leave the kibbutz some day.
If I were certain of housing and income elsewhere, I would leave the kibbutz.
I sometimes think of leaving the kibbutz.
If circumstances forced me to leave the kibbutz, I can imagine myself being happy
    elsewhere.

		No.	%	Net %
	No answer	3	1.4	
	Two or three positive answers only—strong inclination to stay in kibbutz	46	21.0	21.3
	One positive answer only—inclination to stay in kibbutz	68	31.1	31.5
	Two or three positive answers with one negative answer—inclination to stay in kibbutz with some desire to leave	10	4.6	4.8
	One positive answer and one negative answer—ambivalence	32	14.6	14.8
	Two or three negative answers with one positive answer—inclination to leave the kibbutz with some desire to stay	3	1.4	1.4
	One negative answer only—inclination to leave the kibbutz	39	17.8	18.1
	Two or three negative answers only—strong inclination to leave the kibbutz	18	8.2	8.3
66	*I prefer work*			
	No answer	7	3.2	
	Which requires me to carry it out alone	146	66.7	68.9

Question Number	Question Content	No.	%	Net %[a]
	Which requires me to carry out some of it alone	61	27.9	28.8
	Which does not require me to carry it out alone	5	2.3	2.4
67	*I prefer work*			
	No answer	4	1.8	
	Which requires me to decide completely independently	115	52.5	53.5
	Which requires me to decide somewhat independently	94	42.9	43.7
	Which does not require me to decide independently	6	2.7	2.7
68	*I prefer work*			
	No answer	7	3.2	
	Which requires much physical effort	14	6.4	6.6
	Which requires little physical effort	38	17.4	17.9
	Which requires normal physical effort	160	73.1	73.1
69	*I prefer working*			
	No answer	5	2.3	
	Entirely alone	39	17.8	18.2
	Mostly alone, but occasionally with others	88	40.2	41.1
	With less than 10 others	72	32.9	33.6
	With 11 to 25 others	10	4.6	4.7
	With more than 25 others	5	2.3	2.3
70	*Members of the kibbutz*			
	No answer	83	27.9	
	See me as a social, responsible person	80	36.5	58.8
	Do not see me as a social, responsible person	56	25.6	41.2
71	*The branches with the highest prestige are*			
	No answer	26	11.9	
	Factory	111	50.7	57.5
	Field crops	22	10.0	11.4
	Hothouses	6	2.7	3.1
	Dining room	1	.5	.5
	Other branches	40	18.3	20.7
	There are no differences in the prestige of branches	13	5.9	6.7
72	*The branches with the lowest prestige are*			
	No answer	46	21.0	
	Factory	1	.5	.6
	Field crops	4	1.8	2.3
	Sanitation	30	13.7	17.3
	Dining room	35	16.0	20.2
	Kitchen	38	17.4	22.0
	Other branches	47	21.5	27.2
	There are no low prestige branches	18	8.2	10.4
73	*Factors contributing to satisfactions at work*			
	Feeling of achievement; satisfaction; creativity	73	20.3	20.3
	Relationships with other workers in same branch	40	11.1	11.1
	Relationships with people other than workers in same branch, including consumers of product or service	37	10.2	10.2

Question Number	Question Content	No.	%	Net %[a]
	Pleasure in work; fitted to task; work desired	34	9.4	9.4
	Variety/interest	25	6.9	6.9
	Profitability of branch to kibbutz	24	6.7	6.7
	Independence	22	6.1	6.1
	Importance of the work and the way it is valued by others	21	5.8	5.8
	Pace of work; time pressure	20	5.6	5.6
	Participation in decision making; possibility of use of initiative	17	4.7	4.7
	Use of skills	15	4.2	4.2
	Possibilities of advancement, learning, acquiring useful experiences	11	3.1	3.1
	Working conditions, including hours	11	3.1	3.1
	Permanence in branch	2	.6	.6
	Other factors	8[b]	2.2	2.2
74	*Factors contributing to dissatisfactions at work*			
	Relationships with other workers in same branch	32	12.3	12.3
	Relationships with people other than workers in same branch, including consumers of product or service	31	11.9	11.9
	Working conditions, including hours	30	11.5	11.5
	Importance of the work and the manner in which it is regarded by others	25	9.6	9.6
	Lack of feeling of achievement; satisfaction; creativity	21	8.1	8.1
	Nonpermanent workers in branch	21	8.1	8.1
	Monotony of work	19	7.3	7.3
	Unpleasant work; not fitted to task	11	4.2	4.2
	Profitability of branch to kibbutz	10	3.8	3.8
	Lack of cooperation from other organs of the kibbutz; lack of budget	10	3.8	3.8
	Lack of participation in decision making	10	3.8	3.8
	Lack of possibilities of advancement, learning, acquiring useful experience	7	2.7	2.7
	Lack of permanence in branch	7	2.7	2.7
	Lack of independence at work	6	2.3	2.3
	Lack of planning; disorganization	4	1.5	1.5
	Other factors	16[b]	6.2	6.2
75	*Changes in work branch desired by members*			
	Outside factors			
	Relationship of branch to factors outside of branch	16	5.3	5.3
	Scope and methods			
	Budget changes	9	3.0	3.0
	Improvements and enlargement	38	12.7	12.7
	Automation	14	4.7	4.7
	Content			
	Pretraining	22	7.3	7.3
	Advanced training	10	3.3	3.3

Question Number	Question Content	No.	%	Net %[a]
	Arrangements			
	Physical conditions	54	18.0	18.0
	Structure			
	Organization; planning	19	6.3	6.3
	Division of tasks and responsibility	5	1.7	1.7
	Rotation of work coordinator	16	5.3	5.3
	Participation in decisions, rules, meetings	11	3.7	3.7
	Composition			
	Changes in composition of work group; replacement/elimination of hired workers	11	3.7	3.7
	More permanent workers in branch	11	3.7	3.7
	More younger members in branch	14	4.7	4.7
	Additional manpower in branch	18	6.0	6.0
	Relationships			
	Changes in relationships among workers in branch	7	2.3	2.3
	Other factors			
	Liquidate the branch; replace the workers; examine fitness for branch	7	2.3	2.3
	No changes			
	No changes needed	18[b]	6.0	6.0
76	*Changes in kibbutz desired by members*			
	Physical changes			
	Cleanliness, landscaping, roads	14	3.0	3.0
	Kitchen, dining room, children's rooms	19	4.1	4.1
	Housing	16	3.5	3.5
	Work			
	Structure and conditions	10	2.2	2.2
	Reduce hours	8	1.7	1.7
	Manpower changes in branches	19	4.1	4.1
	More efficiency; automation	27	5.6	5.6
	Education			
	General education; raise intellectual level	20	4.3	4.3
	In-service training; vocational education	5	1.1	1.1
	Standard of living			
	Changes in standard of living	16	3.5	3.5
	Increase personal budgets	21	4.5	4.5
	Institutions			
	Changes in kibbutz institutions; rotation in offices	23	5.0	5.0
	Changes in decision-making processes	20	4.3	4.3
	More personal freedom	28	6.1	6.1
	More personal responsibility	11	2.4	2.4
	Intrapersonal changes			
	More patience, tolerance; less indifference	18	3.9	3.9

Question Number	Question Content	No.	%	Net %[a]
	Increased concern for work	14	3.0	3.0
	Ideological changes; increased faith in kibbutz	17	3.7	3.7
	Equality; treating others equally	21	4.5	4.5
	Interpersonal changes			
	More concern for and opportunity to the younger generation	8	1.7	1.7
	Changes in relationships	44	9.5	9.5
	Sharing responsibility with/by the younger generation	25	5.4	5.4
	Membership			
	Replace (some) members	5	1.1	1.1
	Culture			
	Changes in cultural and sport activities; establish discotheque	27	5.8	5.8
	Other			
	Other changes needed	21	4.5	4.5
	No changes			
	No changes needed	5[b]	1.1	1.1
77	*Why some kibbutz members work harder than others*			
	Personality	35	9.6	9.6
	Satisfaction, pleasure, interest in work	34	9.4	9.4
	Sense of responsibility and initiative	59	16.2	16.2
	Conscience, energy, ability	58	16.0	16.0
	Desire for prestige; to impress; lack of ability to advance; competitiveness	21	5.8	5.8
	Lack of ability to properly organize work; impact of work group	12	3.3	3.3
	Health, age, nervousness	10	2.7	2.7
	Ideology, education, consciousness of importance of work, identification with work	22	6.1	6.1
	Nature of the work	63	17.4	17.4
	Encouragement and recognition by others; lack of equality	14	3.9	3.9
	Lack of manpower; physical conditions	14	3.9	3.9
	Other factors	10	2.7	2.7
	No members work harder than others	11[b]	3.0	3.0

a. Excludes nonrespondents.
b. Totals more than number of respondents since each respondent could give more than one response.

SOURCES

Adams, A. V. "The American Work Force in the Eighties: New Problems and Policy Interests Require Improved Labor Force Data." *Annals of the American Academy of Political and Social Science* 453 (1981): 123-129.

Adams, L. P. *Public Attitudes Toward Unemployment Insurance: A Historical Account with Reference to Alleged Abuse.* Kalamazoo: Upjohn, 1971.

Aitkin, M. and J. Hage. "Organizational Alienation: A Comparative Analysis." *American Sociological Review* 31 (1966): 497-507.

Allardt, E. *Dimensions of Welfare in a Comparative Scandinavian Study.* Helsinki: University of Helsinki, 1975.

Anderson, N. *Dimensions of Work: The Sociology of a Work Culture.* New York: McKay, 1964.

Andras, R. K. "Introductory Speech," in *Work in a Changing Industrial Society.* Paris: Organisation for Economic Co-operation and Development, 1975.

Ansbacher, H. L. and R. R. Ansbacher (eds.) *The Individual Psychology of Alfred Adler.* New York: Harper & Row, 1956.

Anthony, P. D. *The Ideology of Work.* London: Tavistock, 1978.

Antonofsky, A., H. Antonofsky, and N. Biran. *Social Life in the Kibbutz.* Jerusalem: Institute for Applied Social Research, 1970. (Hebrew)

Arendt, H. *The Human Condition.* Chicago: University of Chicago Press, 1958.

M. Argyle, *The Social Psychology of Work.* Harmondsworth: Penguin, 1972.

Argyris, C. "The Individual and the Organization: An Empirical Test." *Administrative Science Quarterly* 4 (1959): 145-167.

Arian, A. *Ideological Change in Israel.* Cleveland: Western Reserve University, 1968.

Arnold, M. G. and G. Rosenbaum. *The Crime of Poverty.* Skokie, IL: National Textbook, 1973.

Athanasiou, R. "Job Attitudes and Occupational Performance: A Review of Some Important Literature," in J. P. Robinson, R. Athanasiou, and K. B. Head, *Measures of Occupational Attitudes and Occupational Characteristics.* Ann Arbor: University of Michigan, Institute for Social Research, 1969.

Ball, R. M. *Social Security Today and Tomorrow.* New York: Columbia University Press, 1978.

Barfield, R. E. and J. N. Morgan. *Early Retirement: The Decision and the Experience and a Second Look.* Ann Arbor: University of Michigan, 1969.

Bar-Gal, D. "Domains of Work and Methods of Work of Occupational Welfare Officers: An Exploratory Study of an Emerging Role." *Journal of Social Service Research* (in press).

Barlow, R. "Motivation of the Affluent," in G. G. Somers (ed.) *Manpower and Its Motivation.* New York: Industrial Relations Research Association, 1967.

———— H. E. Brazer, and J. N. Morgan. *Economic Behavior of the Affluent.* Washington, DC: Brookings, 1966.

Bass, B. M. and G. V. Barrett, *Man, Work, and Organizations: An Introduction to Industrial and Organizational Psychology.* Boston: Allyn & Bacon, 1972.

Bell, D. "The Future That Never Was." *Public Interest* 51 (1978): 35-73.

Ben Menachem, D. "A Proposed Programme for the Social Absorption of Immigrants from Russia, India, and North Africa in Dimona." *Adult Education in Israel* 24 (1974): 8. (Hebrew)

Bensusan-Butt, D. M. *On Economic Man.* Canberra: Australian National University Press, 1978.

Berg, I. *Education and Jobs: The Great Training Robbery.* Boston: Beacon, 1971.

_____ "Foreword," in S. Parker, *The Future of Work and Leisure.* New York: Praeger, 1971.

_____ M. Freedman, and M. Freeman. *Managers and Work Reform: A Limited Engagement.* New York: Free Press, 1978.

Bernard, S. E. *Fatherless Families: Their Economic and Social Adjustment.* Waltham, MA: Brandeis University, 1964.

Bernardo, R. M. *The Theory of Moral Incentives in Cuba.* University: University of Alabama Press, 1971.

Best, F. "Preferences on Worklife Scheduling and Work-Leisure Tradeoffs." *Monthly Labor Review,* 101 (1978): 31-37.

Bindra, D. and J. Stewart (eds.) *Motivation.* Harmondsworth: Penguin, 1973.

Bird, C. *The Invisible Scar.* New York: Pocket Books, 1966.

Black, B. J. "Vocational Rehabilitation," in *Encyclopedia of Social Work.* New York: National Association of Social Workers, 1965.

Boisvert, M. P. "The Quality of Working Life: An Analysis." *Human Relations* 30 (1977): 155-160.

Bolweg, J. F. "The Quality of Working Life: An Industrial Relations Perspective," in *Proceedings of the Thirty-Third Annual Meeting.* Madison: Industrial Relations Research Association, 1980.

Bowles, S. and H. Gintis. *Schooling in Capitalist America: Educational Reform and the Contradictions of Economic Life.* New York: Basic Books, 1976.

Brayfield, A. and W. Crockett. "Employee Attitudes and Employee Performance." *Psychological Bulletin* 52 (1955): 396-424.

Brightbill, C. K. *Man and Leisure.* Westport, CT: Greenwood, 1961.

Brim, O. G. Jr., and S. Wheeler. *Socialization After Childhood.* New York: John Wiley, 1966.

British Broadcasting Corporation. *The Chips Are Down.* Television documentary film, 1979.

Bronfenbrenner, U. "The Changing American Child—A Speculative Analysis," in R. C. Coser (ed.) *Life Cycle and Achievement in America.* New York: Harper & Row, 1969.

Brown, G. E. (ed.). *The Multi-Problem Dilemma: A Social Research Demonstration with Multi-Problem Families.* London: Metheun, 1968.

Brown, H. P. *The Inequality of Pay.* Oxford: Oxford University Press, 1977.

Bruce, M. "Thirty Years on the Politics of Welfare." *Social Service Quarterly* 52 (1978): 5-8.

Bruyn, S. T. *The Human Perspective in Sociology.* Englewood Cliffs, NJ: Prentice-Hall, 1966.

Buckingham, W. *Automation.* New York: Mentor, 1961.

Burton, R. *The Anatomy of Melancholy.* London: Chatto and Windus, 1907.

Campbell, A., P. E. Converse, and W. L. Rodgers. *The Quality of American Life: Perceptions: Evaluations, and Satisfactions.* New York: Russell Sage, 1976.

Campbell, J. P. and R. D. Pritchard. "Motivation Theory in Industrial and Organizational Psychology," in M. D. Dunnette (ed.) *Handbook of Industrial and Organizational Psychology.* Chicago: Rand McNally, 1976.

Caplow, T. *The Sociology of Work.* New York: McGraw-Hill, 1954.

Carey, A. "The Hawthorne Studies: A Radical Criticism." *American Sociological Review* 32 (1967): 403-416.

Carey, J. L. and P. F. Otto. "Output per Unit of Labor Input in the Retail Food Store Industry." *Monthly Labor Review* 100 (January 1977) 42-47.

Carnes, R. B. "Laundry and Cleaning Services Pressed to Post Productivity Gains," *Monthly Labor Review* 101 (1978): 38-42.

———— and H. Band. "Productivity and New Technology in Eating and Drinking Places." *Monthly Labor Review* 100 (September 1977): 9-15.

Cass, M. *Development, Employment and the Environment: Is There a Conflict?* Curtin Memorial Lecture delivered at the University of Western Australia, October 11, 1974.

Champoux, J. E. "The World of Nonwork: Some Implications for Job Re-Design Efforts." *Personnel Psychology* 33 (1980): 61-75.

Chandrasekar, K. "Productivity and Social Indicators." *Annals of the American Academy of Political and Social Science* 453 (1981): 153-167.

Cheek, N. H., Jr. "Toward a Sociology of Not-Work," in T. B. Johannis, Jr., and C. N. Bull (eds.) *Sociology of Leisure*. Beverly Hills, CA: Sage, 1971.

Cherns, A. B. and L. E. Davis. "Assessment of the State of the Art," in L. E. Davis and A. B. Cherns (eds.) *The Quality of Working Life: Problems, Prospects, and the State of the Art*. New York: Free Press, 1975.

Cherrington, D. J. and J. L. England. "The Desire for an Enriched Job as a Moderator of the Enrichment-Satisfaction Relationship." *Organizational Behavior and Human Performance* 25 (1980): 139-159.

Cherviss, C. *Professional Burnout in Human Service Organizations*. New York: Praeger, 1980.

Clayre, A. *Work and Play: Ideas and Experience of Work and Leisure*. New York: Harper & Row, 1974.

Coburn, D. "Job Alienation and Well-Being." *International Journal of Health Services* 9 (1979): 41-59.

———— "Work and General Psychological and Physical Well-Being." *International Journal of Health Services* 8 (1978): 415-435.

———— "Job-Worker Incongruence: Consequences for Health." *Journal of Health and Social Behavior* 16 (1975): 198-212.

Colvard, R. "Interaction and Identification in Reporting Field Research: A Critical Reconsideration of Protective Procedures," in G. Sjoberg (ed.) *Ethics, Politics and Social Research*. Cambridge, MA: Schenkman, 1967.

Constitution of the Union of Soviet Socialist Republics 1936. Article 12, 1936.

Criden, Y. and S. Gelb. *The Kibbutz Experience: Dialogue in Kfar Blum*. New York: Herzl Press, 1974.

Csikszentimihalyi, M. *Beyond Boredom and Anxiety*. San Francisco: Jossey-Bass, 1975.

Cumming, E. and W. E. Henry. *Growing Old: The Process of Disengagement*. New York: Basic Books, 1966.

Cummings, T. G. and E. S. Molloy. *Improving Productivity and the Quality of Work Life*. New York: Praeger, 1977.

Cunningham, R. L. *The Philosophy of Work*. New York: National Association of Manufacturers, 1964.

Curtis, C. "They Can't Be Workaholics—They're Having Too Much Fun." *New York Times* (March 30, 1975): 30.

Dale, E. (ed.). *Readings in Management: Landmarks and New Frontiers*. New York: McGraw-Hill, 1975.

Daniels, A. K. "The Low Caste Stranger in Social Research," in G. Sjoberg (ed.) *Ethics, Politics and Social Research*. Cambridge, MA: Schenkman, 1967.

Dasgupta, S. "Facing the New Era: A Plea for a New Approach to Human Well-Being," in *Human Well-Being: The Challenge of Continuity and Change*. New York: International Council on Social Welfare, 1978.

Davis, L. E. and A. B. Cherns (eds.). *The Quality of Working Life: Problems, Prospects and the State of the Art*. New York: Free Press, 1975.

De Grazia, S. *Of Time, Work and Leisure*. New York: Twentieth Century Fund, 1962.

Denison, E. F. *Accounting for Slower Economic Growth: The United States in the 1970s*. Washington, DC: Brookings, 1979.

Deutscher, M. "Adult Work and Developmental Models." *American Journal of Orthopsychiatry* 38 (1968): 882-892.

De Vos, G. A. *Socialization for Achievement: Essays on the Cultural Psychology of the Japanese*. Berkeley: University of California Press, 1973.

DeVries, P. *Reuben, Reuben*. New York: Bantam, 1965.

Drucker, P. F. "Frederick W. Taylor: The Professional Management Pioneer," in E. Dale (ed.) *Readings in Management: Landmarks and New Frontiers*. New York: McGraw-Hill, 1975.

_____ *Management: Tasks, Responsibilities, Practices*. New York: Harper & Row, 1973.

Dubin, R. "Industrial Workers' Worlds: A Study of the Central Life Interests of Industrial Workers," in A. M. Rose (ed.) *Human Behavior and Social Processes*. London: Routledge & Kegan Paul, 1962.

_____ *The World of Work*. Englewood Cliffs, NJ: Prentice-Hall, 1958.

Dubno, P. and R. D. Freedman. "Birth Order, Educational Achievement and Managerial Attainment." *Personnel Psychology* 24 (1971): 63-70.

Dudycha, G. J. and M. M. Dudycha. "Some Factors and Characteristics in Childhood Memories." *Child Development* (1933-1934): 265-278.

Duke, J. "New Car Dealers Experience Long-Term Gain in Productivity." *Monthly Labor Review* 100 (March 1977): 29-33.

Dyer, J. S. and M. Hoffenberg. "Evaluating the Quality of Working Life—Some Reflections on Production and Cost and a Method for Problem Definition," in L. E. Davis and A. B. Cherns (eds.) *The Quality of Working Life: Problems, Prospects and the State of the Art*. New York: Free Press, 1975.

Dyer, W. G. "Family Reactions to the Father's Job," in A. B. Shostak and W. Gomberg (eds.) *Blue-Collar World: Studies of the American Worker*. Englewood Cliffs, NJ: Prentice-Hall, 1964.

Dymmel, M. D. "Technology in Telecommunications: Its Effect on Labor and Skills." *Monthly Labor Review* 102 (1979): 13-19.

Easterlin, R. A. "Does Money Buy Happiness?" *Public Interest* 30 (1973): 3-10.

Eisenstadt, S. N. *Israeli Society*. London: Weidenfeld and Nicolson, 1967.

Employment and Unemployment, May 1977. Canberra: Bureau of Statistics, 1977.

Etzioni, A. *Modern Organizations*. Englewood Cliffs, NJ: Prentice-Hall, 1964.

Falbo, T. "The Only Child: A Review." *Journal of Individual Psychology* 33 (1977): 47-61.

Faunce, W. A. and R. Dubin. "Individual Investment in Working and Living," in L. E. Davis and A. B. Cherns (eds.) *The Quality of Working Life: Problems, Prospects, and the State of the Art*. New York: Free Press, 1975.

Fein, M. "Motivation to Work," in R. Dubin (ed.) *Handbook of Work, Organization, and Society*. Chicago: Rand McNally, 1976.

Ferkiss, V. C. "Technological Man," in J. A. Inciardi and H. A. Siegel (eds.) *Emerging Social Issues: A Sociological Perspective*. New York: Praeger, 1975.

Field, F. "Making Sense of the Unemployment Figures," in F. Field, *The Conscript Army*. London: Routledge & Kegan Paul, 1977.

Fischer, J. "Is Casework Effective? A Review." *Social Work* 18 (1973): 5-20.

_____ "Has Mighty Casework Struck Out?" *Social Work* 18 (1973): 107-110.

Fish, D. H. *A Study of the Turnover and Separation of Social Workers in Public Welfare Agencies.* Ramat Gan, Israel: Bar-Ilan University School of Social Work, 1976.

Fogarty, M. P., R. Rapoport, and R. P. Rapoport. "Dual-Career Families," in D. Weir (ed.) *Men and Work in Modern Britain.* Bungay, Suffolk: Fontana, 1973.

Franke, R. H. "The Hawthorne Experiments: Re-View." *American Sociological Review* 44 (1979): 861-867.

———— and J. D. Kaul. "The Hawthorne Experiments: First Statistical Interpretation." *American Sociological Review* 43 (1978): 623-643.

Freedman, M. K. "The World of Work," in *Young People and the World of Work.* New York: National Federation of Settlements and Neighborhood Centers, 1963.

Freud, S. *Civilization and Its Discontents.* New York: Paperback, 1958.

Friedmann, E. A. and R. J. Havighurst. *The Meaning of Work and Retirement.* Chicago: University of Chicago Press, 1954.

Fuchs, V. R. and J. A. Wilburn. *Productivity Differences Within the Service Sector.* New York: Columbia University Press, 1967.

Galper, J. "Private Pensions and Public Policy." *Social Work* 18 (1973): 5-22.

Garrett, J. F. and B. W. Griffis. "The Economic Benefits of Rehabilitation for the Mentally Retarded." *Welfare in Review* 9 (1971): 1-7.

Garson, R. *All the Livelong Day: The Meaning and Demeaning of Routine Work.* Harmondsworth: Penguin, 1975.

Gellerman, S. W. *The Management of Human Relations.* New York: Holt, Rinehart & Winston, 1966.

Gerard, D. "Democracy—A Fiction?" *Social Service Quarterly* 52 (1978): 24-27.

Gershuny, J. *After Industrial Society: The Emerging Self-Service Economy.* London: Macmillan, 1978.

Gil, D. G. *Unravelling Social Policy.* Cambridge, MA: Schenkman, 1973.

Gilbert, N. and H. Specht. *Dimensions of Social Welfare Policy.* Englewood Cliffs, NJ: Prentice-Hall, 1974.

Gilson, T. Q. and M. J. Lefcowitz. "A Plant Wide Productivity Bonus in a Small Factory: Study of an Unsuccessful Case." *Industrial and Labor Relations Review* 10 (1957): 284-296.

Glaser, E. M. "Productivity Gains Through Worklife Improvement." *Personnel* 52 (1980): 71-77.

Glickman, A. S. and Z. H. Brown. *Changing Schedules of Work: Patterns and Implications.* Kalamazoo: Upjohn, 1974.

Gluskinos, U. M. and B. J. Kestelman. "Management and Labor Leaders' Perception of Workers' Needs as Compared with Self-Reported Needs." *Personnel Psychology* 24 (1971): 239-246.

Goffman, E. *The Presentation of Self in Everyday Life.* Garden City, NY: Doubleday, 1959.

Goldner, F. H. "Role Emergence and the Ethics of Ambiguity," in G. Sjoberg (ed.) *Ethics, Politics and Social Research.* Cambridge, MA: Schenkman, 1967.

Goldthorpe, J. H., D. Lockwood, E. Bechhofer, and J. Platt. *The Affluent Worker: Industrial Attitudes and Behaviour.* Cambridge, England: University Press, 1968.

Gooding, J. *The Job Revolution.* New York: Collier, 1972.

Goodman, P. S. "Quality of Work Life Projects in the 1980s." *Proceedings of the 1980 Spring Meeting of the Industrial Relations Research Association.* Madison, WI: Industrial Relations Research Association, 1980.

Goodwin, L. *Do the Poor Want to Work? A Social-Psychological Study of Work Orientations.* Washington, DC: Brookings, 1972.

Gorn, G. J. and R. N. Kanungo. "Job Involvement and Motivation: Are Intrinsically Motivated Managers More Job Involved?" *Organizational Behavior and Human Performance* 26 (1980): 265-272.

Gottlieb, N. *The Welfare Bind.* New York: Columbia, 1974.

Grant, P. C. "A Model for Employee Motivation and Satisfaction." *Personnel* 56 (1979): 51-57.

Green, A. "The Middle Class Male Child and Neurosis." *American Sociological Review* 11 (1946).

Greenberg, L. *A Practical Guide to Productivity Measurement.* Washington, DC: Bureau of National Affairs, 1973.

Griffiths, D. *Whither Work.* Bundoora: Preston Institute of Technology Press, 1977.

———— *The Waiting Poor: An Argument for Abolition of the Waiting Period on Unemployment and Sickness Benefits.* Fitzroy, Victoria, Australia: Brotherhood of Saint Laurence, 1974.

Grimaldi, D. L. "Distributive and Fiscal Impacts of the Supplemental Security Income Program." *Review of Social Economy* 26 (1978): 175-196.

Gross, A. M. "Appropriate Cost Reporting: An Indispensable Link to Accountability." *Administration in Social Work* 4 (1980): 31-41.

Guion, R. M. and F. J. Landy. "The Meaning of Work and the Motivation to Work." *Organizational Behavior and Human Performance* 7 (1972): 308-339.

Gutman, H. G. *Work, Culture and Society in Industrializing America.* New York: Knopf, 1976.

Hackman, J. R. and G. R. Oldham. "Motivation Through the Design of Work: Test of a Theory." *Organizational Behavior and Human Performance* 16 (1976): 250-279.

Hale, W., Jr. "Sensing the Rhythm." *Infection Control and Urological Care* 4 (1979): 19-20.

Hansen, M. L. "The Third Generation in America," in H. D. Stein and R. A. Cloward (eds.) *Social Perspectives on Behavior.* New York: Macmillan, 1958.

Hare, M., E. E. Ghiselli, and M. E. Gordon. "A Psychological Study of Pay." *Journal of Applied Psychology Monograph* 51 (1967).

Heckhausen, H. *The Anatomy of Achievement Motivation.* New York: Academic, 1967.

Henderson, R. F. *Poverty in Australia.* Volume One. Canberra: Australian Government Printing Service, 1975.

Herrick, N. Q. and M. Maccoby. "Humanizing Work: A Priority Goal for the 1970s," in L. E. Davis and A. B. Cherns (eds.) *The Quality of Working Life: Problems, Prospects and the State of the Art.* New York: Free Press, 1975.

Hertz, J. H. (ed.). *The Pentateuch and Haftorahs.* Philadelphia: Jewish Publication Society, 1917.

Herzberg, F. *Work and the Nature of Man.* Cleveland: World, 1966.

———— B. Mausner, and B. B. Snyderman. *The Motivation to Work.* New York: John Wiley, 1959.

Hess, R. D. "The Transmission of Cognitive Strategies in Poor Families: The Socialization of Apathy and Underachievement," in V. L. Allen (ed.) *Psychological Factors in Poverty.* Chicago: Markham, 1970.

Hill, W. F. "Activity as an Autonomous Drive." *Journal of Comparative and Physiological Psychology* 49 (1956): 15ff.

Hoagland, J. H. "Charles Babbage: His Life and Works in the Historical Evolution of Management Concepts." Ph.D. dissertation, Ohio State University, 1954.

Hobsbawm, E. J. *Industry and Empire: An Economic History of Britain Since 1750.* London: Weidenfeld, 1968.

Hoffman, L. W. and F. I. Nye. *Working Mothers.* San Francisco: Jossey-Bass, 1975.

Hofstede, G. *Culture's Consequences: International Differences in Work-Related Values.* Beverly Hills, CA: Sage, 1980.

Homans, G. C. *The Human Group*. London: Routledge & Kegan Paul, 1951.

Hoppock, R. "A Twenty-Seven Year Follow-Up on Job Satisfaction of Employed Adults." *Personnel and Guidance Journal* 38 (1960): 485-492.

House, R. J. and L. A. Wigdor. "Herzberg's Dual-Factor Theory of Job Satisfaction and Motivation: A Review of the Evidence and a Criticism." *Personnel Psychology* 20 (1967): 369ff.

Huizinga, G. *Maslow's Need Hierarchy in the Work Situation*. Gronigen: Wolters-Noordhoff, 1970.

Hulin, C. L. and M. R. Blood. "Job Enlargement, Individual Differences, and Worker Responses." *Psychological Bulletin* 69 (1968): 41-55.

Hunnius, G. "On the Nature of Capitalist-Initiated Innovations in the Workplace," in T. R. Burns, L. E. Karlsson, and V. Rus (eds.) *Work and Power: The Liberation of Work and the Control of Political Power*. Beverly Hills, CA: Sage, 1979.

Ingham, G. K. *Size of Industrial Organization and Worker Behaviour*. Cambridge, England: Cambridge University Press, 1970.

Itskhokin, A. "The Dual System." *American Journal of Sociology* 85 (1980): 1317.

Jerusalem Post. "Productivity in the Prisons." July 17, 1981.

Jerzier, J. M. and L. J. Berkes. "Leader Behavior in a Police Command Bureaucracy: A Closer Look at the Quasi-Military Model." *Administrative Science Quarterly* 24 (1979): 1-23.

Kafry, D. and A. Pines. "The Experience of Tedium in Life and Work." *Human Relations* 33 (1980): 477-503.

Kagan, J. and M. Berkun. "The Reward Value of Running Activity." *Journal of Comparative and Physiological Psychology*, 47 (1954): 108.

Kahn, R. L. "The Meaning of Work: Interpretation and Proposals for Measurement," in A. Campbell and P. E. Converse (eds.) *The Human Meaning of Social Change*. New York: Russell Sage, 1972.

―――― "Value, Expectancy, and Mythology," in G. G. Somers (ed.) *The Development and Use of Manpower*. Washington, DC: Industrial Relations Research Association, 1967.

Kaplan, M. *Leisure: Theory and Policy*. New York: John Wiley, 1975.

―――― *Leisure in America: A Social Inquiry*. New York: John Wiley, 1960.

Kateb, G. *Utopia and Its Enemies*. New York: Schocken, 1963.

Katona, G. *The Mass Consumption Society*. New York: McGraw-Hill, 1964.

Katz, D. and R. L. Kahn. *The Social Psychology of Organizations*. New York: John Wiley, 1978.

Katz, E. and B. Danet (eds.) *Bureaucracy and the Public: A Reader in Official-Client Relations*. New York: Basic Books, 1973.

―――― "Petitions and Persuasive Appeals: A Study of Official-Client Relations," in E. Katz and B. Danet (eds.) *Bureaucracy and the Public: A Reader in Official-Client Relations*. New York: Basic Books, 1973.

Katz, E. and S. N. Eisenstadt. "Observations on the Response of Israeli Organizations to New Immigrants." *Administrative Science Quarterly* 5 (1960): 1ff.

Katz, R. and J. Van Maanen. "The Loci of Work Satisfaction: Job, Interaction, and Policy." *Human Relations* 30 (1977): 469-486.

Katzell, R. A., P. Bienstock, and P. H. Faerstein. *A Guide to Worker Productivity Experiments in the United States 1971-1975*. New York: New York University Press, 1977.

Kelman, H. C. *A Time to Speak: On Human Values and Social Research*. San Francisco: Jossey-Bass, 1968.

―――― "Processes of Opinion Change," in W. G. Bennis, K. D. Benne, and R. Chin (eds.) *The Planning of Change*. New York: Holt, Rinehart & Winston, 1964.

Kendrick, J. W. "Productivity Trends and the Recent Slowdown," in W. E. Fellner (ed.) *Contemporary Economic Problems*. Washington, DC: American Enterprise Institute, 1979.

———— *Understanding Productivity: An Introduction to the Dynamics of Productivity Change*. Baltimore: Johns Hopkins University Press, 1977.

Kershaw, J. A. "The Attack on Poverty," in M. S. Gordon (ed.) *Poverty in America*. San Francisco: Chandler, 1965.

Kogut, A. and S. Aron. "Toward Full Employment Policy: An Overview." *Journal of Sociology and Social Welfare* 7 (1980): 85-99.

Kohen, M. L. and J. A. Clausen. "Parental Authority Behavior and Schizophrenia." *American Journal of Orthopsychiatry* 26 (1956): 297-313.

Kohn, M. L. "Social Class and Parent-Child Relationships: An Interpretation," in R. L. Coser (ed.) *Life Cycle and Achievement in America*. New York: Harper & Row, 1969.

———— and C. Schooler. "Occupational Experience and Psychological Functioning: An Assessment of Reciprocal Effects." *American Sociological Review* 38 (1973): 97-118.

Kornhauser, H. *Mental Health of the Industrial Worker*. New York: John Wiley, 1965.

Kranzberg, M. and J. Gies. *By the Sweat of Thy Brow*. New York: Putnam, 1975.

Kreinin, M. E. *Israel and Africa: A Study in Technical Cooperation*. New York: Praeger, 1964.

Kreps, J. M. "Some Time Dimensions of Manpower Policy," in E. Ginzberg (ed.) *Jobs for Americans*. Englewood Cliffs, NJ: Prentice-Hall, 1976.

Kulpinska, J. "Workers' Attitudes Towards Work," in M. R. Haug and J. Dofny (eds.) *Work and Technology*. Beverly Hills, CA: Sage, 1977.

Kutscher, R. E., J. A. Mark, and J. R. Norsworthy. "The Productivity Slowdown and the Outlook to 1985." *Monthly Labor Review* 100 (May 1977): 3-8.

Lampman, R. C. "Employment versus Income Maintenance," in Ginzberg, E. (ed.) *Jobs for Americans*. Englewood Cliffs, NJ: Prentice-Hall, 1976.

Lasson, K. *The Workers*. New York: Grossman, 1971.

Lauterbach, A. *Men, Motives and Money: Psychological Frontiers of Economics*. Ithaca: Cornell, 1959.

Lawler, E. E. III and L. W. Porter. "The Effect of Performance on Job Satisfaction," in G. A. Yukl and K. N. Wexley (eds.) *Readings in Organizational and Industrial Psychology*. New York: Oxford University Press, 1971.

Lawler, E. E. and J. L. Suttle. "Expectancy Theory and Job Behavior." *Organizational Behavior and Human Performance* 9 (1973): 482-503.

Le Monde, May 28, 1981.

Leon, D. *The Kibbutz: A New Way of Life*. London: Pergamon, 1969.

Leontiff, W. "The Future of the World Economy." *Socio-Economic Planning Sciences* 2 (1977): 171-182.

Levinson, H. *The Great Jackass Fallacy*. Boston: Harvard, 1973.

Levy, J. *Play Behavior*. New York: John Wiley, 1978.

Lewin, K., R. Lippitt, and R. K. White. "Patterns of Aggressive Behavior in Experimentally Created 'Social Climates.'" *Journal of Social Psychology* 10 (1939): 87.

Likert, R. *New Patterns of Management*. New York: McGraw-Hill, 1961.

Locke, E. A. "The Nature and Causes of Job Satisfaction," in M. D. Dunnette (ed.) *Handbook of Industrial and Organizational Psychology*. Chicago; Rand McNally, 1976.

———— "Personnel Attitudes and Motivation." *Annual Review of Psychology* 26 (1975): 457-480.

———— "Job Satisfaction and Job Performance: A Theoretical Analogy." *Organizational Behavior and Human Performance* 5 (1970): 484-500.

———— D. B. Feren, V. M. McCaleb, K. N. Shaw, and A. T. Denny. "The Relative Effectiveness of Four Methods of Motivating Employee Performance," in K. D. Duncan, M. W. Gruneberg, and D. Wallis (eds.) *Changes in Working Life*. Chichester: Wiley, 1980.

Macarov, D. "Use of the Task Force in the Human Services: A Documented Experience." *Administration in Social Work,* in press.

――――― "Work and the Prospect of Social Development: In the West and Elsewhere." Paper presented at the Seminar on Social Development, Institute of Social Studies, The Hague, Netherlands, May 1981.

――――― "Humanizing the Workplace as Squaring the Circle." Paper presented at the Second World Congress on Social Economics, Jerusalem, August 1981; *International Journal of Manpower,* forthcoming.

――――― *Work and Welfare: The Unholy Alliance.* Beverly Hills, CA: Sage, 1980.

――――― *The Design of Social Welfare.* New York: Holt, Rinehart & Winston, 1978.

――――― "Management in the Social Work Curriculum." *Administration in Social Work* 1 (1977): 135.

――――― "Social Welfare as a By-Product: The Effect of Neo-Mercantilism." *Journal of Sociology and Social Welfare* 4 (1977): 1135-1144.

――――― "Reciprocity between Self-Actualisation and Hard Work." *International Journal of Social Economics* 3 (1976): 39-44.

――――― "Israel's Social Services: Historical Roots and Current Situation," in D. Thursz and J. L. Vigilante (eds.) *Meeting Human Needs: An Overview of Nine Countries.* Beverly Hills, CA: Sage, 1975.

――――― "Work Without Pay: Work Incentives and Patterns in a Salaryless Environment." *International Journal of Social Economics* 2 (1975): 106-114.

――――― *Work Incentives in an Israeli Kibbutz.* Jerusalem: Paul Baerwald School of Social Work, the Hebrew University, 1973. (Hebrew)

――――― *Incentives to Work.* San Francisco: Jossey-Bass, 1970.

――――― and G. Fradkin. *The Short Course in Development Training.* Ramat Gan, Israel: Massadah, 1973.

Macarov, D. and N. Golan, "Goals in Social Work: A Longitudinal Study." *International Social Work* 16 (1973): 68-74.

Macarov, D. and B. Rothman, "Confidentiality: A Constraint on Research?" *Social Work Research and Abstracts* 13 (Fall 1977): 11-16.

McClelland, D. C. *Motivating Economic Achievement.* New York: Free Press, 1975.

――――― "Sources of *n* Achievement," in D. C. McClelland and R. S. Steele (eds.) *Human Motivation: A Book of Readings.* Morristown, NJ: General Learning Press, 1973.

――――― *The Achieving Society.* New York: Free Press, 1961.

McCord, W. and J. McCord. *Origins of Alcoholism.* London: Tavistock, 1960.

McCullough, C. *The Thorn Birds.* New York: Harper & Row, 1977.

McFarland, K. "Why Men and Women Get Fired." *Personnel Journal* 25 (1957): 307.

McGaughey, W., Jr. *A Shorter Workweek in the 1980's.* White Bear Lake, MN: Thistlerose, 1981.

McGregor, D. *The Human Side of Enterprise.* New York: McGraw-Hill, 1960.

Machlowitz, M. M. *Workaholics: Living with Them, Working with Them.* New York: Mentor, 1981.

――――― "The Workaholic." Yale University, 1976. (mimeo)

McKeachie, W. J. "Motivation, Teaching Methods and College Learning," in D. C. McClelland and R. S. Steele (eds.) *Human Motivation: A Book of Readings.* Morristown, NJ: General Learning Press, 1973.

Macy, B. A. "The Bolivar Quality of Work Life Program: A Longitudinal Behavioral and Performance Assessment." *Proceedings of the Thirty-Second Annual Meeting.* Madison, WI: Industrial Relations Research Association, 1979.

Maddi, S. R. *Personality Theories.* Homewood, IL: Dorsey, 1968.

Maier, N. R. F. *Psychology in Industrial Organizations.* Boston: Houghton Mifflin, 1973.

Mallet, S. "The Class Struggle: Death and Transfiguration at Caltex," in E. Shorter (ed.) *Work and Community in the West*. New York: Harper & Row, 1973.

Manchester, W. *The Glory and the Dream*. Boston: Little, Brown, 1973.

Mann, S. Z. "The Politics of Productivity: State and Local Focus." *Public Productivity Review* 4 (1980): 352-367.

Marrus, M. R. (ed.). *The Emergence of Leisure*. New York: Harper & Row, 1974.

Marshall, R. "Selective Employment Policies to Achieve Full Employment," in B. D. Dennis (ed.) *Proceedings of the Thirtieth Annual Winter Meeting*. Madison, WI: Industrial Relations Research Association, 1978.

Martin, J. M. *Lower-Class Delinquency and Work Programs*. New York: New York University Press, 1966.

Maslow, A. H. *Motivation and Personality*. New York: Harper & Row, 1954.

Massey, G. M. "Book Review." *American Journal of Sociology* 85 (1980): 1446-1449.

Mayo, E. *The Human Problems of an Industrial Civilization*. New York: Viking, 1933.

Mazlish, B. *The Wealth of Nations: Representative Selections*. New York: Bobbs-Merrill, 1961.

Melman, S. "Managerial versus Cooperative Decision Making in Israel," in *Studies in Comparative International Development*. New Brunswick: Rutgers, 1970.

Mendelssohn, K. *The Riddle of the Pyramids*. London: Sphere, 1977.

Menninger, K. "Work as Sublimation." *Bulletin of the Menninger Clinic* 6 (1942): 170-182.

Meyer, H. J., E. F. Borgatta, and W. C. Jones. *Girls at Vocational High*. New York: Russell Sage, 1965.

Michelotti, K. "Multiple Jobholding Rate Remained Unchanged in 1976." *Monthly Labor Review* 100 (June 1977): 44-48.

Miller, D. R. and G. E. Swanson. "Child Training in Entrepreneurial and Bureaucratic Families," in E. Katz and B. Danet (eds.) *Bureaucracy and the Public*. New York: Basic Books, 1973.

Miller, S. M. "Productivity and the Paradox of Service in a Profit Economy," *Social Policy* 9 (1978): 4-6.

Mintzberg, H. *The Nature of Managerial Work*. New York: Harper & Row, 1973.

Mirels, H. L. and J. B. Garrett. "The Protestant Ethic as a Personality Variable." *Journal of Consulting and Clinical Psychology* 36 (1971): 40-44.

Misgav, M. *The Relationship Between Job Satisfaction Factors and Job Behavior*. Ramat Gan, Israel: Bar-Ilan University, Department of Psychology, n.d. (Hebrew)

Mitchell, A. "Human Needs and the Changing Goals of Life and Work," in F. Best (ed.) *The Future of Work*. Englewood Cliffs, NJ: Prentice-Hall, 1973.

Monthly Labor Review. 102 (March 1979): 91, 107.

_____ "Current Labor Statistics." 104 (January 1981): 103.

Moore, H. *Psychology for Business and Industry*. New York: McGraw-Hill, 1942.

Mortimer, J. T. and J. Lorence. "Work Experience and Occupational Value Socialization: A Longitudinal Study." *American Journal of Sociology* 84 (1979): 1361-1385.

Mueller, E. *Technological Advance in an Expanding Economy*. Ann Arbor: Institute for Social Research, University of Michigan, 1969.

Munts, R. and I. Garfinkel. *The Work Disincentive Effects of Unemployment Insurance*. Kalamazoo: Upjohn, 1974.

Mussan, A. E. "Technological Change and Manpower: An Historical Perspective." *International Journal of Manpower* 1 (1980): 2-5.

Neff, W. S. *Work and Human Behavior*. New York: Atherton, 1968.

Neider, L. L. "An Experimental Field Investigation Utilizing an Expectancy Theory View of Participation." *Organizational Behavior and Human Performance* 26 (1980): 425-448.

Neugarten, B. "A Developmental View of Adult Personality," in J. E. Birren (ed.) *Relations of Development and Aging*. Springfield, IL: Charles C Thomas, 1964.

Neulinger, J. "The Need for and the Implications of a Psychological Conception of Leisure." *Ontario Psychologist* 8 (1976): 13-20.

———— *The Psychology of Leisure: Research Approaches to the Study of Leisure*. Springfield, IL: Charles C Thomas, 1974.

———— "Leisure and Mental Health: A Study in a Program of Leisure Research," in T. B. Johannis, Jr., and C. N. Bull (eds.) *The Sociology of Leisure*. Beverly Hills, CA: Sage.

New York Times. "Letters to the Editor—Workaholics." October 24, 1976.

Oates, W. F. *Confessions of a Workaholic*. New York: Abingdon, 1971.

Opsahl, A. L. and M. D. Dunnette. "The Role of Financial Compensation." *Psychological Bulletin* 66 (1966): 94-118.

Organisation for Economic Co-operation and Development. *Work in a Changing Industrial Society*. Paris: Author, 1975.

———— *Main Economic Indicators: Historical Statistics, 1955-1971*. Paris: Author, 1973. (Also, *Supplements 1, 2, and 3;* May, August, and November, 1977.)

Orpen, C. "The Effects of Job Enrichment on Employee Satisfaction, Motivation, Involvement, and Performance: A Field Experiment." *Human Relations* 32 (1979): 189-217.

O'Toole, J. *Work, Learning, and the American Future*. San Francisco: Jossey-Bass, 1977.

Overbeck, T. J. *The Workaholic*. Chicago: Loyola University, 1977.

Ozawa, M. N. "Issues in Welfare Reform." *Social Service Review* 52 (1978): 37.

Parker, S. *The Future of Work and Leisure*. New York: Praeger, 1971.

Parnes, S. and M. Rosow. *Productivity and the Quality of Working Life*. Scarsdale: Work in America Institute, 1978.

Parrington, V. L. *Main Currents in American Thought*. New York: Harcourt Brace Jovanovich, 1927.

Patruchev, V. A. "The Problems of Organizing Spare Time of Society in Conditions of the Scientific and Technological Revolution," in M. R. Haug and J. Dofny (eds.) *Work and Technology*. Beverly Hills, CA: Sage, 1977.

Personnel Psychology. 33 (1980): 259-300.

Pierce, J. L. "Job Design in Perspective." *Personnel Administrator* 25 (1980): 67-75.

Plattner, M. F. "The Welfare State *vs.* the Redistributive State." *Public Interest* 55 (1979): 28-48.

Porket, J. L. "Old Age Pension Schemes in the Soviet Union and Eastern Europe." *Social Policy and Administration* 13 (1979): 22-36.

Poverty. 39 (1978): 7.

Power, E. *The Cambridge-Somerville Youth Study*. New York: Columbia, 1951.

Quinn, R. and L. Shepard. *The 1972-1973 Quality of Employment Survey*. Ann Arbor: Institute for Social Research, University of Michigan, 1974.

Quinn, R. P. et al. "Evaluating Working Conditions in America." *Monthly Labor Review* 96 (1973): 32-43.

Raskin, A. H. "Toward a More Participative Work Force," in C. S. Sheppard and D. C. Carroll (eds.) *Working in the Twenty-First Century*. New York: John Wiley, 1980.

Rees, A. *The Economics of Work and Pay*. New York: Harper & Row, 1979.

Reynolds, B. C. *Learning and Teaching in the Practice of Social Work*. New York: Holt, Rinehart & Winston, 1942.

Ribeaux, P. and S. E. Poppleton. *Psychology and Work: An Introduction*. London: Macmillan, 1978.

Robbins, L. "The Accuracy of Parental Recall of Aspects of Child Development and Child Rearing Practices." *Journal of Abnormal and Social Psychology* 66 (1963): 265-276.

Robins, L. N. *Deviant Children Grow Up*. Baltimore: Williams and Wilkins, 1966.

Robinson, H. A. and J. E. Finesinger. "The Significance of Work Inhibition for Rehabilitation." *Social Work* 2 (1957): 22.

Robinson, J. P. "Occupational Norms and Differences in Job Satisfaction: A Summary of Survey Research Evidence," in J. P. Robinson, R. Athanasiou, and K. B. Head, *Measures of Occupational Attitudes and Occupational Characteristics*. Ann Arbor: University of Michigan, 1969.

Rodgers, D. T. *The Work Ethic in Industrial America 1850-1920*. Chicago: University of Chicago Press, 1974.

Roethlisberger, F. J. and W. J. Dickson. *Management and the Worker*. Cambridge, MA: Harvard University Press, 1939.

Rosen, B. C. "Family Structure and Achievement Motivation." *American Sociological Review* 28 (1961): 574-585.

_____ and R. D'Andrade. "The Psycho-Social Origins of Achievement Motivation." *Sociometry* 22 (1959): 185-218; also in U. Bronfenbrenner (ed.) *Influences on Human Development*. Hinsdale, IL: Dryden, 1972.

Rosow, J. M. "Human Values in the Work Place Support Growth of Productivity." *World of Work Report* 2 (June 1977): 62.

Rossi, A. S. "Equality Between the Sexes: An Immodest Proposal," in R. L. Coser (ed.) *Life Cycle and Achievement in America*. New York: Harper & Row, 1969.

Rotenberg, M. *Damnation and Deviance: The Protestant Ethic and the Spirit of Failure*. New York: Free Press, 1978.

Rothman, D. J. *The Discovery of the Asylum*. Boston: Little, Brown, 1971.

Rubin, L. B. *Worlds of Pain: Life in the Working Class Family*. New York: Basic Books, 1976.

Salvendy, G. "Can the Slow Worker Go Faster?" *Industry Week* 168 (March 1971): 43.

Samant, S., S. Sawant, and B. Talati. *Distribution of Fertilizers in Ralnagiri (India) District*. Tel Aviv: Foreign Training Department, Ministry of Agriculture, 1970. (mimeo)

Sarason, S. B. *Work, Aging and Social Change: Professionals and the One Life-One Career Imperative*. New York: Free Press, 1977.

Scanlan, B. K. "Determinants of Job Satisfaction and Productivity." *Personnel Journal* 55 (1976): 12.

Schechter, G. "Influence of the Protestant Ethic on Patterns of Achievement and Loneliness within Different Ethnic Groups in Israel." MA thesis, Hebrew University, Jerusalem. (Hebrew)

Schiltz, M. E. *Public Attitudes Toward Social Security 1935-1965* Washington, DC: Department of Health, Education, and Welfare, 1970.

Schmitt, N., B. W. Coyle, J. Rauschenberg, and J. K. White. "Comparison of Early Retirees and Non-Retirees," *Personnel Psychology* 32 (1979): 327-340.

Schrecker, P. *Work and History: An Essay on the Structure of Civilization*. Gloucester, MA: Peter Smith, 1967.

Schumacher, E. F. *Good Work*. New York: Harper & Row, 1979.

Seashore, S. E. "Defining and Measuring the Quality of Working Life," in L. E. Davis and A. B. Cherns (eds.) *The Quality of Working Life: Problems, Prospects and the State of the Art*. New York: Free Press, 1975.

_____ and T. D. Taber. "Job Satisfaction Indicators and Their Correlates," in A. D. Biderman and T. F. Drury (eds.) *Measuring Work Quality for Social Reporting*. New York: John Wiley, 1976.

Segalman, R. "The Protestant Ethic and Social Welfare." *Journal of Social Issues* 24 (1968): 125-141.

Shamir, B. "Between Service and Servility: Role Conflict in Subordinate Service Roles." *Human Relations* 33 (1980): 741-756.

Shepard, J. M. "On Alex Carey's Radical Criticism of the Hawthorne Studies." *Academy of Management Journal* 14 (1971): 23-32.

Shipley, P. "Technological Change, Work Scheduling, and Individual Well-Being," in K. D. Duncan, M. M. Gruneberg, and D. Wallis (eds.) *Changes in Working Life*. Chichester: Wiley, 1980.

Shostak, A. B. "Educational Reforms and Poverty," in A. B. Shostak and W. Gomberg (eds.) *New Perspectives on Poverty*. Englewood Cliffs, NJ: Prentice-Hall, 1965.

Singer, E. "Adult Orientation of First and Later Children." *Sociometry* 34 (1971): 328-345.

Sjoberg, G. (ed.) *Ethics, Politics and Social Research*. Cambridge, MA: Schenkman, 1967.

Smith, C. P. "The Influence of Testing Conditions and Need for Achievement Scores and Their Relationship to Performance Scores," in J. W. Atkinson and N. T. Feather (eds.) *A Theory of Achievement Motivation*. New York: John Wiley, 1966.

Smith, P. C., L. M. Kendall, and C. L. Hulin. *The Measurement of Satisfactions in Work and Retirement: A Strategy for the Study of Attitudes*. Chicago: Rand McNally, 1969.

Sommer, J. J. "Work as a Therapeutic Goal: Union-Management Clinical Contribution to a Mental Health Program." *Mental Hygiene* 53 (1969): 263-268.

Spitze, G. D. and L. J. Waite. "Labor Force and Work Attitudes: Young Women's Early Experiences." *Sociology of Work and Occupations* 7 (1980): 3-32.

Stagner, R. "The Affluent Society Versus Early Retirement." *Aging and Work* 1 (1978): 25-31.

Stendahl, K. "Religion, Mysticism, and the Institutional Church," in D. Bell (ed.) *Toward the Year 2000: Work in Progress*. Boston: Beacon, 1967.

Stollberg, R. "Job Satisfaction and Relationship to Work," in M. R. Haug and J. Dofny (eds.) *Work and Technology*. Beverly Hills, CA: Sage, 1977.

Stone, E. F. "The Moderating Effect of Work Related Values on Job Score-Job Satisfaction Relationship." *Organizational Behavior and Human Performance* 15 (1976): 147-167.

Strauss, A. "Transformations of Identity," in A. M. Rose (ed.) *Human Behavior and Social Processes*. Boston: Houghton Mifflin, 1962.

Strauss, G. "Book Review." *American Journal of Sociology* 85 (1980): 1467-1469.

———— "Job Satisfaction, Motivation, and Job Redesign," in *Organizational Behavior: Research and Issues*. Madison, WI: Industrial Relations Research Association, 1974.

———— "Workers: Attitudes and Adjustments," in J. M. Rosow (ed.) *The Worker and the Job: Coping with Change*. Englewood Cliffs, NJ: Prentice-Hall, 1974.

Strodtbeck, F. L. "Family Interaction, Values, and Achievement," in D. C. McClelland, A. L. Baldwin, U. Bronfenbrenner, and F. L. Strodtbeck (eds.) *Talent and Society: New Perspectives in the Identification of Talent*. Princeton, NJ: Van Nostrand, 1958.

Strumpel, B. "Economic Life-Styles, Values, and Subjective Welfare," in B. Strumpel (ed.) *Economic Means for Human Needs: Social Indicators of Well-Being and Discontent*. Ann Arbor: University of Michigan, 1976.

Strumpfer, D. J. "Failure to Find Relationships Between Family Constellations and Achievement Motivation." *Journal of Psychology* 85 (1973): 29-36.

Sumner, W. G. *Social Darwinism*. Englewood Cliffs, NJ: Prentice-Hall, 1963.

Sykes, A. J. "Economic Interest and the Hawthorne Researches: A Comment." *Human Relations* 18 (1965): 253-263.

Szalai, A. (ed.) *The Use of Time*. The Hague: Mouton, 1972.

Tamuz, M. *Work Role Centrality, Role Strain and Organizational Commitment: A Study of Social Workers in Public Welfare*. Ramat Aviv, Israel: Tel Aviv University School of Social Work, 1977.

Tawney, R. H. *The Acquisitive Society*. New York: Harcourt Brace Jovanovich, 1948.

Taylor, F. W. *The Principles of Scientific Management*. New York: Harper & Row, 1911.

Taylor, G. C. "Executive Stress," in A. A. McLean (ed.) *To Work Is Human*. New York: Macmillan, 1967.

Taylor, J. and D. G. Bowers, *Survey of Organizations: A Machine-Scored Standardized Questionnaire Instrument*. Ann Arbor: Institute for Social Research, University of Michigan, 1972.

Terkel, S. *Working*. New York: Random House, 1972.

Thibaut, J. W. and H. H. Kelley. *The Social Psychology of Groups*. New York: John Wiley, 1959.

Toffler, A. *The Third Wave*. New York: Bantam, 1980.

Toman, W. *Family Constellation*. New York: Springer, 1976.

Tooney, B. T. "Work Ethic and Work Incentives: Values and Income Maintenance Reform." *Journal of Sociology and Social Welfare* 7 (1980): 148.

U.S. Department of Agriculture. *The Secret of Affluence*. Washington, DC: Author, 1976.

U.S. Department of Health, Education, and Welfare. *Social Security Programs Throughout the World, 1977*. Washington, DC: Author, 1977.

_____ *Social Security Bulletin, Annual Statistical Supplement, 1975*. Washington, DC: Author, 1975.

_____ *Work in America*. Cambridge: MIT Press, 1973.

van Assen, A. and P. Wester. "Designing Meaningful Jobs: A Comparative Analysis of Organizational Design Practices," in K. D. Duncan, M. M. Gruneberg, and D. Wallis (eds.) *Changes in Working Life*. New York: John Wiley, 1980.

Varga, K. "Marital Cohesion as Reflected in Time-Budgets," in A. Szalai (ed.) *The Use of Time*. The Hague: Mouton, 1972.

Vecchio, R. P. "Individual Differences as a Moderator of the Job Quality-Job Satisfaction Relationship: Evidence from a National Sample." *Organizational Behavior and Human Personality* 26 (1980): 305-325.

Verba, S. *Small Groups and Political Behavior*. Princeton, NJ: Princeton University Press, 1961.

Vernon, G. M. "Religion as a Social Problem," in E. O. Smigel (ed.) *Handbook on the Study of Social Problems*. Chicago: Rand-McNally, 1971.

Vidich, A. J., J. Bensman, and M. R. Stein. *Reflections on Community Studies*. New York: John Wiley, 1964.

Vroom, V. H. *Work and Motivation*. New York: John Wiley, 1964.

Walbank, M. "Effort in Motivated Work Behavior," in K. D. Duncan, M. M. Gruneberg, and D. Wallis (eds.) *Changes in Working Life*. Chichester: Wiley, 1980.

Waldfogel, S. "The Frequency and Affective Character of Childhood Memories." *Psychological Monographs* 62 (1948).

Walfish, B. "Job Satisfaction Declines in Major Aspects of Work, Says Michigan Study: All Occupational Groups Included." *World of Work Report* 4 (February 1979): 9.

Ward, P. and T. Wall. *Work and Well-Being*. Harmondsworth: Penguin, 1975.

Wardwell, W. I. "Critique of a Recent Professional 'Put-Down' of the Hawthorne Research." *American Sociological Review* 44 (1979): 858-861.

Weaver, C. N. "Relationships Among Pay, Race, Sex, Occupational Prestige, Supervision, Work Autonomy, and Job Satisfaction in a National Sample." *Personnel Psychology* 30 (1977): 437-445.

Weber, M. *The Protestant Ethic and the Spirit of Capitalism*. New York: Scribners, 1952.

Weiner, H. J. and S. H. Akabas. *Work in America: The View from Industrial Social Welfare*. New York: Columbia University School of Social Work, Industrial Social Welfare Center, 1974.

Weiner, Y. and J. Vardi. "Relationship Between Job Organization and Career Outcomes: An Integrative Approach," *Organizational Behavior and Human Performance* 26 (1980): 81-96.

Weingarten, M. *Life in a Kibbutz*. New York: Reconstructionist Press, 1955.

Westley, W. A. and M. W. Westley. *The Emerging Worker: Equality and Conflict in the Mass Consumption Society*. Montreal: McGill-Queen's University Press, 1971.

Wheelis, A. *How People Change*. New York: Harper & Row, 1973.

White, J. K. "Individual Differences and the Job Quality-Worker Response Relationship: Review, Integration and Comment." *Academy of Management Review* 3 (1978): 267-280.

Whitsett, D. A. and E. K. Winslow. "An Analysis of Studies Critical of the Motivator-Hygiene Theory." *Personnel Psychology* 20 (1967): 391.

Whyte, W. F. *Organisational Behaviour: Theory and Application*. Homewood, IL: Dorsey, 1969.

————— *Money and Motivation*. New York: Harper & Row, 1955.

World of Work Report. 4 (1979): 8; 4 (1979): 59; 5 (1980): 53; 5 (1980): 72; 5 (1980): 86; 6 (1981): 10; 6 (1981): 16; 6 (1981): 32; 6 (1981): 38.

Wright, J. D. and R. F. Hamilton. "Work Satisfaction and Age: Some Evidence for the 'Job Change' Hypothesis." *Social Forces* 56 (1978): 1140-1158.

Yadov, Y. A. and A. A. Kissel. "Job Satisfaction: Analysis of Empirical Data and Attempt at Their Theoretical Interpretation," in M. R. Haug and J. Dofny (eds.) *Work and Technology*. Beverly Hills, CA: Sage, 1977.

Yankelovich, D. "Work, Values, and the New Breed," in C. Kerr and J. M. Rosow (eds.) *Work in America: The Decade Ahead*. New York: Van Nostrand Reinhold, 1979.

Yearbook of Labour Statistics: Sixteenth Edition; Twenty-Sixth Edition; Thirty-Sixth Edition. Geneva: International Labour Organization, 1956, 1966, 1976, 1978.

Zaleznik, A., G. W. Dalton, and L. B. Barnes. *Orientation and Conflict in Career*. Boston: Harvard, 1970.

Zdravomyslov, A. G., V. P. Rozhin, and V. A. Iadov. *Man and His Work*. White Plains, NY: International Arts and Sciences Press, 1967. (Translated from the Russian by S. P. Dunn.)

AUTHOR INDEX

SUBJECT INDEX

ABOUT THE AUTHOR

DAVID MACAROV is Associate Professor at the Paul Baerwald School of Social Work, the Hebrew University, Jerusalem. He holds a B.S. in psychology from the University of Pittsburgh, an M.S. in social administration from Western Reserve University, and a Ph.D. in social planning from the Florence Heller Graduate School for Advanced Studies in Social Welfare, Brandeis University. He has been a visiting professor at the University of Boston, Virginia Commonwealth University, Adelphi University, University of Pennsylvania, University of Michigan, and Melbourne University. He has participated in the NATO Conference on Changing Patterns of Work in Thessaloniki, Greece, and the International Conference on Leisure Time Policies in Jerusalem. He has presented papers at the annual meeting of the Industrial Relations Research Association in New Orleans, at the Arden House Conference on Administration, the First International Conference on Social Economics in Mexico City, and the Research Seminar in Hong Kong. He is a member of the board of the International Association for Social Economics, and was Director for the Second Conference of that body, held in 1981 in Jerusalem. He is the author of *Incentives to Work* (Jossey-Bass, 1968), *The Short Course in Development Training* (Massadah, 1973), *The Design of Social Welfare* (Holt, Rinehart & Winston, 1978), and *Work and Welfare: The Unholy Alliance* (Sage, 1980), as well as many articles.